BOMBSHELL

BOMBSHELL

THE MANY FACES OF WOMEN TERRORISTS

MIA BLOOM

HURST & COMPANY, LONDON

First published in the United Kingdom by

C. Hurst and Co. (Publishers) Ltd,
41 Great Russell Street, London, WC1B 3PL

Printed in the United Kingdom

The right of Mia Bloom to be identified as the author
of this volume has been asserted by him in accordance with
the Copyright, Designs and Patents Act, 1988.
A catalogue data record for this volume is available
from the British Library.

ISBN 978-1-84904-160-7 *paperback*

www.hurstpub.co.uk

To my loving husband, John,
for everything he does and everything he is

CONTENTS

ACKNOWLEDGMENTS

This book would not have been possible without the support of many people. First and foremost, I want to thank Westwood Creative Artists, in particular Bruce Westwood and Carolyn Forde, for their support and encouragement since the inception of the project. I will always be grateful to Thomas Homer-Dixon, who was a real advocate in seeing the potential for this book. I want to thank everyone at Penguin Canada, and especially my editors Diane Turbide and Jonathan Webb. I am grateful to Scott Steedman and Chandra Wohleber for their significant improvement of my writing, and Sandra Tooze for all of her production assistance. Many thanks to Vijay Vaitheeswaran for suggesting the title. I am also grateful to Roger Haydon at Cornell University Press, the smartest man I know, for his indomitable patience and for allowing me to put other projects on the backburner in order to finish this book. Roger, you are a saint!

Writing can be both a labor of love and an intensely painful process. Ideas come at their own pace and not always at the most opportune times. This can mean crazy hours on my laptop or scrawling notes on bits of paper when coming up with a turn of phrase. The scarcest luxury of all is time. I owe a debt of gratitude to the academic departments who have given me leave to write, and especially to the Office of Naval Research, whose support allowed me to teach a little less and write a little more. I specifically want to thank Ivy Estabrooke and Harold Hawkins for their support of my research projects as well as Jo and Ted for all their hard work. I thank the staff and the director, John Horgan, of the International Center for the Study of Terrorism (ICST) at Penn State, as well as Machelle Seiner and all of my colleagues at ICST. I am grateful to the dean of Liberal Arts, Susan Welch, as well as to Ray Lombra, Denise Solomon, Avis Kunz, Carolyn Sachs, Chris Woods, Trish Alexander, and Chris Bundy for giving me the time to make this book a reality.

I thank all the women who gave me their time to discuss their histories and their feelings about being involved in insurgent and terrorist movements. For obvious reasons, I will not be able to identify all those who offered their time and patience in responding to my questions about such difficult and sensitive issues. There are others, however, that I can thank and mention by name. Pat at Coíste and Evelyn at Tar Anal helped enormously with various introductions in Belfast, and Sree helped locate material about the women of the LTTE. The staff at the Linen Hall Library assisted me tirelessly in sifting through years of historical background material on the Provisional IRA. Alistair Gordon and Ross Moore deserve thanks for everything they did to help me over several visits to the NIPC Collection in Belfast.

Ehud Sprinzak and Chuck Tilly continue to inspire me even in their absence. They both taught me so much and I will always be grateful for having known and studied with them. I am grateful to the research assistance of Shireen Judeh, Yael Miller, Lauren Coffey, Clare Hatfield, Mike Bartenfeld, Kelley Johnson, and Eleonora Rossi, in addition to all of my former students at UGA. Your questions in class often spurred me to delve deeper into this subject matter.

To my research collaborators, Kathleen Deloughery, Alex Downes, David Edelstein, Paul Gill, Ian Roxborough, Tricia Sullivan, and Ike Wilson: it is great working with such a talented team of people. Thank you all.

My friends and colleagues have always been wonderful sounding boards for new ideas. They brave extended discussions replete with all of the gory details about terrorist tactics. I am always grateful for their input and support. Due to the limitations of space I can only list but a few of you who have helped over the years: Farhana Ali, Nichole Argo, Victor Asal, Sammy Barkin, Irina Bazarya, Tore Bjørgo, David Burbach, Dan Byman, Erica Chenoweth, Dara Cohen, Helen Currie, Beth De Sombre, Adam Dolnik, Dan Drezner, Kathy Driehaus, Richard English, Roberto Farneti, James Forest, Boaz Ganor, Dipak Gupta, Chris Harmon, Ron Hassner, Bruce Hoffman, Karyn Holdsworth, Rick and Jennifer Jacobs, Philip Jenkins, Sidney Jones, Jenna Jordan, Keith Karako, Chaim Kaufman, Mike Kenney, Peter Krause, David Lake, Tom Lauth, Roy Licklider, Michael, Carol, and Ed Lipson, Orla Lynch, Bill and Julie Middleton, Judy Miller, Cecilia Mills, Helen Murphy, Alex, Katie, and Roux Novak, Reuven Paz, Ami Pedazhur, Daniela Pisoiu, Chris Preble, David Rapoport, Jean-François Ratelle, Christopher, Lori, and Jack Rudolph, Marc Sageman, Steve Saideman, Prakhar Sharma, Phil Shrodt, Amy Shuster, Marcia Sprules, Zack Taylor, Eileen Trauth, Maurits van der Veen, Leonard Weinberg, Paul and Sue Wilkinson, and Dan Winship. Thank you all for your ideas, insights, comments, critiques, and friendship.

I want to thank my family—my mother, Betty, Samara and Liam Archer-Bloom, Faygie Goldberg, Granda Martin, Louise and Rick Pygman—who are always the best cheerleaders for anything and everything I do.

Last but certainly not least, I thank John for everything. *Tá grá agam duit.*

All errors in this book are my sole responsibility and the views expressed represent those of the author and not of my academic institution, the International Center for the Study of Terrorism, or of the Department of the Navy.

PREFACE

As the number of female terrorists and suicide bombers has increased several hundredfold in the past few years, the trend has been accompanied by a barrage of misinformation and misperception about what is actually going on. Many people have assumed that women could not consciously choose to participate in terrorism of their own volition. The underlying assumption is that *a man made her do it*. In their attempts to explain women's involvement in terrorism for a general audience, journalistic accounts have presented a far too simple and unidimensional account of the phenomenon.

We need to work past gender stereotypes and begin to examine the conditions that really influence female violence. We do not want to excuse the women's behavior, nor do we want to denude their actions of their political motivation. Lots of women are just as bloodthirsty as the male members of terrorist groups, but women's motivations tend to be intricate, multi-layered, and inspired on a variety of levels. Anger, sorrow, the desire for revenge, and nationalist or religious zeal coalesce in ways that make any simple explanation impossible. Given that terrorist groups gain so much from women's participation, it is far easier to understand why terrorist groups seek female activists than to explain why women oblige them by heeding the call to action.

I have attempted to make these complexities accessible for as wide an audience as possible, from the general reader to the counter-terrorism analyst. I aim to clarify the various reasons why women might choose terror and to explain the many roles they take on when they make that choice.

My work has always sought to bridge the divide between political science and policy. To understand what is going on, I have found we need to better understand the past. If we fail to take into account the history of violence, we will never be able to anticipate what is likely to happen in the future.

The stories presented in this book shed light on the conditions under which women are mobilized themselves or mobilize others for terrorism. The book also explains the unique pressures women face during conflict and how they can become involved in the struggle, sometimes against their will. The women presented here encompass a spectrum of involvement and provide an insider's view of the many faces of women and terror.

A few comments regarding names. Where possible, I have used the most common transliterations, although this poses some problems when multiple spellings exist simultaneously. For Russian names, the female patronymic always includes an *a*, and so within the same family, the women's last names will be Ganiyeva, for example, while the men's will be Ganiyev. I have followed standard usage in academic literature and used the *a* rather than the *e* for Russian transliteration—for example, Basayev rather than Basaev or Besaev. Also, where either a *b* or a *p* is used, I have deferred to the *p*, and so, for instance, have used the name Vagapov rather than Vagabov, although both occur in journalists' accounts.

For Chechen names, an additional complication is that Chechens often have official names, which appear on their passports but are rarely used within the family, and nicknames, regularly used at home. For the purposes of consistency, I have provided the reader with both. In many cases the nickname makes sense, and Raisa becomes Reshat, for example; in other cases, however, the nickname has little or no connection to the passport name, and thus Fatima might become Milana.

As for Arabic names, I have used the most common spelling for the names of individuals and organizations, although this too might cause some confusion. Thus the Lebanese terrorist group Party of Allah, more commonly known as Hizb'allah, can be spelled as Hezbollah, Hizbullah, Hizbollah, or Hizballah. I have chosen the most anglicized version, Hezbollah. The same considerations apply to the name Muhammed, which can also be spelled as Muhammad or Mohammed. Where possible, I have provided the reader with the simplest translations of foreign material when I have used sources in Arabic, Dutch, French, German, Hebrew, or Russian.

PROLOGUE

In the early-morning hours of Monday, March 29, 2010, two men and two women left an apartment in central Moscow. They had used the apartment as a base where they had assembled two improvised explosive devices (IEDs) in the form of belts, which the women had then wrapped around their stomachs. Each IED contained between two and three hundred grams of explosive and one was packed with nails to maximize the carnage.

A second apartment in the city housed more explosives—up to one kilo of TNT—for future attacks. The apartment had been rented by Akhmed Rabadanov, who had allegedly accompanied the two women from Dagestan to Moscow and eventually taken them to the Sokolnicheskaya or Red Line subway that traverses the center of the city.[1] Along its route are some of Moscow's most important buildings, including the Russian Duma (parliament), the Kremlin, Red Square, and, significantly, the headquarters of the old KGB, now occupied by its successor, the Federal Security Forces or FSB.

The younger of the two women, Djennet Abdurakhmenova (a.k.a. Abdullaeva), boarded the train headed toward the Ulitsa Podbelskogo station around 8:20 A.M. The rush-hour crowd filled the cars to capacity and she had to stand in the middle of the fifth car for the whole journey. As many as half a million commuters were riding the trains that morning. As people rushed in and out of the car and the train made its way through the center of the city, Djennet looked at her watch nervously. The train was taking longer than usual to reach its destination. Instead of six minutes, it was taking more than twenty minutes, and the delay seemed to agitate her. The attacks were planned to occur consecutively to achieve maximum psychological impact, and Djennet wanted to make sure that she kept as close to schedule as possible.

Djennet wore a bulky purple jacket to hide the bomb, but the jacket looked far too big for her tiny frame. Her exotic Asian features were hallmarks of a mixed Azeri-Kumyk parentage. Muscovites were now chronically afraid of Chechen women, and a few shot nervous glances in her direction, even though it had been five years since a female suicide bomber had launched an attack on the Moscow metro. Djennet's baby face made her look very young, but her strange demeanor and behavior did not match her innocent appearance.

In the middle of the car twenty-three-year-old Sim eih Xing, a Malaysian medical student from Penang, stood behind Djennet and observed her curiously. Djennet's posture was all wrong and her pupils were dilated; she barely blinked at all. Xing assumed that she was on drugs or perhaps mentally ill, and he slowly moved away from her. As he brushed past her, he confirmed that there was definitely something wrong with her. But his thoughts drifted to his impending surgical exams and how tired he was from the challenges of medical school. For reasons that Xing still cannot explain, he decided to exit the train three stops early, at Park Kultury, though he had planned to stay on until Okhotny Ryad. The Red Line trains were stopping and starting every few minutes, frustrating everyone on board. Later, people would realize that the delay had been caused by the first bomb, which rocked Moscow's metro at the Lubyanka station at 7:52 A.M.

As Xing exited the car by the middle door, a massive shock wave hit him from behind and knocked him to the ground. When he regained consciousness seconds later he could not hear anything, but saw bodies all around him. Smoke billowed out of the subway car and the smell of burnt rubber and skin permeated the air. When his hearing returned moments later, he could hear screams and the wail of approaching ambulances on the street above. Bloodied people ran past him as he stood up and walked out of the station in a daze. He looked back over his shoulder at the smoldering subway car and on its floor saw a dozen bodies piled up and various body parts strewn about. On the bloodstained floor lay Djennet's motionless corpse, her severed head a few feet away.

Xing climbed the stairs to the street. In his head he repeated an Islamic prayer over and over again, worrying that there might be a second bomb and hoping the prayer would afford him some protection. As he reached the top of the stairs, he stumbled and fell into the street. There was something on his leg. He lifted his jeans' pant leg to reveal bits of shrapnel and human flesh. The flesh could belong only to Djennet, whose upper body had been blown apart by the bomb. (Other victims were either crushed or killed by shrapnel.) Xing suffered only minor injuries, singed hair, and some cuts and bruises. He was lucky; his impatience and instinct had saved his life. Fourteen people were killed by the blast and dozens more were injured.

Another eyewitness, Angelika Penalgieva, recalled seeing bodies lying all over the platform at the Park Kultury station after the blast. People tried to use their cell phones to call friends and family but most of the calls did not go through. The FSB, worried that the bombs were triggered by cell phones and that there were other bombers on different subway lines, had jammed the cell towers.

Djennet was only seventeen years old when she blew herself up on the Moscow subway. She had grown up in Khasavyurt, a town in northern Dagestan close to the border with Chechnya. She was the widow of Umalat Magomedov (a.k.a. Al-Bara), a jihadi commander for Shariat Jamaat, the largest militant organization in Dagestan, whose founders were trained by Chechen separatist leader Shamil Basayev and fought alongside their Chechen brethren in the wars with Russia. Djennet's father had abandoned the family when she was a little girl. Her mother's brother, the oldest male in the family, was responsible for her, but drank heavily. In short, she came from a broken home and sensed that others in the traditional Kumyk society regarded her as inferior.[2] Marrying a jihadi leader afforded her the respect and status she did not have growing up.

According to Vladimir Markin, spokesman of the Investigations Committee in the Russian prosecutor-general's office, the special operation that led to Umalat's assassination on December 31, 2009, had been one of their most successful. Umalat was killed during a shoot-out with Russian security authorities. After her husband's death, Djennet was interrogated and photographed. Then she disappeared. Markin claimed that Djennet went straight to a Wahhabi training camp for three months of instruction.[3] At the end of the training, she was sent onto the subway as a suicide bomber.

Djennet was a classic Black Widow: a teenaged bride now alone and vulnerable to jihadi recruiters. Russian sources claimed that she was radicalized and recruited only after Umalat's death, but private photos of Djennet and Umalat have emerged in which she holds a pistol in her hand and has a look of fierce determination on her face. She was clearly radicalized before Umalat's death but probably became active only afterward. The Russians believe that Djennet was trained by Shariat Jamaat to avenge Umalat's death.[4] It seems likely, however, that the attack against Moscow's subways was retaliation not just for one man's death, but also for the policy of assassination by which the FSB was picking off jihadi leaders, one by one.

Across town, at 7:45 A.M., Djennet's colleague, Maryam Sharipova, boarded a different train on the Red Line. Maryam was unlike Djennet in every respect. She was older, twenty-eight, and her alleged husband was still alive. More important, for a woman, Maryam was highly educated by Dagestani standards; both her parents were teachers and she had completed high school and then graduated with an honors degree in mathematics and psychology from the Dagestan Pedagogical University in 2005. She was always at the top of her class and received straight As. After graduation, she took a job in her home village teaching computer science for four years, becoming the school's head of information technology prior to the attack.

In order to carry out her mission, Maryam traveled overland for nearly twenty hours straight to reach her target. Her parents claimed to have seen her in Dagestan as late as March 28, the day before the attack. Maryam was such an unlikely bomber that Russian authorities initially stated that the second Moscow bomber was Maria Ustarkhanova, another Dagestani widow of a jihadi fighter. Only when Maryam's father, Magomed-Rasul, recognized the red headscarf she was wearing did Russian authorities change their story. Magomed-Rasul called the authorities after pictures of the bombers were posted on the Internet; Maryam's friends and family had recognized her instantly. He later officially identified his daughter from three photos of her detached head.[5]

The only girl in a family of boys, Maryam was modest and reserved, an ardent Muslim but not radical in her views.[6] She grew up in a small, steel-gated house in Balakhani, a little hillside village with no running water or electricity, typical of Dagestan. Her house was a traditional Avar two-storied home, with low ceilings, spacious rooms, and a small courtyard. Balakhani is sandwiched between bare cliffs overgrown with pines and encircled by orchards that in the spring are cloaked in white apricot blossoms. Magomed-Rasul claimed that his daughter left home on the afternoon of March 28 to visit a girlfriend and never returned.

What her parents didn't know is that Maryam had secretly married a thirty-five-year-old jihadi, Magomedali Vagapov, the leader of the rebel Gubden Jamaat group, which had trained in Pakistan and had been fighting Russian government forces since the 1990s. Vagapov reported directly to Dokka Umarov, the top Chechen rebel, who officially took responsibility for the subway bombings. Once Vagapov grew tired of Maryam (he had two other wives), he persuaded her to become a suicide bomber.

Contrary to Islamic tradition, in which the individual must settle accounts before an act of martyrdom, Maryam did not leave a note or a will, and did not organize her worldly affairs before the operation. This has raised questions about whether she intended to be a bomber or knew that the operation in Moscow would end her life. Al Jazeera reported that she had no history of extremism, although both of her brothers had previously been involved with the Chechen resistance.

The younger one, Ilyas, was detained in 2008 for his connection to insurgent fighters operating out of the North Caucasus.[7] Her older brother, Anvar, had a more complicated past. He had ties to a radical Islamist group from the fortified village of Gimry (founded by Gazimagomed Magomedov, a fellow native of Balakhani) and several of his friends were killed in guerrilla operations while others were on the run. On the one hand, Anvar fought in the first Chechen war, was in the Dagestani underground, and headed the list of believers in the Wahhabite ideology on the police rolls for 2005. He was amnestied in 2006, however, because there was no blood on his hands. He then moved to Moscow, got married, and started a new life, until his sister's explosion at the Lubyanka station.

Maryam's parents remain skeptical that their only daughter would wed in secret. Her father said, "Maryam would never marry without my permission."[8] She was always either at home or at school; there was no opportunity for her to be with her husband. Furthermore, they rebuff the suggestion made by the Russian authorities that Maryam's older brother, Anvar, had helped coordinate the attacks and drove the two women to the subway.

For a long time after the attacks, no journalists, either Russian or foreign, were permitted into Balakhani to investigate or check the official story disseminated by the FSB.[9] One particularly intrepid reporter, Irina Gordienko, managed to get past the checkpoints and interview Maryam's family; she also conducted phone interviews with Anvar. According to Gordienko, Maryam's mother, Patimat, asked in disbelief, "How can they say that my oldest son, Anvar, himself took his sister to the site of the act of terrorism? After these events he could not even talk with me; tears were choking him. I keep constant contact with him and to this day he does not believe that Maryam is gone. I am afraid for my son. What will come of him now?"[10]

Because Maryam's brothers are suspected of having aided and abetted the female terrorist suicide bombers, both are on the federal fugitive list. Both have disappeared.

The Moscow attacks killed 40 people and injured an additional 160. It was the deadliest incident in Moscow since female suicide bombers brought down two planes and attacked the subway in 2004. In May 2010, when the FSB tried to apprehend the men who had escorted Djennet and Maryam to the metro stations, they resisted arrest and were shot and killed. The FSB refused to disclose their names.[11] According to Russian sources, one of the three men killed was Akhmed Rabadanov, grandson of Atsi Muhammed, the local sheikh in Novyy Kostek, Dagestan.

The bombings in the Moscow subway follow a pattern that was established years earlier when Chechen militants first targeted it in 2004. Attacking infrastructure during the workday rush hour is an alarming trend that has spread wherever suicide bombers prolif- erate. Attacks in Madrid on March 11, 2004 (exactly 911 days after 9/11), as well as the multiple bombings on July 7, 2005, against London's underground have become the hallmarks of groups affili- ated with Al Qaeda. By killing many civilians who happen to be in the wrong place at the wrong time, terrorist organizations instill fear, panic, and a sense that the government is helpless to protect them. This is a trend that shows no signs of imminent decline.

A BRIEF HISTORY OF TERROR
AND THE LOGIC OF OPPRESSION

The only position for women in the [movement] is prone.
—Stokely Carmichael, Black Panther leader, 1964[1]

*Protest is when I say this does not please me. Resistance is when
I ensure what does not please me occurs no more.*
—Ulrike Meinhof, female leader of the German Red Army Faction,
May 1968[2]

ASSASSINS, THEN AND NOW

There is a long history of using violence to inspire terror.
Historically, all the major religions—Muslim (Shi'a and Sunni),
Christian, Hindu, Sikh, and Jewish—have employed terrorist
violence, in many regions of the world. As far back as the Old
Testament, Samson brought down the temple of the Philistines,
killing those inside and himself in the process. Members of various
early Christian, Muslim, and Jewish heretical sects were willing to
sacrifice their lives for their beliefs, and occasionally sacrificed the
lives of others as well. These groups used violence to frighten their
enemies and to instill terror among the population with varying
degrees of efficacy. The early groups, although inspired by religious

fervor, were differentiated by their fundamental goals. Some hoped to expel a foreign occupier; others engaged in violence to celebrate their dedication to a cause, an idea, or a particular leader. The (Hindu) Thugs, (Muslim) Assassins, and (Jewish) Zealots all used terror and were principally motivated by religion.[3]

Much of what inspires religious terrorism today is reflected in the history of these early organizations. The early terrorists' desire for publicity, their indoctrination of children, their targeting of foreign occupiers, and attacks against collaborators are all surprisingly similar to the tactics used today in Israel, Sri Lanka, Chechnya, Iraq, and Afghanistan.

Princeton scholar Bernard Lewis has written about the activities of the twelfth-century Nizari, an Ismaili Islamic sect more commonly known as the Assassins. The word *assassin*, which is still used today to describe a politically motivated murderer, can be traced to the Arabic word *hashishiyyin*, because the Nizari reputedly smoked hashish before engaging in acts of terror. Their primary goal was to purify Islam. They inflicted relatively few casualties, although in their heyday they posed a serious threat to the governments of the Seljuk Empire in Persia and the Levant. The account written by Marco Polo in the thirteenth century describes what many present-day Islamic suicide bombers think will be their ultimate heavenly reward. Speaking of the Assassin chief, Polo wrote,

> The King had caused a certain valley between two
> mountains to be enclosed, and had turned it into a garden,
> the largest and most beautiful that ever was seen flowing
> freely with wine and milk and honey and water; and
> numbers of ladies and of the most beautiful damsels in the
> world, who could play on all manner of instruments and
> sung most sweetly, and danced in a manner that it was
> charming to behold. For the Old Man desired to make his

people believe that this was actually Paradise … So when the Old Man would have any Prince slain, he would say to such a youth: "Go thou and slay So and So; and when thou returnest, my Angels shall bear thee into Paradise. And should'st thou die nevertheless even so, I will send my Angels to carry thee back into Paradise." And in this manner the Old One got his people to murder any one whom he desired to get rid of.[4]

From 1090 to 1256 AD, the Assassins terrorized all who opposed them, killing grand viziers, ministers, and kings, and even attacking the Muslim hero Salah ad-Din. They battled the forces of Genghis Khan during the Mongol invasions of the Middle East. To spread their notoriety, they attacked prominent victims at venerated holy sites and at the royal court. They struck on Muslim holy days when crowds were present to maximize the publicity. Lewis explains that their weapon was "always a dagger, never poison, never a missile … and the Assassin usually made no attempt to escape; there was even a suggestion that to survive the mission was shameful."[5]

The Assassins' goal was to return the Islamic community of believers (*umma*) into a single community, as had been the case under the first four rightfully guided caliphs, the successors to the Prophet, in the seventh century. By the twelfth century there were several centers of Islamic thought and devotion, which had been split apart by war and successive invasions. These splinters gave rise to different schools of Islamic jurisprudence and different interpretations of the faith, which pitted Muslims against other Muslims. The Assassins rebelled against the existing political order and sought to establish their own, one that would consist of a series of mountain fortresses and city states. To facilitate cooperation among the states, they established a network of supporting cells in sympathetic neighboring urban centers.

We can draw many parallels between the Assassins and contemporary Islamic fundamentalist groups that employ terror. Like the Assassins, many of the current movements indoctrinate their followers at an early age and rely upon adherents' dedication to charismatic leaders. Like the Assassins, Al Qaeda leaders Osama bin Laden and Ayman Al Zawahiri call for a restoration of the Muslim caliphate and unification of Islam against the nonbelievers. Like the Assassins, Al Qaeda and its offshoot organizations allege that Islam is surrounded by hostile neighbors and under attack and thus they must use any means necessary to fend off the apostates who would undermine their goal of a united community of believers.

Although there are many early examples of using violence to terrorize a population, the first modern suicide bombers, as far as we know, were the Japanese kamikaze pilots of World War II. Beginning in November 1944, young university-educated men used their bodies and their planes to attack the American fleet in the Pacific, especially targeting aircraft carriers and battleships.

Admiral Takijiro Onishi had asked the young men to volunteer for a "special attack" (*tokkotai*) meaning: transcending life and death. Onishi commanded the first squadron, known as *Shinpu Tokubetsu Kogekitai*. His reasoning was that Japan was nearly defeated, short of resources, and had nothing to lose by sending its young pilots on cost-effective suicide missions in the hope of deterring the enemy. Onishi explained that "if they [the pilots] are on land, they would be bombed down, and if they are in the air, they would be shot down. That's sad ... Too sad ... To let the young men die beautifully, that's what *tokkotai* is. To give a beautiful death, that's called sympathy."[6]

In a letter to his parents, Second Lieutenant Shigeyuki Suzuki explained his reasons for volunteering for a kamikaze mission:

People say that our feeling is one of resignation, but they do not understand at all how we feel, and think of us as a fish about to be cooked. Young blood flows in us. There are persons we love, we think of, and many unforgettable memories. However, with those, we cannot win the war ... To let this beautiful Japan keep growing, to be released from the wicked hands of the Americans and British, and to build a "free Asia" was our goal from the Gakuto Shutsujin year before last; yet nothing has changed ... The great day that we can directly be in contact with the battle is our day of happiness and at the same time, the memorial of our death.[7]

In the Battle of Okinawa, from April to June 1945, more than two thousand kamikaze pilots rammed fully fueled fighter planes into more than three hundred ships, killing five thousand Americans in the most costly naval battle in U.S. history.[8] Researcher Peter Hill found that only a minority of the kamikazes actually hit their targets. The Allied fleets deployed radar ships to spot the enemy planes, after which they bombarded them with antiaircraft fire. The Allies also enjoyed air superiority.

Not everyone in the Japanese high command believed that kamikaze attacks were a good strategy. First, it was an extremely expensive tactic to use a trained pilot and his aircraft for a single attack. It conflicted with the basic military principle of inflicting maximum damage on the enemy with the minimum loss to one's own resources. Second, plane-crash attacks lacked sufficient penetrative power to strike a mortal blow to the American aircraft carriers. To be effective, the kamikaze had to strike when the decks were fully laden with aircraft. Third, it was enormously difficult to evaluate the success of missions because the pilots never returned and their commanders had every incentive to overestimate the gains achieved by their men's sacrifice.

Although Japanese pilots committed the vast majority of the kamikaze attacks, similar missions were conducted by other countries. In April 1945, Germany used planes to crash into bridges to impede the Soviet armies closing in on Berlin. The pilots were reported to have signed a declaration saying, "I am above all else clear that the mission will end in my death."[9] There were at least two incidents of American suicide attacks on Japanese ships, one during the battle of Coral Sea in May 1942, the second at Midway that June. In both cases, the planes were either out of fuel or too badly damaged to return to base .

The most significant factor leading to the kamikaze strategy was the fact that Japan could not win against the American juggernaut using conventional forces. The kamikaze attacks inspired terror throughout the American fleet and helped convince American military leaders to deploy nuclear weapons against this nation whose people were so dedicated and so unafraid of death.

However, an attack by a person in uniform against a military target such as a battleship during a declared state of hostilities does not easily fit the current definition of terrorism. The modern definition assumes that the targets are civilians and the perpetrators are non-state actors: terrorist acts are perpetrated by clandestine organizations or illegal groups that are not directly tied to the institutions of government (although they may have support emanating from other countries). According to the strictest interpretation of the term with its emphasis on civilian casualties, several of the most famous attacks against U.S. targets would not constitute acts of terror. The 1983 attack against the U.S. Marine barracks in Lebanon, the attack in 2000 against the USS *Cole* in Yemen, and, to a lesser extent, the attack against the Pentagon on 9/11, all targeted military rather than civilian personnel.

Although there were instances of political violence to overthrow governments and assassinate world leaders from the seventeenth century on (for example, Guy Fawkes's attempt to kill King James I and blow up the British parliament in 1605), the concept of terror as a systematic use of violence to attain political ends was first codified by Maximilien Robespierre during the French Revolution. Robespierre deemed *le terreur* to be the "emanation of virtue" that delivered "prompt, severe, and inflexible" justice as "a consequence of the general principle of democracy applied to our country's most pressing needs."[10] The Reign of Terror, a period of violence that lasted for one year between 1793 and 1794, represented the internecine conflicts between two political foes, the Jacobins and the Girondins, and was punctuated by mass executions of so-called enemies of the Revolution. The more extremist Jacobins exterminated thousands of potential enemies, regardless of their sex, age, or condition, in a battle between competing ideologies.

Our understanding of terrorism has shifted since the French Revolution to mean the deliberate targeting of civilians by non-state agents intending to cause fear and panic and so bring about political change. The U.S. State Department acknowledges, however, that there is no single definition of terrorism. It uses the term to mean premeditated, politically motivated violence perpetrated against noncombatant targets by subnational groups or clandestine agents, usually intended to influence an audience. "International terrorism" means terrorism involving citizens or the territory of more than one country. In their definitions, scholars tend to place more emphasis on terrorists' intention to inspire fear among a target audience; the aim of persuasion transcends the harm caused to the immediate victims.[11]

All of this is to say that, in effect, there is no clear agreement on exactly what terrorism is. Each organization and institution has its own definition, which tends, not surprisingly, to ensure that any attack against it counts as terrorism. The military does not emphasize that the victims have to be civilian, and business definitions do not suggest that an act of terror has to be purely political. By one recent count, there were in excess of 110 different definitions of terrorism and no clear consensus by international legal agencies about which was correct.

For members of anarchist political groups in the nineteenth century, being called a terrorist was a badge of honor. In 1901, anarchists assassinated American president William McKinley. His successor, Teddy Roosevelt, vowed to exterminate terrorism everywhere. He proposed deporting all anarchists back to their countries of origin, although many had not committed crimes and were opposed to terror. In 1919, President Woodrow Wilson authorized Attorney General Palmer to round up all anarchists and ship them to the Soviet Union.[12]

The 1993 and 2001 attacks against the World Trade Center were certainly not the first (or second) occasions when New York's Financial District was targeted. Another anarchist, Mario Buda, blew up a wagon full of explosives there on September 16, 1920. The dynamite-laden wagon passed by lunchtime crowds and stopped across the street from the headquarters of the J.P. Morgan bank at 23 Wall Street, on the Financial District's busiest corner. Its cargo, 100 pounds (45 kg) of dynamite with 500 pounds (230 kg) of heavy, cast-iron sash weights, exploded in a timer-triggered detonation that sent thousands of slugs tearing through the air.[13] The horse and wagon were blasted into small fragments.[14] Forty people were killed and two hundred injured. There was immediate panic and a national emergency was declared. Capitalism survived but it was widely assumed that President Wilson's roundup of anarchists was the motivation behind the blast.

According to UCLA professor David C. Rapoport, "The Russian writer Stepniak described the terrorist as 'noble, terrible, irresistibly fascinating, uniting the two sublimities of human grandeur, the martyr and the hero.' Dynamite, a recent invention, was the weapon of choice for the male terrorist, because it usually killed the person who threw the bomb also, demonstrating that he was not an ordinary criminal."[15] A successful terrorist had to know how to fight and how to die, and the most admirable death occurred after a court trial where he or she accepted responsibility, and used the occasion to indict the regime. One of the earliest anarchists, the Russian revolutionary Vera Zasulich, embraced the term "terrorist." At her trial she indignantly insisted that she was a terrorist, not a murderer. Such distinctions would be difficult to make today.

According to Rapoport, terrorism has changed significantly over the decades. The groups that have emerged and the goals they espouse have adapted to changing global circumstances and, often, to the changing nature of how states deal with them. Rapoport argues that four waves of terrorism have defined the modern world. The first wave began in the 1880s with the anarchists. The second wave, an anticolonial movement beginning in the 1920s and lasting through the 1960s, pitted many small and new states against their colonial masters to help shake off imperial rule. Some forty years later, the New Left wave married terrorism with communism and was particularly popular in Latin America. Finally, beginning in 1979 with the Iranian revolution, which provided both inspiration and, occasionally, funds, a religious wave fused terror with religious justifications for violence.

The anticolonial wave included a wide variety of groups and organizations that not only directed their attacks against the colonial masters at home but also, when they had the means to do so, took the violence to the countries of the imperialists. This wave was the most diverse in the ways it brought together wildly different organizations, ranging from Palestinian terrorist groups to the Huk rebellion in the Philippines and the Mau Mau uprising in Kenya. Some of the leaders of terror groups during the anti-colonial wave became legitimate leaders in their own right when that period ended. The transition from terrorist-cell leader to president or prime minister has resulted in confusion over who is a terrorist and who is a freedom fighter, a distinction that continues to plague our understanding of political violence. This is particularly evident when one considers that more former terrorist leaders than American presidents have won the Nobel Peace Prize.

Most terrorist organizations have understood their goals to be revolution, secession, or national self-determination. The principle that a people should govern itself was a legacy of the American and French revolutions; the concepts of self-determination and national identity played key roles in both upheavals. Later, President Wilson's Fourteen Points, his hoped-for outcome of World War I, emphasized the right of all peoples to self-determination and freedom from colonial rule. To this day, the heads of terrorist movements often see themselves as the future leaders of their people. But the terms "people" and "self-determination" can both be ambiguous.[16] The drive for self-determination may prompt leaders of terrorist movements to dream of a future in which they replace the current regime or government and transform the political landscape. However, this process requires that the population as a whole supports what the group does in its name.

Most terrorist organizations begin quite small, as a dedicated group of true believers, existing on the outer edges of society, who use violence to spread their message. They begin by engaging in criminal activity—drug-smuggling, bank-robbery, hostage-taking, and the like—to fill their war chests. Once they obtain the money to acquire more sophisticated weapons, they raise the stakes by challenging the government, their rivals, or the institutions of the state such as the army or the police. With every attack they launch, the organizations hope that the state will reveal its brutality. When governments overreact, this plays right into the terrorists' hands.

Many civilians die as a result of heavy-handed counter-terrorist responses, and those individuals who couldn't decide which side they were on initially begin to migrate toward the terrorist groups. Without the violent overreaction by the government forces, terrorist groups could not possibly hope to replenish the ranks of lost operatives.

For rebels seeking publicity or hoping to spread their message, terrorism, and suicide terrorism in particular, may succeed when traditional methods of insurgency fail. In a world in which, according to media lore, "if it bleeds it leads," terrorism bleeds a lot, and suicide terrorism even more so. However, most groups do not begin their campaigns against the state using suicide terrorism. There was no suicide terrorism in the first Chechen war. The first Palestinian intifada did not include suicide terrorism among the many clashes between Palestinians and Israelis. The first World Trade Center attack was a truck bomb, not a suicide mission. Suicide terrorism is frequently the option of last resort when groups are especially weak.

Even as a weapon of the weak, it remains a highly effective tactic for terrorist groups seeking publicity or hoping to cause a high number of casualties on the other side. It is effective because it is extremely difficult to guard against an attack by someone so completely dedicated to a cause that he or she is willing to sacrifice his or her life. The suicide bomber is the ultimate smart bomb, a thinking and breathing missile that can change directions, cross a street, or delay detonation depending on the circumstances. While most terrorist attacks require extensive planning, both for the operation itself and for the safe retreat of the attacker, the suicide attack requires only half as much forethought. The attacker does not expect to survive and, in fact, the success of the attack is defined in part by his or her death. While there is a lively debate about whether terrorists ever really achieve their goals of independence or of putting an end to the presence of foreign troops, part of the goal of terrorist leaders is to terrify large numbers of people by killing only a handful.

In recent years, the goal of killing a few to terrorize many has been replaced by some of the messianic terrorist organizations with a new goal of killing as many people as possible. In the minds of groups that believe in the end of days, the violence they wreak will help expedite the end they look forward to. Groups like the Aum Shinrikyo in Japan and several of the radical Salafi groups advocate huge numbers of casualties for every operation. These groups seek and use weapons of mass destruction. The Salafi groups—which experts say encompass some of the deadliest organizations today, including Al Qaeda, Hamas, and the violent splinter groups from the Muslim Brotherhood (*al Ikhwan al Muslimun*)—aim to re-create the perfection of the early Islamic period. Salafism is associated with the beliefs of Wahhabism (fundamentalism in Saudi Arabia) and fundamentalist interpretations of Islam throughout the Islamic world. Such groups advocate the use of violence and emphasize the smaller jihad against the nonbeliever over the more important and larger jihad within each individual. Salafism differs from Islamism in that it rejects any Western ideologies or constructs such as consti-tutions, political parties, and elections, which Islamists support (as long as Islamic parties benefit).

It is also important to distinguish between the defensive and offensive jihad. According to political scientist Nelly Lahoud, the ideological engine that drives jihadis is the belief that they are engaged in defensive, not offensive, jihad; the defensive nature of the battle today makes jihad lawful. More to the point, during defensive jihad it is every (emphasis on "every") Muslim's individual duty (*fard 'ayn*) to participate. Based on the opinions advanced by the classical/medieval Islamic jurists, Palestinian jihadi 'Abdallah Azzam concluded that the classical defensive doctrine of jihad applies today. Thus he was able first to rally Arabs to volunteer for jihad in Afghanistan against the Soviets and then to pave the way for the foundation of Al Qaeda. Azzam argued that when the land of Islam is invaded, jihad is required for every Muslim, and the need "to seek permission" (from parents, husbands, or authorities) becomes void. Accordingly, "a son is permitted to go out to fight without his father's permission, *a wife without her husband's*, and he who is in debt without his creditor's [italics added for emphasis]."[28]

WOMEN WHO BLOW THEMSELVES UP

Female suicide bombers are even more effective than men for a variety of reasons. At least until recently, their use as operatives has been completely unexpected. Soldiers and security personnel have been guided by profiles and stereotypes of terrorists as men. Terrorist organizations have deliberately used these preconceptions to their advantage by employing operatives who do not fit the conventional profile. They widened the field in which they look for volunteers, and found them among women and even children. Israel's restrictive checkpoints and closely monitored borders proved fairly effective against Palestinian insurgent organizations inside the Occupied Territories in the past. Since the mid-1990s, it has been almost impossible for unmarried men under the age of forty to get travel permits to cross the border into Israel—even if they are sick, wounded, or riding in an ambulance. However, women don't arouse suspicion the way men do, and blend in more effectively with Israeli citizens. The use of the least likely suspect is the most likely tactical adaptation for a terrorist group under scrutiny.[18]

Attacks perpetrated by women have tended to be especially successful where the terrorist planners needed the perpetrator to blend in with the Israeli "street." These female terrorists Westernize their appearance, adopting modern hairstyles and short skirts.[19] For attacking civilians, the best possible operative is one who resembles the target. Alternatively, when the women are not trying to blend into Israeli society by wearing midriff-baring halter tops and short skirts, the conservative loose, billowing clothing that many women wear in the Middle East and South Asia is perfect for concealing the IED. When women strap the explosives around their midsection, the bulge often gives the impression of late-term pregnancy, lulling security forces into thinking they are harmless expectant mothers. When the military or members of the security forces invasively search women at checkpoints, however, their action outrages the population, who feel that their women are being harassed and abused by foreigners. This feeds the propaganda machine that urges men to step up and help protect their women's honor.

Women bombers also tend to be more successful than men. They have higher kill rates and can penetrate the target more deeply than many men, who might get stopped at the entrance of a bus or restaurant. The ability to get deep inside a location increases the effectiveness both of the explosive materials and of the shrapnel packed into the IED. A bomb exploding in a confined space eliminates much of the oxygen, which is consumed as the incendiary device explodes. In essence, the deeper the bomber can get into a room or inside a bus or train, the more violently the enclosure will implode. "Suicide attacks are done for effect, and the more dramatic the effect, the stronger the message; thus a potential interest on the part of some groups in recruiting women."[20] A growing number of insurgent organizations have adopted suicide bombing, not only because of its superiority over traditional guerrilla warfare but also because it garners significant media attention, especially when perpetrated by women and young girls.

Young women who combat Israel by blowing up their bodies generate a powerful symbol that creates publicity throughout the world. The image of women defying tradition to sacrifice their lives for the Palestinian cause has drawn international attention to the despair of the Palestinian people. On average, an attack perpetrated by a woman gets eight times as much press attention as a similar attack by a man. The Al Aqsa Martyrs' Brigades has drawn propaganda mileage from their female bombers. This tactic also makes them appear more dangerous because it has erased the barriers between combatants and noncombatants, terrorists and innocent civilians.

The female suicide bomber is not a recent or new phenomenon. The first terrorist who killed herself while trying to kill others was Dalal Al Maghribi, a female commander of the Palestinian resistance movement Fatah. Dalal hijacked a bus in 1978 and killed herself and thirty-six passengers on the Jerusalem–Tel Aviv road. Her mode of attack was so novel that it was not recognized as a tactic of "suicide terrorism" at the time. Only in retrospect, after suicide bombings became relatively common, was Al Maghribi's martyrdom seen by some to belong in this category. Technically, the tactic was only invented on November 10, 1980, when Hossein Fahmideh, a thirteen-year-old member of the Iranian People's Army (Basiji) used his booby-trapped body to blow up an Iraqi tank.[21]

By most accounts, the first official female suicide bomber was a seventeen-year-old Lebanese girl, Sana'a Mehaydali, who was sent by the Syrian Socialist National Party (the SSNP or PPS), a secular, pro-Syrian Lebanese organization, to blow herself up near an Israeli convoy in Lebanon in April 1985. Women took part in twelve of the suicide attacks conducted by the SSNP during the 1980s. From Lebanon, the phenomenon of female bombers spread to other countries—from Sri Lanka to Turkey, Chechnya, Israel, and, most recently, Iraq and Afghanistan.

There has been a significant public-relations payoff and financial benefit to sending, for example, eighteen-year-old Ayat Akras into the Kiryat HaYovel supermarket in Jerusalem to set off a bomb.[22] The underlying message conveyed by female bombers is: terrorism is no longer a fringe phenomenon and the insurgents are all around you. Akras's death demonstrated that the Palestinian militant groups were not all composed of religious fanatics who believed that they would be granted entrance to paradise or that God would reward them with seventy-two virgins (*houris*). Nor are the organizations' leaders gripped by a burning desire to see all women locked behind black veils. This is a political war, not a religious war, and the suicide bombings are being carefully planned and executed as part of a precise political strategy.[23]

MAKING SENSE OF SENSELESS ACTS

Even terrorist organizations have a rationally calculated strategy when they plan attacks and campaigns against their enemies. Modern armies have at their disposal arsenals and trained cadres of military recruits. States can call upon stores of weapons and destroy their enemies on the battlefield. Terrorist organizations, however, rarely have access to the same kinds of firepower as states and thus must adapt their strategies to account for this imbalance. The use of terrorism and suicide terrorism can be considered an example of the law of comparative advantage. In modern states where the technology is available, states can take a high-tech approach to war. Most terrorist organizations, however, have few resources besides cheap labor and dedicated individuals willing to die for the cause. In the words of Ahmad Yassin, the founder of Hamas, the militant Islamic organization that has perpetrated hundreds of attacks inside Israel: "Once we have warplanes and missiles, then we can think of changing our means of legitimate self-defense. But right now, we can only tackle the fire with our bare hands and sacrifice ourselves."[24]

When conventional military strategies are not available or fail, the rebels resort to guerrilla warfare; when guerrilla war fails, they resort to terror; when traditional methods of terror fail, they resort to suicide terrorism and acts of increasing barbarism against their enemies. In all the cases examined in this book, a group (or groups) is fighting against an overwhelmingly powerful enemy and has no choice but to resort to terrorism if it is to continue its struggle. Even so, much of the success of terrorism hinges on whether the larger community that the terrorists say they represent approves of or rejects the use of violence.

If their own community supports and appreciates the blood-shed, we will see a literal explosion of violence and of groups that use terror to compete for the public's attention and approval. However, if the public rejects violence, or if the terrorists go too far and kill too many civilians or too many members of their own community, the groups will have to switch gears. This has been the case in Spain, where Euskadi Ta Askatasuna (or ETA, meaning roughly "Basque Homeland and Freedom") attacks ended in so many civilian casualties that the organization implemented new operating procedures in which it promised it would give advance warning before detonating a bomb. This was also true of the Provisional Irish Republican Army (PIRA), which tried unsuccess-fully to implement a homicidal car-bomb campaign in the spring of 1990, only to have hundreds of staunch supporters accuse the organization of making them look like those "fanatics" in the Middle East. The PIRA faux suicide-car-bomb campaign began and ended on the same day; when the leadership realized that using such extreme tactics would alienate their base, they went back to using traditional car bombs that allowed the driver to escape with his life.

Inasmuch as the population can demand that even terrorist leaders demonstrate restraint, the population can also be the driving force behind increasing violence against the state and its constitu-ents. Not all civilians will reject civilian casualties on the other side.

If during the course of fighting a war on terror, the government demonstrates its sheer disregard for the other side and sacrifices civilian lives in the pursuit of the terrorists, the propaganda by terrorist leaders begins to resonate with the population upon whose support the insurgent group relies. When the government targets enemy civilians in aerial bombardments or uses helicopter gunships or drones, the civilians on the other side become legitimate targets. In interviews for my previous book, *Dying to Kill*, many Palestinians said, in effect, "If our civilians are not safe from harm, neither will Israel's civilians be safe." Thus any state or government fighting a war on terror must remember that its actions have consequences and that if its actions are unrestrained, the terrorists' will be too.

Just as terrorists adhere to a logic that grows out of their situation, so too does the state—acting to suppress or destroy the rebel movement—develop a rationale to justify its actions. This rationale may be as simple as a democratic state using legitimate force to eliminate an insurgency. The state may identify the rebel forces as foreign, or as members of a race they want to eliminate, sequester, or assimilate into the population. The relative freedom that the state enjoys in pursuing its policy of oppression varies according to a number of factors, including democratic accountability, sensitivity to international opinion, transparency to scrutiny, and the power of the ideology driving the action.

The case studies that follow tend to show that the ferocity of the oppression provokes a reaction from the terrorists more or less equal in ferocity. For example, in May 2009, the government of Sri Lanka used brutal force to eradicate the Liberation Tigers of Tamil Eelam (LTTE). The international community alleged that the government had perpetrated massive human rights abuses and that thousands of innocent civilians were caught in the crossfire. The Sri Lankan air force bombarded villages suspected of LTTE support, and thousands of women and children who were not members of the terrorist groups perished in the process. In the aftermath of the violence, Amnesty International, Doctors Without Borders, the Red Cross, the International Crisis Group, Human Rights Watch Asia, and scores of other NGOs called for an international investigation into alleged war crimes. The government of President Mahinda Rajapaksa refused, and limited international access to the region. For the government, this was how to end the scourge of terrorism. The cases in this book argue the opposite: terrorism does not end with the barrel of a gun; rather, this kind of state brutality gives rise to new generations vowing to fight again in the near and distant future.

Modern military technology provides the state with mobility (helicopters, tanks, planes, forward-operating bases); an extraordinary surveillance capability (satellites, unmanned drones, video, night vision); and overwhelming firepower. The state is also likely to control or have considerable influence over the media, therefore determining the level of support the policy of oppression enjoys. The terrorist has a range of options in attempting to counteract the state's advantages. These include attempts to influence public opinion by use, say, of the Internet or other new media (Twitter, Facebook, etc). They also include sniper attacks, acts of sabotage, ambushes, and bombings. In dire conditions, the terrorist may rationally conclude that he or she can strike a blow against the state only by giving up all hope of escape. In this sense, if the terrorist is sufficiently motivated, the suicide mission appears to be a rational choice. More often than not, suicide terrorism is a tactic of last resort. It is rarely the first choice for insurgent organizations; after all, the cost of suicide terrorism may be the loss of the best and the brightest of their supporters. It is also a tactic of weakness. Like the kamikaze attacks of World War II, the tactic appears rational only when all other options have failed. Under such conditions, the organizations create mechanisms and manipulate cultural mores to justify suicide (which might be contrary to their religious beliefs), and use intense propaganda and indoctrination to convince their populations that they have more to offer when dead than alive.

The logic of terror and oppression drives the terrorists to action and shapes the form of their reaction. But the actual motivation of individuals in specific cases is enormously complex. These motivations can be viewed on a continuum ranging from positive to negative. The strongest positive motivation is *belief in a cause*. In Northern Ireland, the goal was home rule; in Palestine, a separate independent state; in Sri Lanka, an independent Tamil homeland. Those committed to the cause believe in it utterly. These true believers are willing to pay any price to accomplish their goals.

A *history*—incidents of abuse, injustice, pogroms, all manner of grievances, heroic acts, and so on—feeds into belief in the cause. For Palestinians, the Sabra and Shatilla massacres and the First and Second intifadas form part of a history of grievance at the hands of the Israelis. For the Tamils, the memories of the pogroms in 1983, in which thousands of Tamils died, and, more recently, the 2009 war crimes perpetrated against them, constitute an inspirational record of abuse. For Chechens, the history includes distant memories of Stalin's purges and expulsions from their homeland during which tens of thousands perished, as well as more recent instances of violent oppression. For the Irish Republicans, the memories of Bloody Sunday and the hunger strikers inspired generations willing to die for the cause.

Terrorists and potential terrorists are often pressured into action by their peers and by *shared experiences*, including shared humiliation at the hands of their enemies. Many Palestinian men recall the humiliation of their fathers at checkpoints as the precise moment when they decided to join a militant organization. The shared experience of military occupation has increased the degree to which terrorist messages and propaganda resonate with the community. Although not every person under occupation joins the terrorists, the shared humiliation often means that the terrorists enjoy widespread support in their operations against the occupying forces.

Knowledge of and admiration for a pantheon of *heroes and martyrs* is a factor motivating many recruits to radical political movements. The Tamil Tigers published booklets featuring those who had given their lives as suicide bombers, dying for the vision of liberation and self-rule.[25] The Palestinians have produced trading cards with the likenesses of martyrs on them; children trade them like baseball cards in the streets of Jenin. In Northern Ireland, Sinn Féin, the political arm of the Provisional Irish Republican Army, distributed playing cards with photos of well-known Irish martyrs, hunger strikers, and those shot down in cold blood by the British security services. Murals along the Falls Road in Belfast were covered with their images and conveyed the message to never forget those who had sacrificed their lives for others' sake. In the same spirit, charismatic leaders may provoke and embolden their followers into action. Osama bin Laden is a hero to his Muslim followers in the Middle East. Until his death in May 2009, Velupillai Prabhakaran was a cult-like leader among Tamils. Hunger striker Bobby Sands was elected to parliament while he lay starving himself to death in a prison outside Belfast. Across regions and countries, the ability to inspire young people to take their own lives requires charismatic leaders who embody the cause and the fighting qualities of their supporters.

Institutions such as schools, camps, and prisons play a role in indoctrinating would-be fighters. The *culture of martyrdom* plays a causal role in the terrorist groups' ability to "market martyrdom."[26] Instead of posters of Michael Jordan, Ronaldo, or Jim Morrison on their walls, young Palestinian boys place posters of martyrs like Yahya Ayyash or famous suicide bombers like Muhammed

Siddique Khan. The young girls cover their walls with photos of Wafa Idris, the first known Palestinian female suicide bomber. Terrorist organizations name parks and streets after the bombers, making those they are named for far more famous in death than they would have been in life. It is a powerful lure for young people who want to make a difference. In this book you will see how at least one young Iraqi girl, Raniya Ibrahim Mutlaq (Mutleg), who wanted to grow up and become a doctor, was convinced by her extended family that she could do far more as a suicide bomber.

Family traditions, family relationships, and marriage ties preserve memories and provide moral comfort to fighters. These family traditions mean that women are often under intense family pressure to participate in clandestine activities. More often than not, women are involved in a variety of capacities, as couriers or recruiters, and occasionally, they become frontline fighters in the war. Family traditions have also meant that women can be manipulated under current codes of conduct to engage in violence.

Willing participation shades into *coercion*—family and peer pressure exerted with menace or the threat of ostracism. Not all women who participate in terrorism are coerced into it. When families join as a unit, the women can be just as ardent as the men in their lives. However, if the women are specifically targeted for abuse by the security forces or by their own people, they can be shamed into participating in terrorist violence.

In some societies, and in extreme circumstances, there is no question that women are coerced into undertaking suicide missions. When women in traditional societies violate (or are thought to have violated) the rules which govern their sexual behavior, or when they are compromised against their will, becoming a suicide bomber might seem to be a rational choice. Several women involved in terrorism joined because of an illicit love affair gone bad, or because they refused to marry the men chosen for them in an arranged marriage, or because they had cheated on their husbands, or had a child out of wedlock. In one case, a woman's inability to have a child meant that her husband left her and she became a pariah in her community. There are many ways in which women can be seen to bring shame to their families, while there may be only one way to restore pride after they have transgressed—by making the ultimate sacrifice.

In too many cases of women's involvement, the woman has been *abused, victimized, or targeted* in ways that leave her little choice but to join the terrorists in hope of reclaiming her honor. For the Tamil women raped at government checkpoints, their future marriage options disappear. For Iraqi women raped either by soldiers of the occupation or by members of the Ansar Al Sunnah terrorist group, there is no way to escape death at the hands of their family for violating the honor code. By becoming suicide bombers, they manage to reinvent themselves in one fell swoop. With one act of violence they go from being a source of family shame to a source of family pride.

NOT THE WEAKER SEX

In this book, we look at what has driven women to participate in terrorist activities as members of terrorist organizations. And then we look specifically at what has driven women to participate in suicide missions. In the following chapters I introduce the reader to several women and examine in detail how they came to be terrorists and what motivated them to kill. Some of the women have changed their worldviews while others remain as radicalized as they ever were. The women are members of terrorist organizations around the world. They have been plotters, propagandists, and pawns as well as, in some cases, suicide bombers.

Historically, the Provisional Irish Republican Army was a male-dominated organization. Nevertheless, Irish women played a crucial role in planting bombs and in luring British soldiers to their deaths, and even as hunger strikers. Women have been instrumental in Chechen terrorist organizations, especially the Riyadus Salikheen, the Martyrs' Brigade, which has been responsible for attacks in Moscow and Dagestan. The Chechen Black Widows have often been victimized and coerced into becoming bombers, and only a few have willingly blown themselves up for the cause. The Islamic Revival Movement, Hamas, is a traditional and conservative terrorist organization operating in Israel, the West Bank, and Gaza. One would not expect a woman to be among its most important operatives and yet this book introduces you to Ahlam at-Tamimi, a Hamas planner responsible for one of the deadliest attacks in Israel's history. Her rise to prominence and ability to influence others shows beyond a shadow of a doubt that women are not the weaker sex or inherently more peaceful than their male counterparts. Among the Liberation Tigers of Tamil Eelam, women were some of the most experienced fighting units and even constituted their own suicide squad, the Suthanthirap Paravaikal, or Freedom Birds. Women were involved in more than half of the LTTE suicide attacks and successfully killed presidents and prime ministers.

Finally, the book introduces you to the women of Al Qaeda. While international attention has focused on Osama bin Laden and Ayman Al Zawahiri, a new generation of women is emerging to help ensure the group's survival after all the drones and missiles have attacked the current leadership. The women of Al Qaeda, some operating in Europe and the United States, use the Internet to radicalize and recruit scores of male jihadis and send them to their deaths.

Women's participation in terrorism may be a natural progression from their involvement in the radical and revolutionary struggles of the past. The women of the nineteenth-century Russian terror group Narodnaya Volya were considered more willing to die than their male comrades.[27] Women in radical organizations have engaged in anticolonial and revolutionary struggles in the Third World for decades. Beginning in 1968, women became involved in all manner of terrorist groups, from Marxist organizations in Europe to nationalist movements in the Middle East. Female terrorists came from all parts of the globe and from all walks of society—they were part of Italy's Red Brigades, Germany's Baader-Meinhof group, the American Black Panthers and Weathermen, and the Japanese Red Army; occasionally they were leaders in their own right. Women also played essential roles in several Middle Eastern conflicts, notably the Algerian Revolution (1958–62), the Iranian Revolution (1979), the First Lebanon War (1982), the First Palestinian Intifada (1987–91), and the Second or Al 'Aqsa Intifada (since 2000).

Forty years of research on terrorism has revealed little about what motivates men and women to commit acts of terror. The majority of books portray women as the victims of terror,[28] and only a handful have examined women as the perpetrators. The books perpetuate the stereotype of women as mere pawns or victims. After an attack by a female operative, terrorism experts, journalists, psychologists, and analysts frequently develop a so-called psychological autopsy, examining where the perpetrator grew up, where she went to school, and what went wrong to make her turn to violence.

The media fetishizes female terrorists. This contributes to the belief that there is something really unique, something *just not right* about the women who kill. We make assumptions about what these women think, why they do what they do, and what ultimately motivates them. Women involved in terrorist violence are demonized more than male terrorists. One former bomber told me that the enemy was so angry that women were involved in the organization that they would humiliate the female fighters more than their male counterparts just to teach them a lesson.[29] For men in certain traditional societies, having women flout their authority, let alone defeat them in battle, is intolerable. After all, perpetrating acts that cause wanton destruction, death, and disorder seems incompatible with the traditional stereotype of what is expected of women—to be nurturing, caring figures who provide stability. The common assumption is that female terrorists must be even *more* depressed, *crazier*, *more* suicidal, or *more* psychopathic than their male counterparts. This runs contrary to the view of British journalist Eileen MacDonald, who found that women revolutionaries have stronger characters, more power, more energy, and are far more pragmatic than their male counterparts.[30]

Regardless of their initial motivation, what we know for a fact is that women are now more essential to terrorist organizations than ever before. The "exploding womb" has replaced the "revolutionary womb" that produced and supported young extremists in the past. Leaders of terrorist movements routinely make cost-benefit calculations to select the most effective tactics, targets, and operatives. Their analysis has shown that women are deadly.

2

THE BLACK WIDOW BOMBERS

And we will take with us the lives of hundreds of sinners. If we die, others will come/follow us—our brothers and sisters who are willing to sacrifice their lives (in God's way) to liberate their nation ... We are more keen on dying than you are on living.

—Chechen videotape delivered to Al Jazeera, October 21, 2002[1]

I guarantee you and guarantee all the Russians who send and support all those special services, which are sent here and commit ... atrocities—your bandit groups are on our territory of the Caucasus— this is not the last operation. These operations will continue. They will continue on your territory, insh'Allah.

—Dokku Umarov, in his YouTube video statement after the March 29, 2009, Moscow subway bombings[2]

THE CHECHEN WARS

Chechnya had always been a desolate backwater in the northern Caucasus, the mountain range that forms the geographical divide between Europe and Asia. The mountains average 10,000 feet above sea level and stretch 650 miles from the Caspian to the Black Sea. This rugged terrain is made all the more formidable by the steepness of the mountains' craggy slopes. A number of peoples and tribes have populated the region, including the Avars, Tatars, Kabardians, Laks, Khazars, Ossetians, Alans, and the Vainakh. Their relative isolation has insulated them from outside authority and influence.

The Chechen people, historically called the Vainakh, have always resisted outsiders, be they from Persia, Saint Petersburg, Constantinople, or, more recently, Moscow. Invasions and attempted invasions by the Romans, Mongols, Ottoman Turks, and Russians were all repulsed. At the same time, the region was subjected to generation after generation of neglect and, on occasion, attempted ethnic cleansing campaigns. Violence has been an integral part of its history.

The Chechens converted from the pagan Vainakh religion to Islam and developed unique Sufi Naqshbandi traditions insulated from both Mother Russia's Orthodox Christian influence and the urban centers of Islamic jurisprudence (*fiqh*). Their ancient customary laws (*adat*), differed from tribe to tribe. Many Chechen traditions violated the basic tenets of Islamic faith. They stored wine jars in their villages (*aouls*) despite Islam's prohibition against alcohol, and rarely paid their tithes (*zakat*) or went on the pilgrimage to Mecca (the *hajj*). It was only in very recent times that the strictest interpretations of Islamic Wahhabi thought and Salafi traditions took hold, as Saudi Arabia poured men and resources into the area.

The region was first subjected to Russian domination by Grozny Ivan (Ivan the Terrible) in 1559. Chechen resistance can be traced to 1732, when Russian colonial forces were defeated in the village of Chechen-aoul by the Noxche tribe. In 1783, Catherine the Great, then seventy, sent her twenty-five-year-old lover, Prince Platon Zubov, to conquer the region as part of a campaign to convert all the Muslims in the Caucasus to the Christian faith.

Prince Zubov described the Chechens as having a particular "enthusiasm for brigandage and predatory behavior, a lust for robbery and murder, perfidy, a martial sprit, determination, savageness, fearlessness, and unbridled insolence."[3] Catherine looked on them as a barbaric people whom she could subjugate by controlling Georgia to the south. The region was annexed to the empire in 1859. However, the first great Chechen Islamic leaders, Sheikh Mansour and, later, Imam Shamil, emerged during the Caucasian wars of 1817–64 and united the disparate tribes. Shamil's conflict with the Russians, remembered as the Jihad of Imam Shamil, set the tone for future waves of Chechen resistance.[4] Shamil's Muslim warriors (*murids*) preferred death to defeat; no *murid* was ever taken alive.[5] When Chechen women in cliff-top villages perceived that defeat and capture were imminent, they reputedly threw their children over the precipice and jumped after them.[6]

According to Harvard professor Richard Pipes:

The Chechens ... were always, from the Russian point of view, a troublesome element. Unassimilable and warlike, they created so much difficulty for the Russian forces trying to subdue the North Caucasus that, after conquering the area, the government felt compelled to employ Cossack forces to expel them from the valleys and lowlands into the bare mountain regions. There, faced by Cossack settlements on one side, and wild peaks on the other, they lived in abject poverty tending sheep and waiting for the day when they could wreak revenge on the newcomers and regain their lost lands.[7]

During the Russian Revolution, Chechens fought on both the Bolshevik and Menshevik sides and, once Lenin and his gang prevailed, select Chechens were co-opted into the Communist

Party. The Chechen autonomous province (*oblast*) was established in 1922 and Chechnya and neighboring Ingushetia were made autonomous Soviet republics in 1936. However, during World War II, German troops occupied Chechnya in 1943 and 1944, and Chechen leaders allegedly collaborated with the Nazis.[8]

Stalin used the charge of collaboration as justification for dissolving the Chechen-Ingush autonomous republic in 1944 and in what can only be described as ethnic cleansing, three-quarters of the Chechen population (more than a half-million people) were rounded up and physically removed from their homeland— deported in boxcars to Kazakhstan. Nearly half the deported Chechens (between one and two hundred thousand) perished en route; others were killed by Stalin's firing squads. Many of the survivors ended up as slave labor in the mines of Karaganda in Kazakhstan.[9] Survivors were finally allowed to return after Stalin's death in 1957.

It was against this historical backdrop that intense feelings of nationalism and xenophobia developed among the Chechens, reinforced by traditional tribal and family structures. The Chechen clan (*teip*) endured and perpetuated Chechen culture even under the direst circumstances. The *teip* system also bolstered the authority of tribal chiefs, headmen, and, within the family, fathers and husbands. A system of blood feuds (*kanli*) ensured that even the slightest transgression was never forgotten. No wrong could go unpunished and a vendetta culture developed. "The oral tradition abounds in tales of feuds sparked by the theft of a chicken, culminating in the death of an entire *teip*."[10] The young were trained rigorously in the art of warfare as honor and strength became highly prized. It was said, "No Chechen girl would consent to marry a man unless he had killed at least one Russian, could jump over a stream twenty-three feet wide, and over a rope held at shoulder-height between two men."[11]

With the dissolution of the USSR under Mikhail Gorbachev and the balkanization of the Russian empire, Chechnya followed Estonia, Latvia, and Lithuania in its quest for autonomy. Under the leadership of Dzhokhar Dudayev, the all-national congress of the Chechen people stormed a session of the Chechen-Ingush parliament with the aim of asserting independence. The Chechen nationalists pulled down the statue of Lenin in the main square in the capital city of Grozny, drove the KGB out, and threw the first secretary of the Communist Party, Vitaly Kutsenko, out of a third-story window. Dudayev declared Chechnya's independence in 1991. Unable to control the situation and end the violence in the region, Gorbachev's successor, Boris Yeltsin, declared a state of emergency on November 8, 1991.

Dudayev's support surged among Chechens while Yeltsin was criticized by all sides: Russian reformers accused him of going too far, conservatives of not going far enough. The average Russian was angered by stories of Chechen abuse of local Russians and saw Chechnya as a dangerous center of mafia activities. As ethnic Russians fled the region, the economy and industry suffered. In February 1994, Russia signed a treaty with Tatarstan affirming Russian sovereignty in exchange for domestic autonomy. Tatarstan had been the only republic other than Chechnya that had refused to sign the March 1992 federal treaty. Dudayev refused to enter into negotiations until Russia recognized Chechnya as an independent state.

Dudayev's erratic and authoritarian behavior, the severe economic slump, and increasing crime, corruption, and clan rivalry led to political infighting, attempted coups, countercoups, and mounting opposition to his leadership. He finally dissolved the Chechen parliament and introduced direct presidential rule. On November 29, 1992, Yeltsin issued an ultimatum to all the warring factions in Chechnya ordering them to immediately disarm and surrender. When the government in Grozny refused, the Russian president ordered his army to restore constitutional order by force.

In December 1994, Russia began aerial bombardment of Chechnya, including the capital city of Grozny. Russian forces assumed that every Chechen was the enemy and no one was spared. Thousands of civilians died as a result of carpet bombings and rocket artillery barrages. As civilian losses mounted, the Chechen population—even those opposed to Dudayev—became increasingly hostile to the Russian forces. Highly mobile units of Chechen fighters caused severe losses to Russia's demoralized troops. By summer 1996, the Chechen rebels had managed to split the Russian forces into a dozen isolated pockets. Over a period of one week, the rebels were able to fend off the Russian forces and send them fleeing.

The First Chechen War culminated in the Battle of Grozny, also known as Operation Jihad, in August 1996, a bloody siege in which more than 27,000 Chechen civilians died in the first five weeks (some estimates suggest the number exceeded 35,000, including 5,000 children). The bloodbath shocked Russians and the outside world, resulting in severe criticism of the war and waning domestic support among Russians. The total number of civilian deaths in the war is estimated to have been between 30,000 and 100,000, with as many as 200,000 more injured and more than 500,000 people displaced by the fighting. Yeltsin finally called for a ceasefire in 1996 and signed a peace treaty, the Khasav–Yurt Accord, the following year.

The peace agreement was short-lived. In August 1999, Yeltsin nominated Vladimir Putin, a relatively unknown former security service agent, to head the government. Shortly thereafter a series of bomb attacks destroyed several apartment blocks in Moscow and other Russian cities, claiming hundreds of victims. Although the perpetrators were never properly identified and there were many indications that the FSB was responsible, Putin used the bombings as an excuse to once again undertake a full-scale military mobilization against Chechnya. Appealing to Russian chauvinism, Putin's Unity Party swept into office on a wave of nationalist rhetoric and hyperbole.

In the period between the peace treaty and the resumption of hostilities, Chechnya had become the new focal point of the global jihad. As the Taliban consolidated their control of Kabul, many mujahideen fighters migrated to Chechnya, bringing with them the same techniques that had succeeded against the Russians in Afghanistan. Arms and money flowed to Chechnya as Arab mercenaries were integrated into the separatist units. Secular nationalists embraced Islam as a means of exploiting the new allies and resources. Warlords like Salman Raduyev and Arbi Barayev emerged in a region increasingly characterized by its lawlessness. Those Chechen groups not taking money from the jihadis engaged in campaigns of kidnapping and hostage-taking; more than 1,300 people were kidnapped and held for ransom. In August and September 1999, Chechen leader Shamil Basayev (in association with an Arab jihadi, Ibn Al Khattab) led two armies of two thousand Chechen, Dagestani, Arab, and international mujahideen and Wahhabi militants from Chechnya into the neighboring Republic of Dagestan and so precipitated the Second Chechen War.

Putin responded with massive aerial bombardments intended to wipe out the militants and flatten Grozny. The air campaign was followed by a new ground war. In the notorious *zachistka* (mopping-up) operations, Russian units would cordon off a village and prevent anyone from entering or leaving. In Chechnya, it was *normal* for people to disappear. The disappearances would take place either during the mopping-up operations or at the police checkpoints, which were set up on the roads leading in and out of every city. Over the course of several days, the Russians would violently interrogate Chechen civilians. Often the men and boys were killed and dumped in open pits that were subsequently blown up to obliterate all trace of the bodies.[12] The women who found themselves in police custody were vulnerable to sexual preda- tion.[13] Tens of thousands were arrested, tortured, or disappeared. According to the 2001 annual report by Amnesty International:

> There were frequent reports that Russian forces indiscrimi-
> nately bombed and shelled civilian areas. Chechen civilians,
> including medical personnel, continued to be the target of
> military attacks by Russian forces. Hundreds of Chechen
> civilians and prisoners of war were extra judicially executed.
> Journalists and independent monitors continued to be
> refused access to Chechnya. According to reports, Chechen
> fighters frequently threatened, and in some cases killed,
> members of the Russian-appointed civilian administration
> and executed Russian captured soldiers.[14]

The Chechens began to use suicide terrorism against govern- ment targets in 2000. Russian troops had been instructed to focus their attention on men between the ages of seventeen and forty, so Basayev opted to use female bombers. Two women, one aged twenty-two and the other sixteen, perpetrated the first attack, against Russian checkpoints. The twenty-two-year-old was Khava Barayeva, sister of the warlord Arbi Barayev, and soon to be a model for Chechen women and girls throughout the region. Basayev used women in several more operations, to great effect. At the outset his attacks were directed against Russian military and police but, as the conflict raged on, Basayev began to target civilians. In 1995 he took over a hospital in the Russian city of Budyonnovsk; in 2000 he attacked the Russian military base at Vedeno; and finally, he and his lieutenant, Arbi Barayev, began to hatch their most shocking plan to date: to target civilians in Moscow. The two men narrowed down possible targets: the Bolshoi Ballet, the Stage Theater, the Central House of Youth, and another theater, the Dubrovka House of Culture. They agreed that the Dubrovka was likely to have the most Russians (and fewest foreigners) in the audience, and so chose it as their target. Barayev did not get to put the plan into action, however; he was killed by Russian special forces in June 2001.

Notorious for his viciousness, Arbi Barayev was an inspiration to his twenty-five-year-old nephew, the rebel leader Movsar. Arbi boasted that he had personally killed more than 170 people while leading the Chechen Islamic Special Units and the Special Purpose Islamic Regiment (SPIR). He was infamous for shooting six members of the International Red Cross (ICRC) in 1996, and for beheading four foreign telecommunications workers—three British citizens and one New Zealander—in 1998. (Osama bin Laden allegedly paid Arbi thirty million dollars for the feat, outbidding by ten million the Russian police's offer for their safe return.)[15] To honor Arbi's memory, Movsar adopted his name and joined with Shamil Basayev to commemorate the first anniversary of his uncle's assassination in fitting fashion.

DUBROVKA: THE HOUSE OF CULTURE

The lights in Moscow's House of Culture flickered on and off to signal the end of intermission and the beginning of the second act. Ladies decked out in jewels and furs and men in designer suits hurried back to their seats as the orchestra readied the audience for Georgy Vasilyev's sold-out performance of the hit musical *The Two Captains*. The Nord Ost players took their places on the darkened stage. More than 850 people[16] eagerly awaited the play's conclusion. The musical was about love and intrigue during World War II. The elaborate set design and complicated staging had amazed critics: firecrackers and rockets boomed and a real aircraft landed onstage during every performance. It was a stereotypically Russian plot with singing bombers, dancing pilots, and folk music. There were few non-Russians and only a handful of foreigners in the audience.

Five minutes into the second act, an armed man appeared on the stage. This was the reborn Arbi Barayev, a.k.a. Movsar Suleimenov, and the AK–47 in his hands was no stage prop. He announced that he was taking the audience and the actors hostage. At first, many members of the audience assumed the armed man was part of the show. Their smiles faded as Barayev fired several shots into the air. A half-dozen terrorists had been seated in the orchestra; now they pulled black hoods and masks over their heads, drew machine guns from under the seats, and stood to join the other armed Chechen men and women—more than forty in total—who filtered into the crowd. The men wore fatigues and clutched automatic rifles in their hands. F–1 hand grenades dangled from their belts. The women switched out of their sweaters and jeans and covered themselves from head to toe in black Islamic veils and robes. All you could see were their kohl-lined eyes, the Makarov pistols in their hands, and the improvised explosive devices strapped to their bodies.

Onstage, Barayev said: "Take out your cell phones, call your friends and family, call the media and tell them that you have been taken hostage."[17] Then he told the captives to place their hands on top of their heads. Some people remained calm while others panicked. Several women began to cry and some even fainted. It was 9:05 P.M. Moscow time on October 23, 2002, and what would turn into a three-day siege had just begun.

The hostage-taking was originally scheduled for October 29. It was meant to be the culmination of a series of attacks, including car-bomb strikes on a McDonald's and the Russian Duma (parliament).[18] However, the explosives packed into the car (a Lada Tavria) parked outside the McDonald's on October 25 failed to cause sufficient damage to satisfy the rebels,[19] and the attack on the Duma fizzled out when the bomb failed to explode at all. Two more attacks, including one against the Moscow subway (which finally occurred in February 2004), were deferred. The arrest on October 22 of Aslan Murdalov, one of Barayev's co-conspirators, forced the team to speed up their schedule by a week. Barayev was not sure they were ready, but some of their number had begun filtering into Moscow on October 2, and the women had arrived by October 19. On the night of October 23 he left three vehicles— a Chevrolet SUV, a Ford SUV, and a VW Gazelle microbus[20]— with their engines running outside the theater, in case the initial takeover was unsuccessful and the team had to make a hasty retreat. No one noticed the driverless vehicles idling outside the theater until it was too late.[21]

Onstage, Barayev informed the audience that the rebel group was a suicide squad (*smertniki*) from the 29th Division of the Chechen rebel forces. While the women guarded the hostages, the men assembled bombs from parts hidden around the theater and from the bags they had with them. The entire theater was rigged with two tons of RDX hexogen explosives along with two 152-millimeter fragmentation shells, one in each of two massive metal cylinders. They placed one cylinder in the center of the auditorium in row fifteen, where everyone could see it, and the second in the balcony.[22] If either of these two devices had gone off, the theater's ceiling would have collapsed on the hostages. Twenty smaller bombs were placed throughout the building, in the balconies, under the seats where the audience sat, and in the hall. The female terrorists wore suicide vests packed with three to five kilograms of homemade explosive encased with metal nuts, bolts, and ball bearings. The shrapnel would cause as much devastation as the explosions themselves.

The terrorists called select radio and television stations using the hostages' cell phones. Several members of the international media—including the Italian newspaper *La Repubblica*—as well as reporters from Russian television channels NTV, TVS, and Ren-TV were invited into the theater to talk to the rebels and see for themselves that the hostages were being cared for. The stations broadcast the calls from the siege in real time over the next three days. The hostages pleaded with the authorities not to storm the building as truckloads of police and soldiers accompanied by armored personnel carriers encircled the theater. The terrorists said they were prepared to kill ten hostages for any terrorist casualty or in the event that security forces launched an attack.

In a filmed interview with NTV's Sergey Dedukh, Movsar Barayev said that the rebels had nothing to lose. They had traveled two thousand kilometers to get to Moscow and there was no way back. "We have come to die. Our motto is 'freedom and paradise.' We already have freedom in Moscow. Now we want paradise." Movsar explained that the group had not come to Moscow to kill the hostages or to fight Russian troops. They had had enough fighting in Chechnya. They wanted President Vladimir Putin to publicly declare the end of the war in Chechnya. They wanted Russian forces to immediately withdraw from Chechen territory. They also demanded that an antiwar demonstration be held in Red Square and that artillery and aerial bombardments in Chechnya be terminated. They especially wanted a halt to the notorious *zachistka* operations.

The military had seven days to pull out and if they refused, the rebels would start killing the hostages one by one. "We will kill them all!" a hostage-taker named Abusaid told Tatyana Deltsova, the BBC's Moscow correspondent, in a phone interview. "We came here to die. We are suicide fighters."[23] The terrorists expected Russian special forces to attack on the third day of the siege. One of the Chechen leaders, Abu Said, told Azeri TV: "Yes, the Russians will definitely attack. We are waiting for it."[24]

At 3:30 A.M. on October 24, six hours into the siege, a woman walked into the auditorium. Olga Romanova had sneaked past the police cordons and tried to incite the crowd to overtake the terrorists. She screamed at the hostages, telling them there were only forty hostage-takers and hundreds of them. The terrorists pointed their guns at her. A voice from one of the balconies yelled out, "Shoot her!" Romanova dared them to do it: "Yes, go ahead and shoot me!" They took her from the hall into an adjacent room and fired four bullets into her with a 5.45-mm assault rifle. The bullets penetrated the right half of her rib cage, abdomen, lungs, and left hip bone as she crumpled to the ground, and she was soon dead. It was rumored among the hostages that she had been drunk or on drugs. Others claimed that she might have been an FSB agent. Romanova was the first casualty of the siege.

Back in the main auditorium, the terrorists used the hostages' passports and other forms of identification to separate the foreign hostages from the Russians. They also separated the men from the women. The hostages were split between the main stalls and the balcony. Virtually no contact between the groups was allowed. The terrorists also checked IDs to determine how many police officers or federal agents might be among the crowd. Accounts differ as to what happened next. According to one story, police officers and agents were shot; according to another, after the siege it was found that no agents had been killed. All Muslims, Azeris, and Georgians in the audience were told that they were free to leave, as were those holding foreign passports. Seventy-five people from fourteen different countries were told to go, but then the Russian police negotiators refused to let the crowd be divided along ethnic lines. The Russian authorities did permit the terrorists to release 150 women and children and some of the foreigners, especially those who required medical treatment after the first few hours of the siege. One pregnant Russian suffering from dehydration and anxiety was taken to a local hospital.

The siege became a tense standoff and the hours turned into days as the Russians pretended to negotiate with the hostage-takers. Shortly after midnight on day three, a group of Russian doctors, including Dr. Leonid Roshal, head of the Moscow Institute of Emergency Children's Surgery, entered the theater with several NTV reporters to treat the sick and wounded. Most hostages just needed cough medicine or eyedrops. Roshal reported that the rebels were not beating or threatening any of the captives. Most of the hostages were calm; only two or three needed tranquilizers. The Red Cross also brought in hot food, warm clothes, and medicine.

According to Movsar's father, as part of the negotiations, Vladimir Putin promised to come to the theater. The Kremlin also promised to send General Viktor Kazantsev, a former commander of the Chechen war who wasn't even in Moscow, to negotiate terms.[25] Hoping that a peaceful agreement could be negotiated, Barayev ordered the men to disable the bombs in the auditorium and to take the batteries out of the handheld detonators, so that there would be no accidental explosions. In fact, there were no negotiations in the works. The terrorists had been duped. In the final hours before the security forces took over, the rebels were informed that the Russians would concede to their demands, a lie that appears to have persuaded the Chechens to relax their defences. Russian special forces then leaked information to the media that they planned to storm the theater at three in the morning. Barayev and his men waited for two hours for the assault but nothing happened. They let their guard down again, assuming the tip to have been a hoax.

At 5:00 A.M. members of the Russian Spetsnaz (special-purpose troops) stormed the theater. Shortly before, they had accessed the ventilation system of the building through the gay club Central Station located next door. Inside the theater, the hostages heard a hissing sound like the noise a gas stove makes when you first turn it on. Immediately people felt their senses dulling and started to feel woozy and nauseated. The symptoms were those of classic opium poisoning: dilated pupils, vomiting, loss of consciousness, and eventual asphyxiation from a lack of oxygen. Many of the hostages took the smell to be smoke from a fire, but it soon became apparent that gas was being pumped into the building. Some of the terrorists yelled, "Gas! Gas!" and commanded the women to turn off the air-conditioning. Some of the hostage-takers had gas masks, which they put on. Most of the rest soon lost consciousness.

One of the hostages, Anna Andrianova, who worked for the daily *Moskovskaya Pravda*, called the *Echo of Moscow* radio show at the outset of the FSB's assault. She told listeners: "The government forces are pumping gas into the hall. Please, give us a chance. If you can do anything!" She did not know what the gas was but from the terrorists' reactions she believed that they did not want the hostages to die. The same could not be said of the Russian authorities, who did not seem to want anyone to survive the ordeal. Andrianova screamed: "We see it, we feel it, we are breathing it through our clothes ... Our government has decided that no one should leave from here alive."[26]

After nearly one and a half hours of sporadic gun battles while they waited for the gas to take effect, the Russian special forces blew open the doors to the main hall and poured into the auditorium. They threw in noise and light grenades to disorient the terrorists. When the shooting began, the rebels told their hostages to lean forward in their seats and cover their heads. Movsar was holed up in a windowless room, so the gas did not affect him.[27] The FSB's Alpha Group—a specialized counter-terrorism squad—gunned down the terrorists who were still conscious and systematically executed those who had passed out. Soldiers walked around the auditorium and shot each of the women terrorists in the head. Their orders had been to take no chances. The subdued Chechens were summarily executed at point-blank range. Even if the soldiers saw batteries in the women's hands and empty detonators, indicating that the women's bombs had been disarmed, they ignored this sight and killed the Chechens anyway.

The only hostages who recovered from the gas were the ones who received naloxone, a treatment for opium overdose, within the first few hours of the attack. The gas must have been extremely potent to knock out so many people, especially the Chechen captors, who were young and in good physical shape. Observers identified the gas as fentanyl, but it would have taken tons of regular fentanyl to do the job. Some derivatives of the drug, such as 3-methylfentanyl, might have been used instead. The Russian health minister, Yuri Shevchenko, later said that the FSB had used an opiate derivative of fentanyl that was most likely carfentanyl, produced by taking the basic fentanyl molecule and adding carbon to it, making the drug eighty to a hundred times stronger. Carfentanyl is not intended for use on humans; it is normally used by vets to tranquilize bison or elephants. Lev Fyodorov, a Russian toxicologist, told the Russian newspaper *Gazeta* that the gas was probably produced in a secret laboratory in the Lubyanka, the FSB's headquarters. The Russians have consistently refused to disclose precisely which gas they actually used.[28]

A correspondent from the London newspaper *The Guardian* saw the bodies being pulled out of the theater, "their faces waxy, white and drawn, eyes open and blank."[29] Soon, the street in front of the theater was filled with the bodies of the dead and those unconscious from the gas but still alive. Just seventeen doctors confronted almost a thousand casualties. Within minutes they were completely overwhelmed. Few ambulances were standing by and city buses were brought in. It took the commandos more than an hour to evacuate the theater, during which time many of the hostages died. The soldiers, inexperienced in first aid, dragged people outside and piled them up like sacks. Many of the victims choked to death on their own vomit or swallowed their own tongues.

The hostages' coats were in the theater's cloakroom and they had no outside clothing to protect them from the elements; it was a snowy night and many of them suffered from exposure when they were left unattended in the street. There were reports that members of the security services and police rummaged through their pockets, helping themselves to the victims' money and jewels.[30] Rescue workers on the scene had not brought enough naloxone for everyone. The stricken hostages got no relief when they were transferred to the local hospitals, where staff were expecting to treat victims of explosions and gunshot wounds, not victims of an unknown chemical agent.

The following day, the surviving hostages found themselves under virtual house arrest. The FSB posted armed guards at the hospitals and doctors were ordered not to release anyone in case some of the militants were hiding among them. Families panicked as the government refused to release any information about which hospitals were treating the casualties or to disclose the names of those who had died. The official number of the dead rose by the hour while the government maintained the fiction that the assault had been launched when the rebels started executing captives. The final body count was 41 terrorists killed[31] and 129 hostages dead as a result of the gas and the inadequate response by the medical teams. Among the dead were several children and 18 members of the cast. Moscow's health committee chairman, Doctor Andrei Seltsovsky, contradicted official reports and admitted that all but three of the hostages who had been killed in the raid had died of the effects of the unknown gas rather than from gunshot wounds. None of the three people killed by the terrorists were hostages. They were individuals who had entered the siege after it started and were assumed to be FSB agents. It is worth noting that the terrorists took extra care to make sure that the hostages did not die at their hands.

THE BLACK WIDOWS OF DUBROVKA

Al Jazeera satellite television aired a prerecorded video that had been dropped off at their Moscow office a day before the Dubrovka hostage-taking. It showed the Chechen rebels and female Black Widows clad in black abayas with their faces covered in hijabs. The women claimed that they were waiting for a just and humanitarian solution in Chechnya, but that obviously no one cared about the death of Chechen innocents. Old men and children were killed daily and their children's blood flooded the land because of the Russian occupation.[32] One of the women spoke defiantly to the camera: "We might as well die here as in Chechnya however we will die taking hundreds of nonbelievers with us."[33] The terrorists in the video all swore by Allah that they desired death more than the Russians wanted life. Each one of them was willing to sacrifice himself or herself for the sake of God and the independence of Chechnya.[34]

In most Chechen towns, the Russians had completely destroyed all infrastructure, including the systems for water, electricity, and gas, making it impossible for people to live a normal existence and causing a massive refugee flow out of Chechnya into neighboring republics. Now the Chechens would bring the fight to the heart of Russia, a few miles from the Kremlin itself. A female *shahida* (martyr) summed up the reasons for their willingness to sacrifice themselves:

> People are unaware of the innocents who are dying in
> Chechnya: the sheikhs, the women, the children and the
> weak ones. And therefore, we have chosen this approach.
> This approach is for the freedom of the Chechen people and

there is no difference where we die, and therefore we have decided to die here, in Moscow. And we will take with us the lives of hundreds of sinners. If we die, others will come and follow us—our brothers and sisters who are willing to sacrifice their lives, in Allah's way, to liberate the nation.[35]

Despite such statements, some of the men at Dubrovka may have hoped to get out of the theater alive. Only the women wore suicide vests, not the men. Movsar Barayev had several forged passports in his possession along with a large amount of foreign currency.[36] Like Basayev when he attacked the Budyonnovsk Hospital seven years earlier, Barayev might have expected to survive to fight another day. Several of the male terrorists had return bus tickets to Khasavyurt. According to his father, Bukhari, Movsar had not made the usual Islamic preparations for his death prior to the attack. He had unpaid debts and there were other indications that some of the men at Dubrovka did not assume that this was their final operation. However, several of the women had settled their affairs. Rajman Kurbanova returned her wedding presents and said good-bye to her friends in the weeks before the operation.

There appeared to be a double standard for the men and the women at the theater. While the men secured the perimeter, the women circulated throughout the crowd. They were tasked to make sure that the audience did not panic and to see to their needs and make them a bit more comfortable. They distributed water, blankets, and chewing gum. The women ate dried dates and shared them with the hostages. They found chocolates and candies in one of the theater's backrooms, which they distributed. There were a few children attending the performance that night and the female terrorists visited the mothers and asked if their children needed anything. One hostage reported that the women acted more like nuns ministering to the sick than terrorists. They allowed people to go to the toilet without queuing in line. Despite these efforts, after the first few hours, the whole orchestra pit became one giant outhouse.

As the female terrorists mingled with the audience, several hostages got to know their captors a little better. It is from those hostages that we have the most information about the female terrorists' state of mind and motivation. Many of the female hostages showed signs of Stockholm syndrome: they identified with the hostage-takers and empathized with their plight. Tamara Starkova, a forty-two-year-old pediatrician who lost her husband and daughter at Dubrovka, recalled watching the Chechen men running around shouting and screaming at the hostages, but the women were different. The women said "please" and "thank you." They were surprisingly polite under the circumstances. The women did not discuss politics. Tamara listened to the women's stories of Russian atrocities and understood what had led them to Dubrovka. One woman explained that her whole family had been killed by the Russians. She had buried all her children and was now forced to live in the forest. She had nowhere to go and nothing to live for. Another of the *shahidat* confided to Tamara that she had lost her husband and child, and Tamara thought to herself that any mother would be capable of terrible acts under similar provocation.[37]

The hostages were struck by one of the terrorists, named Asya, most likely Aset Gishnurkayeva from Achkoy-Martan, who reassured them that the terrorists' motives were actually peaceful. Asya hoped that there would be a negotiation with the government and that the crisis would end well. She was involved in this mission so that her children could grow up in peace. Asya was particularly helpful during tense moments when the men onstage started shooting their weapons into the air.[38] She tried not to frighten the hostages and begged them not to worry. She explained that it was their war, not the hostages'. Asya's friend, Madina Dugayeva, also helped her calm the hostages. Madina had studied to be an actress at Chechen State University and was exceptionally pretty. Another terrorist, Sekilat Aliyeva, was a teaching assistant in the university's history department. Hostage Irina Filipova, found herself sympathizing with the female terrorists and concluded that the women must all have different motives: for some true believers it might have been a divine mission; some of the others might have been drugged; she wondered whether the younger girls had been forced.[39]

While some of the hostage-takers made repeated references to Islam and Allah during the fifty-seven-hour ordeal and the men placed a banner with the words *"Allahu Akbar"* (God is great) over the stage, many of the women were not well versed in Islam. Several mispronounced their prayers in Arabic and could not answer the most basic questions about the tenets of the faith. When asked questions about Islamic doctrine or practice, the women had no idea how to respond. Most of the terrorists just talked about the persecution that they suffered at the hands of the Russian forces in Chechnya. Their ignorance suggested that they had only recently been taught about Islam. Several wore their Islamic garb incorrectly. In one case, a female terrorist had tied her headscarf improperly and had to get help from one of the hostages to fix it.

More important, several of the women would have been disqualified as *shahidat* according to the strictest interpretation of Islam: one, Koku Khadjiyeva, was mentally ill and another, Medna Baraykova, was sick with tuberculosis and constantly coughing up blood. Russian survivors said some of the women in the group had talked of their eagerness to get home to Chechnya because they were pregnant. In May, four months after the attack, the official autopsies were completed and the Russian weekly *Moskovsky Novisti* revealed that three of the women—Amnat Isueva and two sisters, Raina and Ayman Kurbanova—were indeed pregnant. According to Islamic law, these women would not have been permitted to go on a martyrdom operation.

It's hard to know if these stories are true. It is likely that the Russian security apparatus disseminated disinformation to make the terrorists seem even more monstrous than the events suggested. According to her cousin Usman, Ayman Kurbanova (known as Rajman within her family) could not possibly have been pregnant. Usman reported that her first husband had left her after only a few months of marriage because she was infertile. Usman explained how Rajman's first husband had dishonored her; he literally shoved her out of the house and, in the process, broke her heart. The experience devastated her and left her forever changed. Like so many other Chechen women, in her despair she connected with the Islamists and, at forty, she married her second husband, a jihadi warrior.

Many of the Chechen women clearly suffered from post-traumatic stress disorder and were emotionally fragile. "You're having a bad day, but we've had a bad ten years," one Chechen Black Widow barked at the hostages. Another survivor, Nastya Kruglikova, recalled that one of the women had placed a grenade between her, her cousin, and her aunt. Kruglikova asked: "What is going to happen, are you going to blow us up?" The terrorist assured her that everything would be all right. However, after a few seconds of thought, she seemed to change her mind, and said: "Well, maybe you will be blown up but at least you won't know anything about it. You won't regret it. You don't know what's happening in Chechnya. You can't know what your soldiers have done there to our people. You can't have any idea how terrible our lives are."[40] She said she had left behind a child, but *inshallah* (God willing), God would look after him. Most of the *shahidat* were so fragile, they cried as they related the stories of their childhood and the years of war. The hostages remembered how the female terrorists tried to hide their tears. Many of them looked no more than sixteen years old.

On several occasions the hostages asked whether they could go to the bathroom. Each time, the women terrorists asked the men for permission. It seemed as if the women were not really in charge. One of the hostages claimed that the men controlled all the detonators, including the ones for the bombs attached to the women. Other hostages recalled seeing the women carrying their own suicide-belt detonators but still asking permission for their every move. The women bombers of Dubrovka appeared not to be in control of the situation even though they, not the hostages, were the ones with guns. Unlike female terrorists in other parts of the globe, they seemed weak.

One terrorist, Zura Barayeva, appears to have been an exception. She is reported to have been at ease with what was going on in the theater and more in control than the others. During the siege she took off her bomb belt and slung it nonchalantly over her shoulder. This may be because Zura was Movsar's aunt and one of the widows of Arbi Barayev. She is alleged to have trained the other women for the mission and may have recruited some of them. One of the hostages recalled that Zura seemed normal. She would ask people if they had children. She would always say, "Everything will be fine. It will finish peacefully." She seemed to take pleasure in the situation, particularly in how people were listening to what she had to say and wanted to know what she thought. She was most pleased about being in charge.[41]

THE SISTERS GANIYEVA

At least three pairs of sisters were among the terrorists at the Dubrovka House of Culture: the sisters Khadjiyeva, Kurbanova, and Ganiyeva. The last-mentioned pair, Larissa (Fatima) and Khadizhat (Milana) Ganiyeva,[42] were part of a large family of six boys and four girls. Two of the boys were killed fighting in the First Chechen War. Another brother was killed during a Russian aerial bombardment in 1999 and the oldest girl had worked as a nurse in Grozny treating the war wounded. She disappeared one day in July 2000, never to be seen again.

Fatima had tried to find her first brother's remains back in 1996, braving checkpoints and harassment by Russian soldiers, but the Russians refused to give up his body for a proper burial. For Fatima, this was just one in a series of humiliations that the family was forced to endure at the hands of the Russian military. The family's next encounter with Russian troops was in October 1999, not long after the outbreak of the Second Chechen War. Russian soldiers entered their village, shot five of the Ganiyevs' cows, and left with two of the carcasses tied to their vehicle. In July 2000, Russian troops returned and robbed them of their most valuable possession, a brand-new videocassette recorder. They also took several lambs and chickens and, just before they left, threw a grenade down into the cellar where the family stored their winter provisions.[43]

The last straw occurred during the summer of 2002. Russian soldiers stormed the Ganiyev house yet again and arrested the youngest son and two of the girls, including Fatima, during yet another *zachistka* operation. They tried to take fourteen-year-old Milana as well, but her mother managed to stop them. The girls' arrest coincided with a new special order, number 12/309, issued by the Russian Duma and known as Operation Fatima. This law instructed the police to detain any women wearing traditional Muslim headscarves (hijab) and to strip-search them at military checkpoints. Under Operation Fatima women were routinely detained and, while in detention, were tortured and raped and subjected to other kinds of sexual abuse to make them "confess" to crimes such as smuggling weapons.[44]

The two girls were gone for three and a half days before their father secured their release by paying the Russian soldiers a bribe of $1,000. When they finally came home, however, they were changed. Both had been beaten, subjected to torture by electric shock, and possibly raped. After they returned home they said, "We are now in shame. We cannot live like this."[45] For days Fatima sat without speaking a word. By her culture's standards she was an old maid, already twenty-six, and now ruined for marriage if her virginity was not intact. The war was killing her friends and potential suitors. Her little sister, Milana, had just turned fifteen and Fatima knew that she would be subjected to the same treatment in the next mopping-up operation. Neither she nor their mother would be able to protect her.

That September a strange woman came to visit the girls. It is unclear whether it was Zura Barayeva (one of Arbi's widows), or another woman recruiter of suicide bombers, Kurbika Zinabdiyeva; both allegedly recruited *shahidat* for the Dubrovka operation. Whichever of the women it actually was, she had been invited there by the girls' surviving older brother, Rustam (Aslan), a well-known jihadi fighter in Shamil Basayev's inner circle, who had promised two of his sisters as suicide bombers for the Chechen cause. Rustam was allegedly paid $1,500 per sister. He had recruited half a dozen women for Basayev's suicide bombing unit, the Riyadus-Salikheen (RAS, the reconnaissance and sabotage unit of the Chechen martyrs). Rustam's infamous protégées exploded at Dubrovka, at the Wings rock concert at Tushino Airfield, and at the Mozdok Airbase in North Ossetia. At Tushino, Zulihan Elihadžieva exploded along with another girl, killing more than a dozen people; she was alleged to have been pregnant by her half brother Žaga (Danilahan Elihadžiev). Rustam himself had trained the Mozdok bombers, Lidya Khaldikhoroyeva and Zarema Muzhakhoyeva , before he was arrested and sentenced to life in Vladikavkaz prison in March 2005. He admitted that his role was to drive the girls to North Ossetia, pretending that they were his wives and then to drop them off at a bus stop. He did this with each of the girls, first with Zarema Muzhakhoyeva and then with Lidya Khaldikhoroyeva. Rustam Ganiyev said that he only learned from the television that civilians, including many women, had died in the bus attack; the toll was nineteen dead and twenty-four wounded.[46]

Fatima and Khadizhat were sent to a rebel camp. They and the other girls spent their days training and reading the *Qur'an* while being regaled with stories of Khava Barayeva's heroic exploits. Diligent students, Fatima and Khadizhat wrote down everything they learned in their exercise books, which were later found after an operation against the rebel base. In their notes they wrote that the *shahida* goes to heaven after her death, where she is transformed into one of the *houris*, the beautiful virgins who serve Allah's warriors in paradise. According to the girls' notes, the perfume of heavenly flowers and eternal paradise were the *shahida*'s reward.

The process of indoctrination was intense and intimidating. Once young women entered the rebels' camp, there was no way out. If you fail to carry out your mission, they were repeatedly told, we will kill your parents, we will kill your children. It was very taxing psychologically.[47] Another recruit reported that she was given in marriage to a jihadi who told her that as she was his gift, he could give her to his friends and colleagues. After she was passed around, and had fainted, she woke up in a strange safe house with several other women being trained for a jihadi mission. One girl refused and the instructors reported that she had been eviscerated and chopped up into several pieces, which were tossed into the trash. If any of the other girls refused to carry out their mission, a similar fate awaited them.

Fatima and Khadizhat had been gone for more than a month and a half when their parents found out that their daughters had been among the terrorists at the theater. Across Chechnya, horrified families recognized the faces of their dead daughters and sisters when the news stations aired the footage from the Dubrovka attack.

Rustam's culpability came to light in the months after the Moscow theater siege, when the remaining Ganiyev daughter allegedly sought asylum from the Russian police. In August, Raisa (Reshat) Ganiyeva begged the FSB to provide her a safe haven because Rustam had promised her for one of the four new suicide operations Shamil Basayev was planning. According to the Russian government, she turned herself in of her own volition, but during a meeting with Sophie Shihab of *Le Monde*, Raisa managed to whisper in the journalist's ear, "They arrested me ..."[48] The FSB relocated Raisa to a safe house in Khankala, east of Grozny, where she remained under police protection for a year and then disappeared altogether.

COERCION AND REVENGE

From the beginning of the second war in Chechnya, women became increasingly involved in the fight. Even the smallest fighting units had female health-aid workers, whom the men respectfully called "sisters."[49] Slain Russian journalist Anna Politkovskaya met dozens of women in Chechnya ready to embark upon suicide missions for the cause. She chronicled Russian human rights abuses in Chechnya in several of her articles and books, including *A Dirty War: A Russian Reporter in Chechnya* and *A Small Corner of Hell: Dispatches from Chechnya*. Politkovskaya painted a picture of a brutal war in which thousands of innocent citizens were tortured, abducted, or killed at the hands of Chechen or federal authorities. Politkovskaya herself was tortured in Chechnya for three days and her children threatened.[50] Flown in from the west coast to help negotiate the end of the Dubrovka crisis, she stated that the nineteen women at the siege were "real heroines" to most Chechens, even though they were likely forced into their actions by men. Polish journalist Andrzej

Zaucha believed that the women were at Dubrovka of their own free will but that many had very personal motives for being there. Politkovskaya concurred that a major motive for the women was to avenge the deaths of their family members. Abu Walid, a Saudi who was reportedly one of the rebel commanders, told Al Jazeera that the women, particularly the wives of the mujahideen who were martyred, were menaced by Russian soldiers who threatened *their honor* in their own homes. The women would not accept being humiliated and living under the occupation. They wanted to serve the cause of God and avenge their husbands and sons.[51]

This desire for revenge and the likelihood of coercion were not mutually exclusive. Many Chechen women were outraged by the war and did lose husbands, sons, and brothers. But Russian behavior toward Chechen women during their mopping-up operations was an additional motivating factor. In Chechen society, men are the head of the household; nearly all issues are decided by them. A Chechen woman lives under the guardianship of her relatives until she marries, when she becomes her husband's responsibility. The woman represents the family's honor, and when an injustice is done to her, it can often be washed off only by spilling blood.[52] Traditionally, the wronged family takes revenge only against the individual(s) involved in the original crime or insult. However, with the many years of war and the increased trauma among Chechen civilians, a generalized revenge directed toward all Russians became increasingly acceptable.[53] In this extreme situation, all Russians were blamed for the actions of their soldiers.

According to Chechen sources, many of the women were victims of rape, which meant that they could never marry or have children. The prospect was so bleak that many concluded that they might as well die.[54] In one documented case, Russian federal forces detained Aset (not her real name) at a checkpoint in June 2003 and accused her of being a suicide bomber. According to relatives, during her interrogation she was chained to a bed and gang-raped every night. When she was released six days later, she was barely able to walk or stand.[55] According to one Chechen woman who abandoned her suicide mission at the last minute, if you sacrificed your life in the name of Allah and killed some infidels, you would go straight to heaven regardless of your previous sins.[56]

Anna Politkovskaya argued that the women in Chechnya were "zombified" by their sorrow and grief. Writing in Moscow's *Zhizn* magazine, Svetlana Makunina endorsed the commonly held Russian view that the women terrorists had all been turned into zombies. They did not actually want to be involved in suicide attacks. They were drugged, raped, and forced. Another journalist, Maria Zhirkova, explained how difficult it was for anyone to understand the position of Chechen women in society. Rape was such a big issue. If a woman was raped and it was photographed or filmed, she could be blackmailed into doing anything because the rape was a disgrace to her entire family.[57]

Wartime rape is a relatively common device used against the women of the other side. However, unlike cases in Darfur, Sierra Leone, and Bosnia, the experience of rape in Chechnya occurred in two very different ways: one, young women were raped by Russian soldiers during detention and as part of the campaign to ethnically cleanse certain areas, and two, women were kidnapped and raped by Chechen fighters. These same-side rapes were occasionally videotaped to make it impossible for the victims to return to their families. Under this kind of pressure, martyrdom seemed like a blessing.[58]

Women sent off for marriage to a neighboring village occasionally found themselves kidnapped and raped. Often the interlocutors (matchmakers) were compensated for making the arrangements. Instead of going to their weddings, the women were funneled into the Chechen jihadi network. Aset (Asya) Gishnurkayeva left her village of Naur to get married. When she got off the bus in Achkhoy-Martan, she was kidnapped and molested by Chechen men. It turned out that her mother had sold her to the jihadis. Aset ended up at the Dubrovka. When confronted by police afterward, her mother insisted that Aset was still alive somewhere in the Middle East, her whereabouts unknown. She refused to acknowledge that her daughter was killed at the Dubrovka even when shown photos from the attack.[59]

Russian authorities have also alleged that the girls were under the influence of drugs. It suits the Russian government to say that drugs, brainwashing, and blackmail are involved. To blame societal dynamics in Chechnya is easier than facing up to the role played by Russian soldiers in radicalizing Chechen women. The authorities do not want people to conclude that the situation in Chechnya is so desperate and the living circumstances so awful that women are driven to suicide and murder. So the Russian media regaled readers with stories of drugged and coerced zombies and implied that responsibility for their condition rested entirely on the Chechens themselves and on radical groups like Al Qaeda.

The claims perpetuated in Russian propaganda are refuted by stories of Russian soldiers laughing as they charge Chechen fathers 300 rubles (about $20) *not* to rape their daughters. According to the humanitarian organization Doctors Without Borders, 85 percent of the women raped in Chechnya were raped by soldiers or police officers and 15 percent of the attackers were Chechens.[60] In Chechnya, rape constitutes "normal conduct" and many of the cases never go to court due to the cultural norms or fear of retribution from the Russian authorities. The human rights violations fall under Russian policies of *bespredel* (without limits or boundaries)—committing atrocities and acting with impunity. The concept originated in Moscow's world of organized crime and was exported to Chechnya; thus soldiers could do anything to Chechens with impunity.[61]

While the situation for women in Chechnya was dire, the truth about how women become involved in suicide operations remains murky. Certainly, Russian actions have played a significant role in traumatizing women and incentivizing them to seek revenge. However, a black-and-white interpretation is complicated by reports that several of the women who participated in the Dubrovka siege were "sold" to the resistance to become suicide bombers—as we have seen in the case of Fatima and Khadizhat Ganiyeva. Several of the women were the sisters (not the widows) of well-known jihadis who had been paid as much as $1,500 per sister to deliver *shahidat*. The families of four of the women (Aset, Raina, Ayman, and Koku) reported that their daughters had been kidnapped and trained to kill against their will.

It is difficult to know for sure. Whatever the truth—whether these women chose their fate willingly or were pushed into participation—the attack against the theater was very much a family affair. The terrorists in the room comprised sisters, aunts, uncles, husbands, cousins, and wives. Thirty-two of the terrorists carried their real passports (which were later used to identify them) and several of the attackers were related to one another.

There is no doubt that recruiters routinely target young women who have lost someone during the war, like a close male relative. As a result of the stress from the war, women are highly impressionable and readily convinced to carry out a suicide mission. The organization instills an intense hatred of Russians for causing the death of her loved ones. The outside world is cast in terms of good and evil and an intense religious indoctrination follows.

Not all of the girls are religious. Most of them have grown up in secular environments, wearing miniskirts, listening to rock and roll, and watching American movies. But the recruiters deliberately misinterpret the *Qur'an* to persuade their recruits to become martyrs. Most of the girls have grown up in large families and are told that as *shahidat* they are the only hope for the families' future and their actions will save the whole clan. The girls' new comrades promise to make sure that their families will be taken care of financially, and promise the girls' families thousands of dollars for their daughters' sacrifice. The girls are placed in a closed environment in which they know no one. The psychological process involves bolstering the girls' self-image while simultaneously cutting it down. So while the women train to be fighters, they are also made to do the men's laundry and cook for them. Some of the girls think that life in the rebel camp will be full of adventure. No longer mere village girls frightened by life, they will be transformed into fighters and future heroines respected by their comrades and celebrated by their communities.

Although not all of the Chechen female bombers fit this profile, the majority were younger than thirty. While not all had lost relatives in the fighting against Russian troops or in the brutal purges of Chechen civilians by Russian security services, many had suffered during the mopping-up operations. Not all of them were raped, tortured, or humiliated by the Russian military, but all could tell tales of degradation under the occupation.[62] Starting with the Second Chechen War, a new culture arose in which the norms of Chechen society and expectations of what women could contribute changed irrevocably. Many girls are convinced that a martyrdom operation is their best option. Recruiters now know that they cannot force the girls to do anything. A coerced bomber is considered "vocationally unsuitable and would blow the operation at any moment." In the end the girls go to their deaths voluntarily.

TERROR AND COUNTER-TERROR

After the siege at the House of Culture, then Deputy Internal Affairs Minister Vladimir Vasilyev pledged publicly to cleanse not only Moscow, but all of Russia of Chechen "filth." The hostage-takers' families bore the brunt of Russia's response. The relatives of the women terrorists were persecuted, kidnapped, and killed. Five weeks after the siege, while the parents of the Ganiyeva girls were with their grandchildren at a neighbor's home watching television, the FSB came to the village of Assinovskaya and blew up their house. The Russian authorities destroyed the houses of all of the terrorists they could identify from the Dubrovka. In retaliation for the attack against the Ganiyevs, the homes of four Russian families in Assinovskaya were burned down three days later. Asya's home, too, was blown up by the Chechen administration and the Russian security services in retaliation for her participation in the siege. That December, the FSB killed Movsar Barayev's brother Adlan. And the cycle of violence—as the Moscow subway bombings in March 2010 demonstrated—continues.

3

THE "PREGNANT" BOMBER

We are prepared to fast to the death, if necessary, but our love for justice and our country will live forever.

—Mairéad Farrell, Margaret Nugent, and Mary Doyle, hunger strikers, Armagh Prison, December 1, 1980[1]

We are actively involved in the struggle at all levels raising the issues of sexism, violence against women, and discrimination, women must fight for their freedom.

—Mairéad Keane, Director, Sinn Féin's Women's Department, July 1990[2]

SIOBHAN

Siobhan[3] sat by herself staring out the window of a bus full of tourists and holidaymakers en route to Belfast International Airport. Her rosy cheeks were flushed with both nervousness and excitement. She was wearing denim overalls, the kind that pregnant women often wear, and concealed underneath them fifteen pounds of Semtex explosives strapped to her waist. Her mission: to plant the explosives at the airport and wait for the Provisional Irish Republican Army (PIRA) to make its warning call to clear the premises. In her mind, she could accomplish this task without any civilians getting killed. However, the economic reverberations of such an attack would be huge: tourism in Northern Ireland would grind to a standstill and make it too expensive for the British government to remain and maintain its presence. By attacking a high-value site like the airport, the PIRA would also show that no target was beyond its reach. Siobhan's mission took the PIRA's use of female bomb smugglers to a new level. In a weekend of heightened bombing activity, with nine bombings and shootings all over the province that very day, in Lisburn, Newry, Derry, and Strabane, Siobhan's ruse—pretending to be an expectant mother—might enable her to successfully carry out her mission without anyone ever suspecting her real identity.[4]

At Templepatrick, near Newry, the airport bus started to pull away from the border customshouse and then jerked to a stop. Without warning, several uniformed police officers boarded the bus. They scanned the faces in the crowd and made a beeline for Siobhan. The other passengers looked on quizzically, not yet alarmed, as patrols often boarded the buses to check ID and travel papers. When they began to question Siobhan, the passengers may have assumed that something had happened to the baby's father or that there was some emergency. She looked at them with big blue eyes, trying to appear calm, but they asked her for her identification papers and immediately escorted her off the bus. When they were on the curb, one of the police officers quickly frisked her. The patrol did not yet know what they were dealing with. He undid the metal buttons fastening her overalls and the bib dropped to her waist, exposing the bomb strapped to her midsection. The officers escorted Siobhan to another area and instructed the driver to move the bus as the passengers looked on with horror. The young woman was not pregnant at all, but carrying a bomb. No one had ever seen anything like this before.

Siobhan was loaded into a police car and driven to the station for interrogation. The special explosive unit defused the bomb slowly and carefully and destroyed it with a controlled explosion. Curiously enough, *An Phoblacht/Republican News,* the official newspaper of Sinn Féin (and the PIRA's mouthpiece according to critics), claimed that the attack was successful, writing in its war news a few days later that an IED had exploded at the customhouse, without mentioning that Siobhan had been caught before her mission was complete. *An Phoblacht* never even mentioned her name.

The Belfast airport bombing by a woman feigning pregnancy did not happen that day. When a Sri Lankan woman emulated the tactic the following year, she managed to blow up herself and former Indian prime minister Rajiv Gandhi in Sriperumbudur in Tamil Nadu, India, on behalf of the Tamil Tigers. History records that Gayatri (Thenmuli Rajaratnam) was the first female bomber to feign pregnancy when, in fact, the women of the IRA had been smuggling explosives in their panties and under the guise of pregnancy for years; they just hadn't been suicide bombers.

Siobhan was sentenced to fourteen years on May 21, 1990. The judge tried to convince her to recognize the authority of the court, take a guilty plea, and throw herself on the court's mercy. After all, she was so young, she could have pled to a lesser charge as a minor. She refused. The authorities and even the defense lawyers then tried to pressure her parents to get her to consent and work with the authorities. Siobhan recalled with a smile that her parents had told them where to go, and how to get there.

THE RISE, FALL, AND RISE OF THE IRA

Religious and sectarian violence began in Ireland as far back as the twelfth century, but it culminated in the 1970s during the Troubles. The Emerald Isle had been invaded by Vikings, Romans, and Normans, but the invaders that stayed were the English.

Beginning in the twelfth century, the English began to assert their control. Gaelic Ireland was completely defeated by 1691, at which time thousands of Scottish and English settlers were brought in to farm its rolling green hills. The Gaelic Irish were Catholic and their new masters were Protestant. This religious divide had both economic and political ramifications, with Irish Catholics banned from becoming members of parliament under the Penal Laws, even though they constituted 85 percent of the population. All economic and political power rested in the hands of the Anglo-settler community for two hundred years and land distribution and access to resources varied depending on people's religion.

In 1798 Wolfe Tone, influenced by ideas from the French and American revolutions, led the Irish Rebellion against English rule. The rebellion possessed some of the worst characteristics of a civil war. Sectarian resentment, fueled by the Penal Laws, resulted in even more repression. Rumors of atrocities and massacres multiplied on both sides. Executions of Protestant Loyalist prisoners were answered by the massacres of captured Catholic rebels. The 1798 rebellion was the most concentrated episode of violence in Irish history, and resulted in thirty thousand deaths over three months.

As a result of the rebellion, the English employed a divide-and-rule strategy, using the sectarian conflict to whip up nationalist sentiment among Protestants. In 1801, in the Act of Union, the United Kingdom formally annexed Ireland, making it part of Britain's colonial empire. While King George III had vetoed emancipation of Catholics, in 1829 his son George IV signed into law the Catholic Relief Act, which sanctioned their participation in parliament. This mitigated the source of conflict, but Ulster, in the north, where most of the British had settled, remained the center of the violence between Catholics and Protestants. Elsewhere, tensions had an economic cause, as a growing divide between landowners and tenant farmers resulted in social unrest. Land allocation and socioeconomic status were often highly connected to religious affiliation and so hostility between the two religions remained high.

Most Catholic families had only enough property to plant a single crop: potatoes. When a blight hit the island, the potato crop failed, and much of the population went hungry. The tensions in the countryside reached a crescendo during the Potato Famine of 1845–49, which resulted in one million deaths and another million Irish emigrants to America, Canada, and Australia. The famine profoundly impacted the political, economic, and social development of the island. The situation became catastrophic when epidemics of typhoid, cholera, and dysentery devastated the population. Most of the little food produced on the island was exported to Great Britain, leaving hundreds of thousands of Irish people starving to death. The growing communities of Irish emigrants living abroad helped found the Irish Republican Brotherhood (IRB) in 1858, a secret society whose goal was the independence of Ireland. This and comparable nationalist groups funneled arms and money to the conflict until the 1980s.

Beginning in the 1880s, a series of "home rule" bills was introduced in the British parliament. Some would have allowed Ireland to govern itself independently from Britain while others called for repeal of the Act of Union. Thousands of Unionists, led by Sir Edward Carson, signed the Ulster Covenant of 1912, pledging to resist home rule. The threat of a civil war loomed large and led to the creation of local militias like the Ulster Volunteers, who resisted home rule, and the Irish Volunteers, who supported it. In small villages in County Cork and County Kerry, Catholics began to organize their opposition. These early groups provided the inspiration for the terrorist organizations that would emerge in the twentieth century. The Irish Volunteers were the forerunner of the Irish Republican Army (IRA), and the Ulster Volunteer Force (UVF) gave rise to half a dozen Protestant militant groups.

Conflict between north and south reached a crisis in the 1916 Easter Rising in Dublin and the subsequent guerrilla campaign. During World War I, the British were pressured by the Woodrow Wilson administration to resolve the Irish problem. The Treaty of Versailles, which formally ended the war, recognized the principle of self-determination for all peoples. However, even with the landslide victory for Sinn Féin, the political party representing Irish republicanism, in the 1918 British general election, Ireland did not achieve independence. Although many in the British political establishment believed that it was time to get out of Ireland, they could not leave because they owed allegiance to "kith and kin" in the north, the Protestant majority, who considered themselves to be British.[5]

Between 1918 and 1921, the Irish Republican Army waged a highly successful guerrilla campaign against British security services in Dublin and police and troops in both the north and south of the island. The insurgency was led by Michael Collins and Eamonn de Valera.[6] In response, the British government reinforced its garrisons in Ireland and began to recruit auxiliary forces, including the dreaded Black and Tans, mostly veteran servicemen, criminals, and mercenaries from World War I. The British prime minister, Lloyd George, sought a compromise. The Government of Ireland Act (1920) partitioned Ireland, creating two states, one for the six northern counties (Antrim, Armagh, Derry, Down, Fermanagh, and Tyrone) and one, the Irish Free State, for the remaining twenty-six. It also allowed for the possibility that at some future date, the island could once again be united. The settlement satisfied neither side.

The Irish parliament, the Dáil, voted 64 to 57 in favor of the treaty in January 1922. This rift over the partition of the island had parallels within the IRA, and Northern Ireland was born amid bloodshed and communal disorder. The pro- and anti-treaty allegiances thrust the island into a bitter civil war that lasted until 1923. Ironically, more Irish killed each other during the civil war than had been killed by the British during the preceding War of Independence. Collins himself was shot and killed by one of his former allies in his native Cork. Sinn Féin reorganized under de Valera and reemerged to contest the 1923 elections.[7]

In the 1930s widespread riots in Belfast and the towns of Larne, Portadown, and Ballymena, some of which involved the IRA, caused yet more deaths. The violence peaked in 1935 when twelve people were killed and six hundred wounded. In the southern Free State, former IRA members were absorbed into state bodies, and the organization was officially declared illegal in 1936. The sectarian violence faded as the economic situation improved, and the organization had virtually disappeared by the 1940s. During World War II, Ireland remained neutral; de Valera officially refrained from joining either the Allies or the Axis.[8]

For much of the 1940s and 1950s, the IRA was virtually absent from the political scene on both sides of Ireland's north–south border. The acronym IRA came to signify the much-touted and contemptuous slogan "I Ran Away."[9] The dreadful failure of an IRA offensive from 1952 to 1962 owed more to apathy than to the competence of law enforcement. The last gasp of resistance ended with a communiqué stating that the IRA would abandon the military struggle altogether and concentrate on political-socialist objectives.

The denunciation of armed struggle seemed to guarantee that the 1960s would be free from Republican violence, but it led instead to a new iteration of sectarian violence with the emergence of a charismatic religious leader (and founder of one of the Protestant paramilitary groups), the Reverend Ian Paisley, among the Protestants in the north.[10] Radical voices within the Protestant Unionist movement outlawed the colors of the Irish flag, and flying the tricolor in West Belfast provoked a riot in 1964. Ian Paisley was head of the Free Presbyterian Church and the Protestant Unionist Party and played the leading role in demanding the removal of all symbols of Irish nationalism or independence. Paisley was opposed to any political reconciliation with the Catholic community.

The response was civil rights marches, beginning in 1968. Catholics, seeking equal employment, good housing, and equality under the law, found themselves at loggerheads with state authorities. The civil rights movement demanded an end to discrimination in jobs and housing, the disbandment of the B Specials (the Ulster Special Constabulary), and an end to the gerrymandering of voting districts. The Northern Ireland Civil Rights Association (NICRA) called for one man, one job, and for one family, one house.[11] Their most important demand was "one man, one vote."[12] In the Northern Ireland parliament, known as Stormont, Catholics remained a minority even though they outnumbered the Protestants in the general population. Without a peaceful and legal framework to achieve civil rights, Catholics believed that they had no alternative but to take to the streets. The success of the civil rights movement in America suggested nonviolent protest as a means to achieve their political goals, but the government's ban on peaceful demonstrations allowed militant voices to emerge and take over the movement.

The campaign became much more radical in 1969. The riots in Belfast in August led to the resurrection of the Irish Republican Army and a political split between the Official Republicans, who believed in nonviolence, and those who came to be known as the Provisionals, who advocated the use of force. The group deliberately used the word "provisional " to emphasize that they were the real heirs to the the Irish provisional government (Rialtas Sealadach na hÉireann) of 1922 and to emphasize that this was a provisional decision until such time that the full General Army Convention could formally vote on the split. The Provisionals maintained the principles of the pre-1969 IRA, and considered both British rule in Northern Ireland and the government of the Republic of Ireland to be illegitimate. The official reason for splitting the IRA was a disagreement that emerged from their annual conference over whether to recognize the Irish or British parliaments. Since partition, the Republican movement had followed a policy of abstentionism. The new policy was to take their seats if they were elected. The Provisionals walked out of the conference, set up their own organization, and called themselves the Provisional Sinn Féin and Provisional IRA. The first Provisional Army Council, composed of Seán Mac Stíofáin, Ruairí Ó Brádaigh, Paddy Mulcahy, Sean Tracey, Leo Martin, and Joe Cahill, issued its first public statement on December 28, 1969:

> We declare our allegiance to the thirty-two county Irish
> republic, proclaimed at Easter 1916, established by the first
> Dáil Éireann in 1919, overthrown by forces of arms in 1922
> and suppressed to this day by the existing British-imposed
> six-county and twenty-six-county partition states.[13]

Unlike the leaders of 1916, who were elite, fairly well-educated men who spoke for all of the people of Ireland, the new generation of leaders were children of the Belfast and Derry ghettos. Most were from urban backgrounds and had suffered from sectarian discrimination. The Provisionals or "Provos" would differentiate themselves from the other Republicans through a campaign of armed and violent resistance: they would employ the language of the gun. After the split, the Provisional IRA began planning for an "all-out offensive action against the British occupation."[14]

The civil rights organization People's Democracy (PD) unilaterally decided to march from Belfast to Derry in January 1969, emulating the Selma to Montgomery marches in the United States, even though the government had outlawed peaceful demonstrations of any kind. The marchers were met with violent opposition at Burntollet Bridge, and this event, along with the emergence of the Provos, destroyed the campaign of nonviolent protest in Ireland. The most strident voices and those with weapons now set the agenda.

Back in Britain there was a change in government in 1970. Harold Wilson's Labour government had implemented some civil rights reforms. In May Labour was replaced by a new Conservative government, led by Edward Heath, who had close links with the Unionists in Northern Ireland. The new British government decided that the answer to Northern Ireland was not more reforms, but punitive military action.

Catholics in Belfast soon felt that they were under siege. To complicate matters, Catholic and Protestant communities lived side by side, intermingled, so a Catholic community would be physically next to a Protestant one. The main Catholic neighborhood was located along the Falls Road. Next to it was an area, known as the Shankhill Road, which was the main Protestant working-class community and headquarters for many of the Protestant militant organizations associated with the Ulster Volunteer Force (UVF). Both the IRA and the UVF had a slew of offshoot organizations from these neighborhoods that engaged in ever-increasing levels of violence.[15] The red hand was the symbol of the Protestant vigilante groups, many of whose members were policemen during the day and killers at night. Because Protestants were the majority in some neighborhoods of the north, and because there was complicity with the security forces, they were able to inflict more damage on the Catholic community than vice versa.

The army, in trying to control events, made matters much worse. Its use of CN (tear) gas and CS (chlorobenzylidene malononitrile) gas, which permanently damaged the heart and liver, dramatically escalated tensions. The Catholics living behind the barricades in their neighborhoods believed that the British government meant to destroy them as a people. As a result, the logic of oppression, responding to the pressure exerted by violent protesters, led to the gassing of civilians, the massacre on Bloody Sunday, mass arrests, and hunger strikes, all of which became powerful recruiting agents for the Provisional IRA. People became convinced that violence was the only answer and young people joined the Provisional IRA in droves.

In July 1970, a year known as the time of the Falls Curfew, the army fired 1,600 canisters of CN gas into the densely populated Falls Road. The violence escalated even more on January 30, 1972, when British forces engaged in an affray with the Catholic community in Derry. During a civil rights march led by the Northern Ireland Civil Rights Association, attended by ten to twenty thousand men, women, and children, soldiers chased stone-throwers and, within minutes, shot thirteen marchers dead, seven of them teenagers. A fourteenth victim died days later. In total, twenty-seven civil rights protesters were shot that day, five of them in the back.

Bloody Sunday, as the day came to be known, was a watershed. It united the Catholic community of Northern Ireland, and British authority completely collapsed. World opinion condemned the shootings while the British tried to whitewash the events despite journalistic accounts and eyewitness reports.[16] According to Bishop Edward Daly, "What really made Bloody Sunday so obscene was the fact that people afterward, at the highest level of British justice, justified it."[17] It was unquestionably a terrific recruiting tool for the PIRA. Their leaders, men such as Gerry Adams and Martin McGuinness, found themselves having to turn people away, so many wanted to join.[18]

Bloody Sunday became a clarion call to Catholics throughout Northern Ireland, summoning them to resistance. What started as a small battle in a single Catholic community became a war that spread throughout Northern Ireland, and was the turning point in the Irish struggle.

MAIRÉAD FARRELL

In Mairéad Farrell's Belfast neighborhood, murals depicting the Irish struggle stand next to images of Picasso's *Guernica,* paintings of Palestinian refugees, and graffiti calling for freedom and human rights. For Republican nationalists, the connection to the American civil rights movement is clear.

Violence was all around Mairéad. As a child, she had to pass through military checkpoints and endure curfews. Her mother recalled that her daughter used to ride her bicycle to school. But on the Blacks Road, Protestant children would try to pull the Catholic kids off their bikes, so Mairéad had to start taking the bus. Soon the bus too was attacked on the Blacks Road, so the driver had to make a four-mile detour to get to the school. Such episodes contributed to Mairéad's radicalization.[19]

Feeling that the Catholic community was constantly under siege, Mairéad joined the IRA when she was only a teenager. She vowed that she would do anything necessary to get the British out of Northern Ireland and end the occupation. She was captured while on active service, planting bombs at the Conway Hotel in Dunmurry, on April 5, 1976. When the three five-pound bombs exploded, they demolished the hotel, started a fire, and caused thousands of dollars worth of damage. No one was hurt because the PIRA had called in a warning fifteen minutes ahead of time and Mairéad and her conspirators had made sure everyone had evacuated the building before detonating the explosives. Within an hour of the blast, she was in police custody.

At her trial, Mairéad refused to recognize the court, give evidence, or make any statement. The judge sentenced her to fourteen years for causing three explosions, possession of three bombs and a Colt 45, and for being a member of an illegal organization. In the women's ward of Armagh Prison, she was weighed, washed, and presented to the assistant governor (warden), who asked her what work she wanted to do while in jail. She refused to do any work, insisted on wearing her own clothes, and demanded her rights as a political prisoner. Mairéad served ten and a half years in Armagh's A Wing. While in jail, she became a leader of the female prisoners and their official Officer Commanding (OC). She also became the PIRA's poster girl for opposition to the British "occupation" of Northern Ireland.

The British legal system reversed the principle of "innocent until proven guilty" for Irish political prisoners at this time. Women arrested had to prove their innocence and since most Republicans refused, as Mairéad had done, to recognize the legitimacy of the British court, their conviction rate rose to 94 percent. The number of women in Armagh multiplied exponentially. According to Father Denis Faul, one of only two priests who were allowed access to the women jailed at Armagh, the prisoners were subjected to the most deplorable conditions.[20]

It was a prison out of Hollywood movies, characterized by iron bars, gray concrete walls, and humorless guards. It was old and falling apart. Each cell housing two prisoners was no more than six feet by nine.[21] It contained two iron beds with the bedsprings soldered to the frames so they could not be detached. The beds were covered with a thin foam rubber mattress, a gray blanket, and a pillow sometimes made of straw.[22] There were no amenities and no luxuries or comforts to speak of. Unlike the other wings of the prison, the A Wing had no educational or recreational facilities. As the numbers of incarcerated women increased, overcrowding worsened and the tensions between the prisoners and the guards intensified.

Mairéad had been arrested at the worst time for Irish political prisoners. In 1976, "special status" for political prisoners was arbitrarily rescinded. Women sentenced after March 1 of that year were thus denied the privileges granted to women sentenced a day earlier. Inmates in Armagh Prison's B Wing enjoyed special status in recognition of the fact that they were political rather than criminal prisoners. They could wear their own clothes; were exempted from prison duties; received a weekly visit, letter, or package from their families; and had access to educational materials. Teachers instructed the women in a variety of subjects, including the Irish language, mathematics, geography, dressmaking, art, music, typing, and even physical education. The women could also sit for their high school equivalency tests.

The women without special status who, like Mairéad, refused to do any prison work were locked in their cells twenty-three hours a day and deprived of any mental and sensory stimulation. They were not allowed to watch television, listen to the radio, or get reading materials. They changed their clothes once every three months: for ninety consecutive days they had to wear the same jeans, sweaters, and underwear. The authorities did not bother to put sheets on their beds.[23]

During their time in jail, the women learned to suppress their feelings to avoid having a mental breakdown. They communicated with one another by tapping on the pipes and during their one hour of exercise in the yard. Given their isolation, they struggled to find ways to keep their sanity. They came up with different activities: bingo, trivia quizzes, singsongs, even the occasional political debate. Their singing was infectious—sometimes even the guards would hum or whistle along. Every night at 9:00 P.M., Mairéad would announce it was time to say the rosary, which they would all recite in Irish.[24] The women survived by forming strong friendships with one another. One woman recalled to me: "It was us against the system. They would try and undermine us and demoralize us but it didn't work. We held on to our beliefs and if anything it made us stronger."[25]

According to her prison mates, Mairéad became a skilled negotiator as the Armagh OC. She knew when to accept clean blankets or lice- and flea-free mattresses that would ensure the women stayed healthy, and when to turn down concessions intended to divide the women from the male prisoners in H Block and from each other. During her years there she maintained unity among the women. Typically, the spirit of every woman arriving in prison had been almost entirely broken by what she had endured during capture and trial. The police had forced most of them to sign some sort of confession, and at times the charges were fabricated. When the women were at their lowest, it was often Mairéad who lifted them up and gave them the strength to face the day.

THE PRISON PROTESTS

Over a period of five years beginning in 1976, the men in Maze prison (known as Long Kesh) engaged in the blanket protest. They were led by one prisoner, Kieran Nugent, who refused to wear his prison uniform. Instead, he wore only a blanket, and many of the newly convicted prisoners followed suit. The blanket protest led to the no-wash protest (which the British derisively termed the "dirty protest") in which the prisoners refused to wash, and smeared excrement all over their cell walls. When the blanket and no-wash protests failed to yield any positive results for the prisoners, they opted for a radical act of self-sacrifice. In 1980 the men began a series of hunger strikes.

During the men's blanket protest the female inmates in Armagh, led by Mairéad Farrell, refused to wear their prison uniforms in hopes of challenging the British government's efforts to criminalize them. Unlike the men, they were not allowed to wear only blankets (which might have been more hygienic than their clothes). The women sang freedom songs in Gaelic—an overt expression of Republican nationalism—and demanded to be treated as prisoners of war and not as criminals.[26]

In addition to the blanket protest, Mairéad led the women in a thirteen-month campaign of passive resistance by refusing to bathe or use the two prison lavatories. According to the women, they did not start the no-wash protest of their own volition. When the women were locked down on February 7, 1980, after an incident in which the guards had ransacked their cells looking for pro-IRA contraband (including every piece of black clothing), the guards refused to provide access to the bathrooms. There were only two baths and two toilets for the thirty-plus female prisoners to begin with. Within a matter of days, the cells' chamber pots (bedpans) were overflowing with waste. Initially the women threw the contents out the windows but then the guards boarded these up, and forbade the inmates from emptying the pots using the facilities. Finally, the women resorted to smearing excrement all over the walls of their cells in protest. Soon the cell walls were covered in feces, urine, and blood. The stench was overwhelming. The women recalled to me that there were days when they woke to find maggots crawling all over their hair and bodies.

Nevertheless they were undeterred. As one woman recollected, "It was amazing what one could endure for your principles, and, after a few days, the smell did not bother us and we were able to tolerate these conditions for over a year."[27] Another described the process: "You would pluck a piece of pooh out of the chamber pot using a tissue that your relatives had smuggled in. Then you would smear it all over the walls. As the shit dried to a yellow or pale brown, it eventually lost most of its smell, but it was the urine, used sanitary napkins, diarrhea, and vomit that made everyone sick. The floors were covered in dust that was actually shedded skin and flies buzzed everywhere, dying in orgies on the uneaten food and excrement."[28] When the women woke, there would be hundreds of flies covering the walls. Woodworms jumped from pile to pile as various infestations spread through the prison population. The women's health deteriorated. They lost weight. They lost their hair. Many developed a variety of internal infections. The accumulating broken nails, flaking skin, and hair transformed the cells into rats' nests.[29] To distance themselves from the conditions, the guards patrolled the halls in nylon blue jumpsuits and white Wellington boots that made them look like astronauts on the moon.

After thirteen months of this, Mairéad Farrell, Mary Doyle, and Margaret Nugent began a hunger strike in solidarity with Bobby Sands and the other men at Long Kesh. The women felt that they had exhausted every other possible source of leverage with the prison authorities and the hunger strike was their last resort. All three were prepared to fast to the death to make their point.[30] Sands wrote of Mairéad, Mary, and Margaret in his diary before his death: "I've been thinking of all the girls in Armagh. How can I ever forget them?"[31] One of the other male hunger strikers, Lawrence McKeown, said that the women's experiences during the prison protests made the men more conscious of Irish gender stereotypes. The women recalled that the men at Long Kesh supported their struggle and wrote them notes of encouragement while the women's movement never did. Large segments of the feminist movement viewed the women of the PIRA with suspicion and, at times, contempt. In fact, within the Irish feminist movement they were called the slaves and dupes of the men. In London, Prime Minister Margaret Thatcher declared the three women were criminals.

Mairéad Farrell agreed with Lawrence McKeown that women in Ireland suffered twice, once as Catholics and once as women. Mairéad was quoted as saying: "I am oppressed as a woman, and

I'm also oppressed as an Irish person. We can only end our oppression as women if we end the oppression of our nation as a whole. I hope I am still alive when the British are driven out. Then, the struggle begins anew."[32] For the women of the PIRA, the Republican nationalist struggle was intertwined with the struggle for equality. For many of them, there was no difference. The fight for freedom and equality was joined with the fight against the Unionists and the British army and crown. At the same time, most PIRA women did not consider themselves feminists. They felt a deep distrust of the women's movement and resented the feminist argument that women's rights came first, before revolution, independence, or freedom from Britain. Mairéad told her cell mates, "Everyone tells me I'm a feminist. All I know is that I'm just as good as others, and that especially means men."[33]

Once in the movement, the women were treated as equals. Seán Mac Stíofáin, former chief of staff for the Provisional IRA, said that in the early 1970s the PIRA had selected a number of women to be trained on the basis of full equality with the men. Some of the best shots he ever knew were women, as were the smartest intelligence officers in Belfast.[34] According to the women themselves, they never felt any kind of sexual discrimination or second-class status. Mairéad recalled that she was treated equally to the men, as were all of the women in the PIRA. "You got doing what the lads did but it depended to what extent you were committed, not measured by what sex you were."[35]

The women's organization Cumann na mBan (Union of Women), founded in 1914 alongside the Irish Citizen Army, was one of the precursors of the IRA. Decades later, women were involved only peripherally in the movement, as support units or as "molls" used to lure British soldiers to an apartment or isolated area to be attacked by the women's colleagues.[36] Women accompanied men on a mission as cover; a couple attracted less attention.

Women also served as couriers, ferrying messages and weapons. The army's difficulty was that they could not properly search women for contraband. The women also picketed at the drop of an insult; according to the women themselves, the British were terrified of them.

The British army often conducted night raids in Catholic neighborhoods, in night squads called Duck Patrols. Women began patrolling the streets in units that became known as Hen Patrols. They would blow whistles, bang garbage-can lids, and make as much of a ruckus as possible to warn of an army incursion. The women of Belfast and Derry became the not-so-secret weapon of the PIRA. They were lookouts who raised the alarm when British soldiers approached. They shielded fugitive gunmen when troops swooped into the Catholic ghettos. Over time, they began carrying weapons and taking part in armed encounters against British soldiers.

As the community was increasingly mobilized, more women and children became involved in the movement. Scotland Yard prophesized that mothers and wives would no longer provide a restraining influence on the men in their families. The women would not only egg the men on, but also join in the fight. But not all Republican women were involved in violence. Many joined the local citizen's defense committees and participated in the anti-internment struggles, lobbying for the release of their husbands, brothers, and sons. Some women supported the PIRA simply by wearing paramilitary dress: black skirt, white blouse, and black beret. Wearing this outfit was sufficient cause to get a woman arrested and questioned for possible membership in a terrorist organization, which was itself criminalized. One woman told me that membership was used as a holding charge, especially if the authorities could not find any evidence against them. "So if you got off on one set of charges, they could prove membership in what they had termed an illegal organization and you would be sentenced anyways."[37]

As the numbers of women active in the PIRA increased, the number imprisoned also grew. There were few women interned at Armagh Prison in 1972, more than one hundred in 1976, and more than four hundred by 1982.[38] More and more women were arrested on weapons charges and "intent to bomb." Hundreds of young girls were dragged out of their homes in the middle of the night and interrogated. Once arrested, the women were forced to sign confessions that were often fabricated; many of the women on the Republican wing of Armagh jail had no real connection to the PIRA, and the actual number of women involved with the movement was much smaller than the number serving sentences.[39]

Allegations of sexual misconduct and impropriety followed. In one notable case in 1975, Margaret Shannon, a prisoner who had been strip-searched, alleged that the guards had threatened to rape her in her cell that night. For four consecutive nights, officers came down to her cell, unlocked the door, and menaced her for hours, shouting obscenities and threatening to come in.[40] Another prisoner at Armagh, Anne Walsh, was beaten so badly in the head that she lost the hearing in one ear.

According to military sources, the army's dossier on women's involvement grew thicker every day, with women playing "an increasingly important role in IRA activities, especially as communications officers." In 1973, the Price sisters, Marian and Dolours, made headlines when they received life sentences for the March London bomb attacks that killed one person and seriously injured 216. The following year, Judith Ward was arrested for a bombing on the M62 highway which caused many civilian casualties, and Roisin McLaughlin was wanted in connection with luring three British officers to their deaths.

The British use of the policy of internment refers to the arrest and detention without trial of people suspected of being members of illegal paramilitary groups. The policy was introduced a number of times during the conflict in Northern Ireland, including from August 9, 1971, until December 1975. During this period a total of 1,981 people were detained, more than 90 percent of them Catholic: 1,874 were Catholic/Republican, and 107 were Protestant/Loyalist.[41] Six months after internment was introduced, nearly three hundred Irish Republican women (but no Loyalist women) had been taken into custody and Armagh Prison was bulging at the seams with female political prisoners. Maire Drumm had always said, for every woman they put in the Armagh jail, there would be fifty more ready to take their place.[42]

Many of the women fighters exceeded even the PIRA's expectations in terms of their skills and lethality. One of the most accurate snipers in the Belfast Brigade was a teenage girl; another young woman was their most experienced expert on booby traps. At times, the women were more ruthless than the men and made credible Rudyard Kipling's assertion that the female of the species is more deadly than the male. Critics used hyperbole to demonize the women, comparing them to the harpies better known as *tricoteuses* who, during the French Revolution, sat knitting before the guillotine, counting their stitches by the severed heads. The women did not want the men accusing them of holding back just because they were women. The critics felt that the women were competing not only against the enemy, but also against the men of their own side to show that women could do anything men could do, and could hate better than the men too. The British military claimed that their troops were reluctant to fire upon women, even when faced with female snipers, although this was not always the case, as the subsequent events in Gibraltar would demonstrate.

Starting in the 1970s, scores of teenage girls bolstered the thinning ranks of the PIRA as men were either killed or jailed by British forces. The organization recruited the girls to carry timed devices, hidden under their clothing, into shops; they hoped that because of the girls' youth, they would receive only cursory examination by security staff.[43] Girls as young as thirteen smuggled bombs into Belfast city center. They targeted women's and children's clothing and toy stores, the kinds of places where a man would stick out like a sore thumb. Some nights, as many as ten devices would be found along Belfast's busy Victoria Street, all timed to explode when the shops were closed and shoppers had gone home, nevertheless disrupting the economic life of the city. Some of the more fashionable girls hollowed out their three-inch platform heels and smuggled weapons, ammunition, and even rifle parts through security checkpoints. Each pair of platforms could carry half a pound of explosives.

Mairéad's involvement in the movement mirrored the evolution of women in the PIRA. She had started out as a young girl, throwing rocks at British soldiers and banging garbage-bin lids to warn the PIRA that British troops were on their way. She acted as a lookout and weapons carrier when she was a teenager and then graduated to active service, throwing petrol bombs and planting the Conway Hotel bombs when she was nineteen. She would come to believe that the Irish people had the legitimate right to take up arms to defend their country against the British occupation and to use any means necessary.[44]

Mairéad's experiences in prison would have hardened anyone and yet she retained a softness and joie de vivre even during the darkest times. Her fellow inmates from Armagh recalled her wonderful sense of humor and uniquely Irish sense of irony. During the hunger strikes the women would sit around, their empty stomachs growling loudly, while Mairéad would regale them with tales of delicious curries in her favorite local pubs and restaurants. They understood the effect that their hunger strikes were having on their family and friends. It broke their hearts to see the worried faces of their fathers and mothers when they visited but there was no other way to defeat a system that treated them as common criminals. Mairéad ignored the guards who tried to humiliate her and laughed at their childish pranks. During the strikes the guards brought overflowing plates of hot food (a rarity at Armagh) three times a day to tempt the women to eat. Yes, they were hungry, but such transparent tactics would not defeat the women. Mairéad laughed in the face of her captors. Her admirers said that this showed the strength of her indomitable spirit.

The day after her release Mairéad Farrell was once again in the spotlight, giving interviews to the media and taking up the cause against the forced strip searches and the sexual humiliation of Irish women in prison. She would demonstrate to the assembled reporters how the guards had strip-searched her. The final insult had been the strip search on the day she was released, which had lasted twenty minutes.

Strip-searching female prisoners became a banner issue and a successful rallying cry for the Provisional IRA. The PIRA and Sinn Féin seized the opportunity to mobilize supporters into the movement by describing in horrific detail the process by which the guards and police used strip-searching to demoralize their community. From the perspective of the women, the use of strip-searching was a form of sexual humiliation intended to punish Republican women for their political activity.[45]

British officials insisted that strip-searching was a necessary precaution and that it was only a visual search. They maintained that at no time was the prisoner entirely undressed. Prison staff did not conduct body-cavity searches although they may have sometimes required prisoners to open their mouths. All prisoners (male and female) were routinely searched when leaving or returning to the prison to inhibit the passage of items such as explosives, weapons, drugs, and other contraband into and out of the prison, in order to reduce the risk of escape and for the general safety of prisoners, staff, and visitors.[46] Hundreds of women told a different story in their testimonies and several in personal interviews. The British government's description contradicts the accounts of the women incarcerated in Armagh and Maghaberry prisons.

According to these women, most of the searches involved highly invasive probing of all orifices, often regardless of the presence of male guards. The searches were repeated several times a day, even when the prisoner had never left the guards' control. One woman told me that she was strip-searched seventy-five times in one week, and several times within a single hour.[47] Another said that it was "clearly intended to break us, [but] it just made us stronger and fight them harder."[48] Another woman explained, "You would have to stand there nude and freezing as the guards felt the inside and outside of your legs. It was a degrading experience."[49] Even young children and babies visiting prisoners were subjected to strip-searching. The searches were so invasive that not even menstruating women were exempt—they had to remove any sanitary napkins and hand them to the guards for inspection, much to the women's disgust. If the women didn't remove their tampons or towels, these were forcibly removed. The women recalled to me that it was utterly humiliating .

Prison did not deradicalize Mairéad. If anything, her experiences as a guest of Her Majesty's prison service made her more focused on freeing Northern Ireland from British control. After her release, Mairéad returned to active service and started planning more bombing operations. Many of the plots to "shake the Brits from their complacency"[50] backfired with deadly repercussions. After the Remembrance Day bombing at Enniskillen, which killed eleven and injured sixty-three civilians,[51] Margaret Thatcher had vengeance on her mind. Even though the Provisional IRA leadership and Sinn Féin denied responsibility for the attack and blamed one rogue brigade that had acted unilaterally, the massacre undermined the positive image the PIRA had enjoyed for several years after the death of Bobby Sands. Even the Irish rock band, U2, condemned the bombing and the organization. In their concert the following day in Denver, Colorado, the band's lead singer, Bono, shouted to the crowd, in the middle of the song "Sunday Bloody Sunday": "Fuck the revolution! Where's the glory in bombing a Remembrance Day parade of old-aged pensioners, their medals taken out and polished up for the day? Where's the glory in that? To leave them dying ... or crippled for life ... or dead under the rubble of a revolution that the majority of the people in my country don't want."[52]

Preventing another attack and killing the most famous female operative in the PIRA was a high priority for the British security services and they went through great efforts to circumvent any legal obstacles to kill Mairéad Farrell rather than capture her alive. Her murder, and that of two other members of the Provisional IRA, Danny McCann and Sean Savage, by agents of the Special Airborne Service (SAS) remains controversial. There is little doubt that the three Irish Republicans were unarmed when they were shot dead in Gibraltar on March 6, 1988. The British government eliminated an enemy but in the process created a martyr whose exploits are celebrated in Ireland to this day.

SIOBHAN

Like many other young women who joined the Provisional Irish Republican Army, Siobhan had been raised in Ardoyne, a West Belfast neighborhood that suffered from the tension and conflict caused by sectarianism. Armed struggle was all around her. Siobhan, like Mairéad before her, felt both the British army and the Loyalist paramilitaries were assaulting her community. As a teenager, she witnessed the British army enter Catholic neighborhoods, and saw how men and women were interned without trial. Siobhan's uncle had been imprisoned as a rebel and shot while trying to escape. He was only wounded at first, but Siobhan said that the British army hunted him down and finished him off as part of their shoot-to-kill policy. The army routinely cut off food supplies to the Catholic areas and set up barriers and checkpoints that disrupted daily routine. Worst of all, both the Royal Ulster Constabulary (RUC) and the British army failed completely to control the Protestant paramilitaries that routinely drove through Catholic areas, shooting or beating anyone in their path, including children.

In the ghettos of West Belfast, political awareness was instilled at an early age. Siobhan recalled being told, as a very young child, which areas were dangerous. There were five streets in her neighborhood that were safe; the rest were rife with what she called "murder and mayhem." Her parents cautioned her that the "Shankhill Butchers" were taking anyone and to be careful. Even as a girl of eight, Siobhan was so affected that she later remembered vividly the impression made on her by the Irish hunger strikers and the election of Bobby Sands to parliament while he sat in prison wrapped in a blanket. Sands's death in 1981 at the age of twenty-seven after sixty-six days of a hunger strike resulted in a recruitment surge for the Provisional IRA. In the days and weeks after Sands died, nine other hunger strikers perished. British prime minister Margaret Thatcher was widely condemned for letting an elected member of parliament die; Her Majesty's government responded by amending the electoral laws so that no prisoner could ever run for office again.

On the day of her failed bombing attempt, April 28, 1990, Siobhan was a young, pretty, and idealistic seventeen-year-old, yet she had already been a member of an active service unit (ASU) of the Provisional IRA for three years. She felt at the time that she was living a double life, as she had never told her parents that she had joined up. Now that she had been arrested, she worried what their reaction might be. Her grandfather had been active against the British during the time of Michael Collins and Eamonn de Valera, but her parents were not political.

Siobhan joined the organization very young, like her mentor, Mairéad Farrell, who had herself been recruited at fourteen by Bobby Storey, a notorious leader of the PIRA, after he had escaped from Crumlin Road jail. As a young girl Siobhan idolized Mairéad and followed her exploits on the pages of *An Phoblacht/Republican News*, Sinn Féin's official newspaper. One of only three women who had been on the hunger strikes[53] with Bobby Sands, Mairéad suffered years of what she called cruel and inhuman treatment at the hands of the British.[54] Sands and the women at Armagh were a source of inspiration for a generation of young women like Siobhan, who grew up wanting to be just like them.

In many ways, Siobhan's life as a terrorist paralleled Mairéad's. Mairéad had taken the young girl under her wing when Siobhan secretly joined the PIRA. Siobhan was still in her first year with the organization when Mairéad was gunned down by the SAS in Gibraltar. Siobhan, only fifteen at the time, was devastated. "To the people of Falls Road Mairéad was a patriot. To the British she was a terrorist. To her family she was a victim of Irish history."[55] To Siobhan she was a friend. Days before Siobhan's bombing attempt, *An Phoblacht* reported on the British government's actions to obstruct the investigation into the Gibraltar killings.[56] The assassination of Mairéad Farrell, the subsequent British cover-up, and a perceived pattern of discrimination and human rights abuses suffered all her life led Siobhan to board the airport bus that day to carry out her mission.

As the uniformed officers lifted the bomb from under her overalls and handed it to the bomb-disposal unit, Siobhan thought to herself that someone had given the authorities information about her mission. They knew too much. They knew that she would be traveling alone, that she would be pregnant (not really), and exactly what her plan was. The Provisional IRA was rife with informers and people who were working with the British security services, MI5, or the RUC. A few years earlier, a high-ranking informer on the IRA's command council had provided the information that saved Prince Charles and Princess Diana from an assassination attempt at London's Dominion Theatre in 1983. Another informer, a double agent code-named Stakeknife, had alerted the authorities to Farrell, McCann, and Savage's mission in Gibraltar. Siobhan counted herself lucky that the officers had not shot her on the spot as part of the dreaded shoot-to-kill policy.

Siobhan was sentenced on May 21, 1990. When, years later, she reminisced about her time in jail, there was no regret or bitterness in her voice. Armagh's green and pink stone walls had made her the person she was now. She felt that it was a tremendous growth experience for her. Like Mairéad, she had entered jail as an idealistic young woman, but her experiences in jail transformed her into a leader. Mairéad had not regretted her time in jail either. Her only regret was getting caught.

The idea that prison could be a learning experience was duplicated in many instances of political incarceration around the world. When Nelson Mandela left his prison cell after twenty-seven years in February 1990, the African National Congress dubbed the prison Robben Island University. It had become a college of resistance, a training school for opposition to apartheid in which the older prisoners cared for and educated the younger ones. In prison they learned to read and write, and became politically aware. Among Palestinian inmates in HaSharon and Megiddo prisons, captured terrorists serving life sentences take classes and complete degrees online. Northern Ireland in the 1990s (once political status was restored) was no different. According to the women, prison broadened their political horizons and sharpened their ability to recognize violence against women both in the family and as a form of economic exploitation. As part of the learning process, the women initiated contacts outside of prison. As a consequence, they identified themselves with women across the globe. They spent hours talking about politics, cooking, and studying. The camaraderie was intense and the friendships Siobhan formed in prison lasted long after she was freed.

While in jail, Siobhan worked out two hours a day and took classes online from the Open University toward her degree in political science. By the time of her release she had read hundreds of books on Irish history and politics and had learned about nationalist struggles in the developing world and injustice in places far and wide. Her experiences differed from those of Mairéad Farrell because special status had been reinstated. She was allowed to wear her own clothes, study, and receive packages and mail. Most important, special status meant that she was not considered an ordinary criminal. This was what Bobby Sands and the other nine men had died for, and why Mary Doyle, Mairéad Farrell, and Margaret Nugent had gone on their hunger strike.

After her release Siobhan once again followed in Mairéad's footsteps, pursuing a degree in political science and sociology at Queen's University in Belfast. She was active in many of the student organizations. Unlike Mairéad, who had become famous in jail, Siobhan rarely shared her personal history with others. Unless people were in the movement, they were unlikely to know who she was. But within her own community, she had rock-star status. When she got out of prison, every man wanted to date her and everyone wanted to buy her a pint. She laughed when she told me she could have gotten any man she wanted. After a few months of the adulation, however, she grew bored. She married a boy in her social circle and settled down to start a family. After school she went to work for several benevolent organizations connected to Sinn Féin. Eventually, she took a job at Sinn Féin headquarters.

Siobhan sat in her office wearing a colorful sundress with tiny red and blue flowers. Her shoulder-length strawberry-blond hair would occasionally fall into her eyes. She looked no more than twenty-five despite her five years in prison (she was released early as part of the Good Friday Agreement in 1995). A picture of two lively children and a handsome husband sat on her desk. She smiled a lot and spoke in an animated fashion of life in the PIRA.

Siobhan felt that she was working for peace and justice for her people, but legally now, helping to raise community awareness, ensuring that everyone had voting rights, and helping Sinn Féin win elections. Was she angry at having spent so many years behind bars? No, she did not feel any anger. Several times she said that everybody has to forgive in order to move the peace process forward. That's what she was doing, working toward a peaceful future for her children.

4

THE SCOUT

I do not recognize the legitimacy of this court, and I do not introduce myself to you by my name or age, I introduce myself with my actions ... I see you all in this court today angry, and it is the same anger that [is] in my heart and the hearts of the Palestinian people ... Where are your hearts when you kill children in Rafah, Jenin and Ramallah, Where is the sense!?

—Ahlam at-Tamimi, 2005[1]

AHLAM

Ahlam at-Tamimi smiled angelically as she recalled the events of the afternoon of August 9, 2001, when twenty-two-year-old Izzedine as-Suheil Al Masri went to the Sbarro pizzeria at the intersection of Jerusalem's King George and Jaffa streets. In Al Masri's guitar case was a fifteen-pound improvised explosive device, which master bomb maker Abdullah Barghouti had packed with nails, screws, nuts, and bolts to maximize the carnage. This trip to the Sbarro pizzeria was not a maiden trip for Ahlam. The twenty-year-old from the village of Nebi Saleh had reconnoitered the street days earlier, studying the neighborhood to ascertain when and where a bomb might do the most damage. Ahlam claims that she chose the Sbarro after seeing the crowds of people who crammed into the restaurant at lunchtime.[2] Israel assassinated Jamal and Omar Mansour and six other people in Nablus on July 31, 2001; the next day, Hamas set in motion their act of revenge. The attack had taken just nine days to plan.

Ahlam pointed out the busy intersection to Al Masri. There were four stoplights and people crisscrossed the street in all directions. It was one of the busiest intersections in all of West Jerusalem, the Jewish part of the city. She first suggested detonating the bomb in the middle of the street, perhaps as a bus was stopped at the traffic light, so he could kill all the passengers inside in addition to the pedestrians. But he opted instead to enter the pizzeria.

Al Masri bore an innocent expression as he walked into the Sbarro and sat down at a table. It was 2:00 P.M. and the two-story restaurant was packed with families and young children eating their midafternoon snack. When the bomb exploded, 15 civilians were killed instantly and another 130 wounded. Half a dozen strollers lay charred on the street where mothers had left them while they ate lunch. When rescuers ran into the restaurant, the blistered bodies were still smoking, so hot that they could not be touched. The first wave of good Samaritans ran in and wrapped the pizzeria's checkered tablecloths around the victims' hair and clothes. Everyone in the restaurant and several passersby had been struck by shards of flying glass when the windows were shattered. Streaks of blood ran down people's arms, legs, and torsos.

According to *The Independent*'s Robert Fisk, who arrived on the scene soon after the blast, one woman lay in a heap, a chair leg run through her,[3] and another lay outside with her brains gushing out of her head. A small child was so mutilated by the bomb that the eyes had been blasted out of his head. Amid the acrid smoke and broken glass, rescue workers pulled bodies from the rubble. Jens Palme, a German photographer from *Stern* magazine, counted ten dead in two minutes.[4]

HERZL'S DREAM

Many people observing Israel-Palestine today assume that its inhabitants have been killing each other since Biblical times. In fact, this is not at all the case. Jews and Arabs got on well for centuries even as Jews were being persecuted in Christian Europe in inquisitions, witch hunts, blood libels, and pogroms. In the golden age of Islam in Spain, both Muslim and Jewish philosophy and science were celebrated. Jews, like Christians and Zoroastrians, were honored as "people of the book" (*ahl al Kitab*), their prophets recognized and respected by centuries of Islamic rulers.

The Islamic world was largely insulated from the religious anti-Semitism of the Middle Ages and the so-called "scientific" anti-Semitism that emerged in the late eighteenth century. Europe penetrated the Middle East in both positive and negative ways, influencing political thought and technological progress. When violence erupted between the Muslim and Jewish communities it was often the result of European instigation.

The story of the current Palestinian-Israeli conflict starts with the Jewish diaspora in Europe during the eighteenth and nineteenth centuries. While religious Zionism (love for the Holy Land) was enshrined in the Jewish faith from the beginning, the desire to create a political entity in the Holy Land developed much later. Various movements in the late nineteenth century began to agitate for a Jewish homeland. One of these, the Lovers of Zion, emerged in 1882 during the Russian pogroms and encouraged emigration to the Holy Land. At the time, Palestine was a neglected backwater of the Ottoman Empire,[5] a narrow strip of land bordering the Mediterranean Sea and characterized by swamps, disease, and deserts. While there had been a continuous Jewish presence in the region since Roman times, it consisted mainly of religious scholars.[6] Small Jewish settlements at Hebron, Tzfat, Tiberius, and Jerusalem were notably poor if not destitute.

In 1894 a seminal event in France would have reverberations throughout the Jewish diaspora. A young Jewish captain, Alfred Dreyfus, was accused of spying for Germany. He was found guilty, publicly stripped of his rank, and sent to Devil's Island. But Dreyfus was innocent, and new evidence that implicated the real conspirator, Ferdinand Esterhazy, was covered up by French intelligence. Dreyfus's religion had made him the ideal scapegoat.

French writer Émile Zola wrote an open letter in the newspaper *L'Aurore* accusing the government of anti-Semitism and suppressing evidence. Most of the French intelligentsia took one side or the other. The home of liberty, equality, and fraternity witnessed some of the ugliest anti-Semitic propaganda from the literati. In attendance at Dreyfus's second trial was the Paris correspondent for the Austrian *New Free Press*, Theodore Herzl. A journalist long assimilated into Austrian culture, Herzl found himself shocked and dismayed by the racist epithets he read and the rallies he witnessed in Paris where many chanted "Death to the Jews!" For Herzl this was an epiphany: if Jews were discriminated against in the home of the French Revolution and the Enlightenment, they would never be safe until they had their own homeland.

Herzl quickly wrote *Der Judenstaat* (*The Jewish State*), which became the basis for political Zionism, in 1896. The next year the first Zionist congress met in Basel, Switzerland, to discuss how and where to create a Jewish state. In the sixth congress in 1903 suggestions mooted for potential sites included Uganda, Kenya, or somewhere in British East Africa. But the majority held fast to the idea that the Jewish state would have to be in the biblical Kingdom of Israel.

Zionist groups and their supporters approached the Ottoman sultan Abdulhamid II about forming a chartered company to develop the area. Europeans used charter companies to establish economic and political domination over the developing world;

South Africa and Rhodesia began as chartered companies, as did the Dutch East Indies and the Belgian Congo. While the sultan refused to sanction large-scale Jewish immigration to the area, he permitted several waves of immigration with the hope that European settlement would provide hard currency and strong trading links, both of which the Ottoman Empire needed badly.

Life was extremely difficult for the first colonists. With little infrastructure and the constant threat of disease, many quickly returned to Europe. The handful who survived were a hearty bunch of settlers whose socialist philosophy impacted their daily lives. They brought in eucalyptus trees to soak up the brackish swamps and create a bulwark against the spread of malaria. They introduced irrigation to make the desert bloom. In the early years, the colonists and the local Arab population cooperated and their children often played together. Moshe Dayan, the man who would grow up to conquer the Sinai and the West Bank in 1967, remembered as a child playing with his Arab neighbors and learning to speak Arabic, unaware that their different ethnicities would one day pit friend against friend and divide the land along confessional and religious lines.[7]

As the numbers of Europeans increased, the Jewish National Fund (JNF) bought more and more land, often from absentee landlords who resided in faraway urban centers like Beirut, Cairo, and Damascus. The tenant farmers (*fellahin*) had little to no contact with the landowners who had consolidated the small independent farms into large estates. Tension between the settlers and the expelled farmers was made worse because many of the new settlers believed that only Jewish labor should be employed on the farm. The two communities no longer benefited mutually from one another and gradually separated along ethnic and religious lines.

The situation came to a head when the Ottomans sided with the Central Powers of Germany and Austria-Hungary in World War I and the Triple Entente began to plan for the eventual dissolution of the Ottoman Empire. The foreign ministers of the three European states in the Triple Entente, Mark Sykes of Great Britain, Georges Picot of France, and Sergey Sazonov of Russia, secretly met and drafted the Sykes–Picot Agreement of 1916. In it, they envisioned a division of the Middle East between direct and indirect spheres of influence through a mandate system, which allowed European domination until such time as the colonies had matured and "were able to stand alone."[8] Britain was allocated what is now Jordan, southern Iraq, and Haifa, to provide access to a Mediterranean port. France would control southeastern Turkey, northern Iraq, Syria, and Lebanon. The czar would control Constantinople, the Turkish Straits, and Armenia.[9] The Holy Land remained a sticking point as both France and Britain wanted the area, so it was agreed that the issue would be settled at some future date; one possibility was internationalizing the region, like the "free city of Danzig" (now Gdansk) in Poland.

Britain found itself in the uneasy position of fighting the war on two fronts, in Europe and in Asia. The dramatic loss to the Ottomans at Gallipoli meant that Britain needed local allies who could distract Turkish forces and make them fight a two-front war. Out of Cairo in 1915, the British high commissioner, Henry McMahon, exchanged a series of letters with Hussein bin 'Ali, the Sharif of Mecca, in which he promised Hussein control of Arab lands in exchange for a revolt against the Turks. The Arab Bureau sent Captain T. E. Lawrence (better known as Lawrence of Arabia) to contact the Hashemi family and investigate whether the Arab tribes could be convinced to blow up the Hedjaz Railway that ferried Ottoman troops from the western to the eastern Mediterranean.[10] As Lawrence consulted Sharif Hussein, the keeper of the keys of the Islamic holy places at Mecca and Medina, the India Office of the Crown pursued closer relations with a young upstart religious leader, Abdul Aziz bin Abdur Rahman al Saud, best known as ibn Saud. The Hashemis and al Sauds were sworn enemies and the British negotiated with each family separately to hedge their bets as to who would prevail in Arabia.

The background to why Britain issued the Balfour Declaration is as complex as the Middle Eastern conflict itself. A mixture of good reasons and faulty assumptions led the British government to preemptively issue a declaration in support of Zionist aspirations in Palestine. This was done quickly, before a similar statement of support could be issued by the Central Powers. Britain hoped to get the United States into the war and the Russians back in. According to historian James Gelvin:

> Two of Wilson's closest advisors, Louis Brandeis and Felix Frankfurter, were avid Zionists. How better to shore up an uncertain ally than by endorsing Zionist aims? The British adopted similar thinking when it came to the Russians, who were in the midst of their revolution. Several of the most prominent revolutionaries, including Leon Trotsky, were of Jewish descent. Why not see if they could be persuaded to keep Russia in the war by appealing to their latent Jewishness and giving them another reason to continue the fight?[11]

In London in November 1917, British foreign minister Lord Arthur Balfour issued his famous statement in a letter addressed to Baron Rothschild, a leader of Britain's Jewish community. The wording of the declaration was deliberately vague, and the French and English versions differed in specificity. The English read:

> His Majesty's government view with favour the establish-
> ment in Palestine of a national home for the Jewish people,

and will use their best endeavours to facilitate the achievement of this object, it being clearly understood that nothing
shall be done which may prejudice the civil and religious
rights of existing non-Jewish communities in Palestine, or
the rights and political status enjoyed by Jews in any other
country.[12]

When the Russian monarchy fell to the Bolsheviks in 1917,
one of the first things V. I. Lenin did was make public all of the
secret agreements negotiated by the czar. Among the documents
released was the Sykes–Picot Agreement. Britain's Arab allies were
triply confused. Sharif Hussein had understood that Britain had
promised Palestine to him as part of a greater Arab homeland,
although the McMahon-Hussein correspondence avoided any
mention of Palestine and excluded "portions of Syria" lying to the
west of "the districts of Damascus, Homs, Hama and Aleppo."
Meanwhile, the Balfour Declaration promised the Holy Land to
the Jews, while the Sykes–Picot Agreement implied that it would
fall under British or French colonial control.

In 1920, the Allied Supreme Council offered Great Britain a
mandate for Palestine. Prince Faisal—Sharif Hussein's son—was
given control over a new entity called Iraq (three Ottoman *sanjaks*
or provinces that had been unnaturally fused together). His brother
Abdullah was installed as king of Trans-Jordan and ibn Saud took
over the Arabian Peninsula in 1924. The Middle East state system
was thus born with new borders devised by British planners who
were now assured that they could ship their oil from the Gulf to
the Mediterranean without ever touching French-controlled soil.

In 1920, the Jewish population comprised roughly 8 percent of
Palestine; nevertheless, the Balfour Declaration was incorporated
into the new entity's mandate, in both the preamble and as
article 6 of the text. Several Arab leaders, such as Hajj Amin al

Husseini, the Mufti of Jerusalem, virulently opposed Jewish immigration. In protest, the Palestinian Arab population refused to participate in the mandate administration.[13]

Knowing that the Arabs would inevitably refuse any cooperation with the British colonial authorities, the Jewish community in Palestine, known as the Yishuv, accepted any concessions the British were willing to offer. As immigration increased, so did Arab opposition, leading to a series of riots from 1922 to 1929. The British responded by issuing several White Papers beginning in 1922, and began to scale down the number of Jews permitted to immigrate. Nevertheless, in the years between 1931 and 1936 the Jewish population in the Holy Land more than doubled, from 175,000 or 17 percent of the population to 370,000 or 27 percent.[14] As a result of the growing hostility between the communities and Arab opposition to both the Yishuv and the British Colonial Office, the Arab Higher Committee called for boycotts and trade embargoes.

The Palestinian Arab revolt of 1936 had three key demands: prohibit future Jewish immigration; prohibit the transfer of Arab land to Jews; and establish a national government responsible to a representative council.[15] The uprising was initially directed against the British and the Jews and included attacks against infrastructure, transportation, and Jewish settlements, neighborhoods, and individuals. The struggle quickly turned into an exercise in self-destruction as Palestinians began killing each other in large numbers, each side accusing the other of collaborating with the British. The Yishuv took a series of defensive actions. The first was to create parallel institutions so that any economic interaction with the Palestinians was unnecessary for Jewish survival. They established the port of Tel Aviv so as not to rely on Jaffa for trade and many Jews offered Britain their assistance in quelling the revolt in hopes of receiving training and weapons for the inevitable clash between the two communities. By the time order was restored in March 1939, more than 5,000 Arabs, 400 Jews, and 200 Brits had been killed.[16]

The final British White Paper, issued in 1939 and known as the MacDonald White Paper after the British colonial secretary at the time, stopped Jewish immigration precisely at a time when a safe haven was most needed, as the political situation worsened in Nazi Germany. European Jews began to enter Palestine illegally and the Jewish community planned for an eventual bid for independence from Britain. The leader of the Yishuv, David Ben Gurion, decided that the best Zionist strategy was to fight the war in Europe as if there was no problem with the British in Palestine and fight the British in Palestine as if there was no war in Europe.

In the aftermath of World War II and the discovery of what Hitler's "Final Solution" really entailed, world public opinion shifted in favor of Jewish settlement in Palestine and many refugees held in deportation camps were repatriated to Palestine. Palestinian Arab leaders worried about the massive influx of Jewish refugees and opted once again for a violent response. Riots broke out in Jerusalem, and Palestinian irregular forces cut off food, water, and fuel supplies to the city during the long siege that followed. There was strife throughout the country, with massacres taking place at Gush Etzion (by Palestinians) and in Deir Yassin (by Jews). Arab Palestinians began leaving their towns and villages in droves to escape the fighting.[17]

By 1947, Britain could no longer tolerate the cost of empire in either lives or treasure. World War II had bankrupted the nation and one by one all of its colonial possessions were becoming independent: Sri Lanka; the "jewel in the crown," India; and, eventually, Palestine. The British brought the Palestinian issue to the fledgling United Nations. In a surprising move, the U.N. voted in favor of partition.

On May 14, 1948, Israel declared itself to be independent and British troops left immediately. The following day the new state was invaded simultaneously by all of its neighbors: Iraq, Jordan, Egypt, Syria, and Lebanon. Israel emerged victorious from the war and with decidedly more territory than had been proposed by the 1947 Partition Plan. Resolution 181 of the United Nations General Assembly recognized the state of Israel. In 1948 and 1949, the U.N. arranged a series of ceasefires to end hostilities. Several armistice agreements were signed but never ratified to become formal peace agreements. The Arab states refused to recognize the existence of the state of Israel and considered the 1948 war to be a great catastrophe; while Israelis call it the War of Independence, Arabs know it as *al Naqbah* (the disaster). Hundreds of thousands of Palestinians went or were forced into exile. The Palestinian areas that remained under Arab control in the West Bank were annexed to the Kingdom of Jordan and the Gaza Strip found itself under Egyptian administrative control.

The origin of the Palestinian refugee problem has long been a subject of intense debate among Israeli scholars and even among Palestinians. Estimates for the number of Palestinian Arab refugees who fled or were forced out of their homes during the fighting vary from 520,000 (Israeli sources) to 726,000 (U.N. sources) to more than 800,000 (Arab sources). Since 1987, when an Israeli freedom-of-information act allowed the war records to be released, many of the accusations Palestinians have leveled over the years about Israelis' deliberate ethnic cleansing campaigns have turned out to be true. Israeli revisionist scholars like Benny Morris, Illan Pappé, and Avi Shlaim have detailed the creation of the refugee problem by emphasizing the deliberate campaigns to clear Palestinians from strategic areas around Jerusalem and Lydda (Lod).[18] Hundreds of thousands of Palestinians were forced to reside in temporary housing, a refugee problem that has still not been fully addressed.

With every war that Israel and Palestine fought, culminating in Israel's greatest victory in the Six Day War of 1967, the refugee crisis worsened and the Palestinian population tended increasingly to radicalization and the pull of violence.

Before 1967, competing Arab governments used the Palestinian refugees in their bid for leadership of the Arab World. The Arab countries were sharply divided between those with monarchies and those with revolutionary regimes. The crisis within the Arab world resulted in a proxy war between Egypt and Saudi Arabia in Yemen, as well as hostile accusations within the Arab League. In 1964 President Gamal Abdel Nasser of Egypt took the initiative and established the Palestinian Liberation Organization (PLO). It was soon recognized as the sole legitimate representative of the Palestinian people, even though its leader, a lawyer named Ahmed Shukairi, was little more than an Egyptian puppet. Several other Arab countries established their own Palestinian groups. Far from the manipulation of Arab leaders, another group, Fatah (Harikat al Tahrir al Watini al Falistini; the acronym, read backwards, meant the Palestinian National Liberation Movement), had been founded in 1954 in the Persian Gulf, where many educated Palestinian engineers and teachers had gone to earn a living. Unlike the other organizations, this group was created by the members of the Palestinian diaspora and remained in the background of the Palestinian movement until after the defeat of 1967. At the Battle of Karameh in March 1968, Fatah fedayeen (guerrilla fighters) were able to repel Israeli forces back across the Jordan River. This small victory in the wake of the agonizing 1967 defeat propelled Fatah to prominence.[19] The group's leader, a young engineer named Yasser Arafat, became the chairman of the PLO in 1969 and launched a new era of armed struggle.

The Palestinian militant groups began to use acts of terrorism to great effect. Arafat created a virtual "state within the state" inside Jordan. As the militias took and did as they pleased in their host country, tension mounted between the Palestinians and the Jordanian monarch, King Hussein bin Talal. Fedayeen raids distressed King Hussein because the Israeli air force responded to every Palestinian incursion with strikes against Jordanian targets. On September 1, 1970, the king narrowly dodged several attempts on his life. Three airplane hijackings on September 6 were the last straw. The king declared martial law and began to eliminate Palestinian officers from the military. The clashes developed into an all-out civil war between Jordanian forces and the Palestinian militias. The neighboring Arab states that had promised to provide air cover to the PLO reneged as the Jordanian air force strafed columns of fleeing Palestinian refugees en route to Lebanon and Syria. The Palestinians were outgunned by the well-equipped Jordanian forces and more than 3,500 of them died in the melee. The events are known as Black September.

The PLO and its leadership left Jordan for Lebanon. Once again Arafat carved out a state within a state, in the southern part of the country. The refugees' presence exacerbated the fragile sectarian balance within Lebanon and led to the Lebanese Civil War (1975–90). After Israel's invasion of Lebanon in 1982, the PLO fled once again, this time to Tunisia. For many Palestinians who resided in the Occupied Territories there was a discernible gap between the jet-setting lifestyles of their leaders and the horrors of their everyday existence. According to Dan Fisher of the *LA Times*: "The youth lost hope that Israel would ever give them their rights. They felt the Arab countries were unable to accomplish anything. They felt that the Palestine Liberation Organization (PLO) has failed to achieve a thing."[20]

By 1987, the disconnect between the Palestinian people and its formal leadership had reached a breaking point. A whole genera-tion of young people had grown up knowing nothing but the

Israeli occupation and felt little or no solidarity with the leadership in Tunis. In December Palestinians launched their first intifada, a "shaking off" of Israeli control. The First Intifada (1987–93) began as an uncontrolled, unplanned explosion of Palestinian frustrations. It started within the Occupied Territories but was soon co-opted by the leadership in Tunis. It also marked a shift in world opinion as Israeli forces increasingly lost sympathy by shooting at children throwing rocks and killing scores of civilians daily. The event that most shifted public opinion was the burial alive of four young Palestinian protesters on February 5, 1988, in the West Bank village of Salim. The Israeli army had ordered them to lie facedown on the ground and then bulldozed dirt over them.[21] Once Israel lost the moral high ground in its fight against terrorism, what people would consider an acceptable response changed dramatically.

While the PLO dominated Palestinian resistance in the 1960s and 1970s, a rival group was emerging from the Society of Muslim Brothers. In Israel's infinite wisdom, it assumed that any challenge to the PLO's leadership was positive and so it pursued a dual strategy of benign neglect and even encouragement of rivals to the organization. Likud, the Israeli right-wing governing party, had watched Arafat's transformation from a revolutionary leader to the "sole legitimate representative" of the Palestinian people, recognized by the Arab League and the U.N. General Assembly in 1974. In response, the party's strategy was to promote an Islamic alternative. According to Arab-American journalist Ray Hanania: "In addition to hoping to turn the Palestinian masses away from Arafat and the PLO, the Likud leadership believed they could achieve a workable alliance with Islamic anti-Arafat forces that would also extend Israel's control over the occupied territories."[22]

Between 1967 and 1987, the number of mosques in Gaza tripled from two hundred to six hundred, all with Israeli government sanction. In trying to undercut the PLO, Israel's leaders,

Menachem Begin and Yitzhak Shamir, created the Village Leagues, local councils composed of Palestinians willing to cooperate with the Israelis. In return, the Israelis put the group's members on their payroll and allowed them to publish a newspaper and set up an extensive network of charitable organizations, which collected funds not only from the Israelis but also from Arab states opposed to Arafat.[23] The Village Leagues were dominated by Sheikh Ahmed Ismail Yassin and his followers within the Al Mujamma' Al Islami (Islamic Center). The organization that emerged from them in 1988 became known as Hamas, an acronym for "Islamic Resistance Movement." It was Hamas that would claim credit for the attack on the Sbarro pizzeria on August 9, 2001.

JUSTIFYING MASS MURDER

As Ahlam at-Tamimi sat answering questions, she was the embodiment of serenity. She wore no makeup and her thick dark hair was neatly tucked under a beige hijab. She wore an earth-toned silk scarf and a long brown *jilbab* (a long, baggy overgarment). Ahlam both personified and led the Hamas women in HaSharon prison, but she had come to represent much more: she was a symbol of the Palestinian resistance and the new feminine face of Hamas.

Ahlam had done more than just accompany the suicide bomber Izzedine as-Suheil Al Masri to the Sbarro pizzeria. Together they had caused one of the most infamous and deadly terror attacks in Israel's history. Ahlam provided the intelligence and was pivotal in planning the operation, choosing the target, and accompanying the bomber. She claims that blowing up the pizzeria was her idea. This was not Ahlam's first mission as a terrorist. On June 30, 2001, a little more than a month before the pizzeria bombing, she had placed an explosive device disguised as a can of beer in a garbage bin at a Jerusalem grocery store on King George Street, then tried to detonate it at a distance using a timer. Security personnel detected the can before it could explode and it caused no damage. Having failed at her first attempt, Ahlam needed to up the ante with the next operation.

Hamas and Ahlam learned some valuable lessons from the failure that June. The first lesson was, use a suicide bomber rather than a timed device. A suicide bomber is a weapon with a brain that can change directions or make adjustments as the situation requires. Because there is no need to plan for the perpetrator's escape route, the hardest part is reaching the target. The suicide bomber is deadlier than other forms of terrorist attacks because of his or her ability to switch targets midmission or, if the detonator fails, to find an alternative way of activating the explosive. Timed devices, although they allow the attacker to survive another day and conduct more operations in the future, are more likely to fail or be discovered.

Part of the lethality of a suicide attack comes from the actual explosive, whose bursting fireball kills anyone near the bomber on impact. Additional casualties result from projectile materials—such as nails, screws, or ball bearings—added to the weapon, all of which tear into the flesh of bystanders. Hamas had also learned that a bomb is even more deadly when it explodes in an enclosed space. As the explosive burns, it gobbles up oxygen: in a confined area, the explosion causes the space to implode under the pressure of the disappearing oxygen. Knowing this, the bomber tries to find a spot away from the doors and windows, which might allow oxygen to fill the vacuum created when the bomb goes off. This is what made Israeli buses attractive targets to Palestinian terrorist groups: during summer all the windows are closed (when the air-conditioning is on) and in winter they're still closed (when the heat is on). And this is probably why Al Masri entered the restaurant rather than explode on the street. That hot day in August, most of the Sbarro customers were crammed into the restaurant, which was air-conditioned, rather than sitting outside in the blazing sun. Fortunately, the building that housed the pizzeria had been recently retrofitted to improve its structural integrity. If not for these improvements, the ceiling might have collapsed, doubling the death toll.

Earlier on the day of the bombing, Ahlam rendezvoused with Al Masri and his lethal guitar case at an intercity taxi stand in the West Bank town of Ramallah. The couple shared the ride with six other passengers going to Jerusalem. At the heavily manned Kalandiya checkpoint outside Ramallah, they briefly separated, and Al Masri passed through security on foot without his guitar case. Ahlam rested the case on her lap in the backseat of the vehicle and watched Al Masri cross to the other side while pretending not to know him. Both wore Western-style clothes, mimicking young Israelis rather than conservative Palestinians. She was in tight blue jeans and a sexy halter top. He had shaven off his beard and his chest and body hair, following the Islamic tradition of preparation for a martyrdom operation, but rather than shave his head as well, he had taken the suggestion of their Hamas handler Hassan, and had dyed his hair platinum blond so he would look more like an Israeli. To complete the look of a hipster, Al Masri sported dark sunglasses, blue jeans, and a T-shirt. No one would give the young "Israeli" couple walking through downtown Jerusalem a second glance.

Hassan had given Al Masri 100 Israeli shekels (about $27) for the cab fare, and had instructed them not to talk to each other until they had cleared the checkpoints. When they did speak, it was only in English. Ahlam carried a camera so that she could pass for a tourist. After the pair successfully traversed Kalandiya, they switched taxis at the Aram checkpoint and continued on toward Jerusalem. The taxi dropped them off at the Damascus Gate near the walls of the old city and Ahlam and Al Masri continued on foot toward the city center. They arrived at the intersection of King

George and Jaffa streets. Ahlam says, "I did not want to blow up that day," so she had asked Al Masri to wait fifteen minutes before detonating the bomb. She wanted to be far from the blast area.

With her head start, Ahlam raced back to the Palestine TV studio where she was a news presenter for the Palestine Authority. She changed into a cream-colored cotton turtleneck and chocolate brown safari jacket for the broadcast. With her long dark hair and tawny lipstick matching her outfit, she was extremely telegenic, the picture of a modern Palestinian woman. Her on-air persona looked nothing like the woman she became later in HaSharon prison. She composed herself and reported the event in which she had played such an intrinsic part. She recalls that it was hard to keep a straight face. "A suicide action took place on Jaffa Street at the Sbarro restaurant," she told viewers. "The result: fifteen dead."[24]

Within hours, several Palestinian groups had claimed responsibility for the attack. The Islamic Jihad, based in Damascus, faxed several news agencies, including Agence France Presse in Beirut, and claimed that the bomber was Hussein Omar Abu Naaseh. Hours later they corrected their mistake, this time claiming that the bomber was Hussein Omar Abu Amsha. Finally, after several hours of confusion and competing claims of responsibility, Ramadan Abdullah Shallah, the Islamic Jihad's secretary general, told a Gulf television station that there had been a mistake: Hussein Abu Amsha was indeed on a suicide mission, but he was not the Sbarro bomber. Shallah explained: "Our fighter Hussein Abu Amsha was en route to carry out a martyrdom operation and when the explosion [in Jerusalem] happened our brothers thought it was him … Abu Amsha is now a *potential* martyr."[25] Shallah had blown Amsha's cover, alerting the Israelis to his name, destination, and intent, and so rendering him virtually useless.

Hamas also claimed responsibility for the attack, identifying the bomber correctly as twenty-two-year-old Izzedine as-Suheil

Al Masri, from Aqaba in the Jenin district of the West Bank. Following the standard operating procedure after a suicide strike, Hamas representatives distributed a pre-attack photo of a bearded Al Masri holding an M16 assault rifle and a copy of an illuminated *Qur'an*[26] in his left hand with explosives strapped around his waist. His green Hamas headband matched the flag behind him and proclaimed in Arabic, *La ilaha il Allah* ("There is no God but God").

Reactions within the Al Masri family varied from joy to sorrow. Al Masri's older brother, Iyad, expressed unadulterated pride, calling the operation unique because of its quality and success. Izzedine had always spoken of martyrdom and now Palestinians everywhere would hold their heads up high.[27] Their father, Suheil, said that he was filled with both pride and sadness. "When I heard about the operation in Jerusalem, I did not doubt that my son did this," he said. "I will weep for him all of my life." And then he added, "I hope that many others follow him."[28] Yet to Barbara Victor, a journalist who interviewed him a few years after the attack, Suheil said that the operation had made him sick to his stomach and "had destroyed him and his family."[29] Another brother, Salahaddin, considered Al Masri a hero, but their mother, Umm Iyad, disagreed. Izzedine was never active politically, unlike the other little boys growing up during the First Intifada. He never threw stones at the Israelis and had not joined any of the militant organizations operating in Jenin. Umm Iyad had never seen anybody from Hamas in the house, and besides, the Al Masri family would not have wanted them there! While many groups had tried to claim Al Masri as their own, Umm Iyad argued that he did not belong to any of them. She even said he would have to have been mentally unbalanced to commit such an atrocity.[30]

Al Masri's mother probably did not know of his activities. Would-be suicide bombers rarely inform their parents of their plans. The terrorist groups deliberately keep the family in the dark for fear that they might try to change the bomber's mind. Procedure dictates that the group isolate the bombers in a safe house for several days before the attack, during which time a minder will sit with them, pray with them, and help them through the various purification rituals. The isolation is intended to focus the bomber's thoughts and instill the clarity required to commit a suicide operation. Despite warnings to keep his mission secret, a few days before the attack, Al Masri asked his very pregnant sister, Hala, whether she would name her unborn child after him if he died a martyr. But since he had no previous record of extremism or political activism, his sister assumed he was kidding.[31]

While the organizers of terrorist operations deliberately keep children away from their parents, they will not go against a family's wishes. Terrorist leaders immediately cancel an attack if a bomber's family learns about the operation. They assume that the family will try to prevent the operation, and might even contact the Palestinian National Authority (PNA) or even the Israeli authorities. "Azam [Fatah] thought that the mothers were the pivot of family opposition, and thought that a mother who supported her son's suicide was insane."[32]

Some parents will feign pride at the martyrdom of their children for the cameras and the community but mourn quietly when the cameras and reporters leave. Mothers are expected to ululate with joy rather than shed tears when their children become martyrs. The women in HaSharon prison say that being the parent of a martyr is life's biggest reward. It is a huge honor for the family. Al Manar television regularly parades women before the cameras to endorse their children's martyrdom. When Umm Nidal's son told her that he wanted to be a martyr for the Islamic Jihad she stated on camera, "May Allah give you the strength and courage. I hope you will become a martyr for Allah. May Allah be thanked, my boy has died for eternal life."[33] Otherwise known as Mariam Farhat, Umm Nidal is also featured in her son's last will and testament video. The video has had a huge impact on other would-be bombers. In Beer Sheba jail, one failed female bomber recalls: "I saw with my own eyes a mother who said good-bye to her son a suicide bomber, and gave him the weapon to perform his action. I dream of being like her. When I have a child I will strap the bomb on him myself."[34]

Farhat capitalized on her son's fame as a suicide bomber. She ran for election on the Hamas ticket in 2006 and won, and is infamous in Gaza for having sent three of her six sons on suicide missions. But Farhat is likely an exception to the rule. Most parents are not happy when they lose a child, and mourn the loss in private. It is considered unnatural when a parent buries a child and reverses the normal order of life. But Palestinian society has placed a high value on martyrdom, and the relatives of martyrs reap great rewards, especially respect in the community.

In contrast to the ambivalent and contradictory reactions in the Al Masri home, the attack was heralded in the Arab press with great fanfare. Editorials in the Arab world promote such activity: "We should bless every Palestinian man or woman who goes calmly to carry out a martyrdom operation, in order to receive a reward in the Hereafter, sacrificing her life for her religion and her homeland and knowing that she will never return from this operation."[35]

In Palestinian areas, suicide bombers are called martyrs—*shahids*—and considered heroes. Hundreds of people attend their funerals and their families receive congratulations rather than condolences. In the village of Aqaba, Palestinian children point to Izzedine Al Masri's house, saying, "*Shahid, shahid*, this way!" The *shahids*' names are memorialized on street signs, in public parks, and even in youth camps. The glossy pre-mission photos of the bombers are reproduced as twelve-by-sixteen-inch posters that Palestinian children put up on their bedroom walls. According to some sources, the amount of space a bomber gets on a poster depends on how many Israelis he or she has killed. Al Masri did not have to share the space: his was one of the deadliest attacks in Israel's history, at the time second only to the Islamic Jihad's attack at the Dolphinarium disco on the Tel Aviv waterfront two months earlier, in which 21 Russian-Israeli teenagers had died and 120 had been injured. Just weeks after the pizzeria bombing, An-Najah University in Nablus mounted an exhibition to commemorate the second anniversary of the Al 'Aqsa Intifada that included a diorama of the attack, replete with fake bodies, blood, and gore.

Israel's secret service agency, the Shabak, arrested Ahlam on September 14, 2001, and charged her with extending logistical support to the Hamas cell responsible for the Sbarro bombing, along with Muhammed Wail Daghlas, another Hamas activist. Using a smuggled cell phone, Daghlas told the television program *Nightline* that militant groups "have to send a message that Israeli children are not safe if they continue killing [Palestinian] children."[36]

At Birzeit University, where Ahlam had been a communications and journalism major, students understood the attack as revenge for the humiliating checkpoints, harsh living conditions, and killing of Palestinian civilians. Sara Helm of the *Sunday Times* interviewed some of Ahlam's fellow students at Birzeit after the attack. They suggested to her that, because Ahlam was reporting on all the suffering at the TV station every day, she felt the pain of the occupation more deeply than others. Mia, the gentlest of girls, bright-eyed in denim dungarees and pink T-shirt, said that "you had to understand how Palestinians were made to feel like animals in order to understand their support for a suicide operation. The Israeli military cages them up." Palestinians feel that Israel has stolen their land. "They have made me feel that when I die, I too want to hurt the person who has hurt me and my family." And the Jewish children? "Yes, the children too," said Mia. "Because the children of the Jews will be the soldiers of the future. They are the ones who will kill us."[37]

An Egyptian newspaper, *Al Masa'a*, published an editorial that endorsed the killing of Israeli civilians, including children, during martyrdom operations. The editor explained that he would not question the legitimacy of such operations against Israel because the suicide attacks were a powerful weapon used by the Palestinians against an enemy with no morality or religion, an enemy who has deadly weapons prohibited by international law and is not deterred from using them against the defenseless Palestinian people. "Even if during [a martyrdom operation] civilians or children are killed— the blame does not fall upon the Palestinians, but upon those who forced them to turn to this modus operandi."[38]

Many people connect the phenomenon of suicide bombing with the ideas of French sociologist Émile Durkheim and his study of altruistic suicide, in which the person embedded within society is convinced that his or her death is the only possible contribution he or she can make. But in most cases of suicide terrorism, altruism does not readily apply. According to Dr Azzam Tamimi (no relation to Ahlam), it is the belief in paradise rather than altruism that plays a key role in martyrdom operations. Nor does the bomber feel guilt for his or her action. By giving his or her own life as part of the sacrifice, the bomber's martyrdom wipes out the moral wrong of killing civilians. This hardly compares to self-immolating Buddhist monks, hunger strikers, or prisoners of conscience, whose own suffering is intended to make a political statement without harming others. Suicide terror is murder in which the perpetrator justifies his or her action by a theological loophole so that he or she can enter paradise.

According to this loose interpretation of Islamic law, the act of self-sacrifice provides the rationale for the killing of innocents, which otherwise is strictly prohibited by the *Qur'an* and the sayings of the Prophet Muhammed (PBUH [peace be upon him]). Verse 5:32 of the *Qur'an* echoes Genesis chapter 4: "If any one slew a person—unless it be for murder or for spreading mischief in the land—it would be as if he slew the whole people: and if any one saved a life, it would be as if he saved the life of the whole people." This justification is widely accepted in Palestine even if it violates both the spirit and letter of orthodox Islamic law.

Umm Anas (her nom de guerre), an eighteen-year-old female Islamic Jihad operative in Gaza interviewed by the BBC, echoes the justifications for killing civilians, including children. For her, all Jews, including the children, have violated Palestinian land as a result of the Occupation. While she acknowledges that children are technically (and according to the *Qur'an*) civilians, they will one day grow up to be soldiers. For Umm Anas, martyrdom permits the Palestinians to level the playing field. Ahlam concurs. The Israeli side is twice as powerful as the Palestinian side, she says. There is no balance of power between the two, so Palestinians need to defend their lands using any means at their disposal. She considers herself to be a daughter of the Palestinian people defending Palestinian lands. She will use any means necessary.[39] This is why terrorist leaders such as the Islamic Jihad's Abdullah ash-Shami routinely claim that suicide bombing is the only Palestinian option: "We have no bombs, tanks, missiles, planes, or helicopters."[40] Martyrs or human bombs allow the Palestinians to capitalize on their comparative advantage in numbers: in the absence of high-tech weapons or nuclear arms, the Palestinians have many people willing to die for the cause. Umm Anas sums up the trade-off: "Jews are scared when we just throw stones. Imagine what happens when body parts fly at them."[41]

Sayyid Hassan Nasrallah, the current secretary-general and leader of the Lebanese Hezbollah, was the first terrorist leader to deploy suicide bombers effectively to leverage an overwhelming military force. The 1983 attack on the U.S. Marine barracks was the deadliest terrorist attack against Americans before September 11, 2001, and helped compel the Americans to leave Lebanon. Asked to explain what goes through the martyr's mind prior to an operation, and why someone like Umm Anas would consider dying to be a gift from God, Nasrallah employs a metaphor to describe the euphoria felt by the would-be *shahid*. Martyrdom provides a huge relief, he explains: "Imagine you are in a sauna and it is very hot, but you know that in the next room there is air-conditioning, an armchair, classical music, and a cocktail. So you pass easily into the next room. That is how I would explain martyrdom to a Westerner."[42]

For Ahlam, martyrdom is a beautiful thing—not for her, for her accomplice. "If there was a poor man and you gave him a lot of money, that would make him very happy, and you would be happy for giving him the life that he wanted so much. I gave this bomber the life he wanted so much. I was amazed by his enthusiasm for this operation and his eagerness to pass into the next world."[43]

Most individuals who plan operations are unlikely ever to volunteer for martyrdom themselves. According to interviews conducted by Tel Aviv University psychologist Ariel Merari, several organizers said that they were reluctant to kill themselves in a martyrdom attack. They explained to him how difficult it would be for them to carry out the operations that they had planned. "If one is destined to organize [suicide attacks] others are destined to perform martyrdom operations. A recurrent theme in the explanations was that their role as organizers was more important than that of the bomber."[44] Yasser, a Hamas organizer, said that he wouldn't be willing to die himself. Presumably, knowing that you are sending others to make the utmost sacrifice, a sacrifice you would be reluctant to make yourself, must generate psychological distress, unless you are utterly cynical and manipulative.[45]

If the Palestinians have worked out their own elaborate justifications for killing civilians, so have the Israelis—the logic of oppression and terror again playing itself out. According to Lieutenant-General Moshe Ya'alon, a former Israeli chief of staff, Israel is at war with an enemy that has no qualms about killing children. That is why Israelis "shoot first and ask questions later." For Ya'alon, Palestinians need to pay the price for their war.[46] Israeli Air Force general Dan Halutz, another former chief of staff, was a key figure behind then Prime Minister Ariel Sharon's policy of targeted killings of suspected terrorists. Halutz gave an interview to the *Washington Post* in which he declared that targeted killing was the most important method Israel had at its disposal in its fight against terrorism.[47] From the beginning of the Second Intifada in September 2000 through June 30, 2008, there were more than 521 deaths from Israeli targeted assassinations, including 233 bystanders, 20 women, and 71 children. Entire families were wiped out with the dropping of a bomb, including women, children, the sick, and the elderly.

A July 2002 incident in Gaza showed how lethal targeted assassinations can be. Halutz ordered an Israeli F-16 to drop a 1,000-kilogram (approximately one-ton) bomb on an apartment block in Gaza City where Salah Shehadeh, the leader of the Izzedine Al Qassam Brigades, Hamas's armed wing responsible for suicide operations, lived with his wife and children. Ya'alon knew Shehadeh's family was there. The bomb killed Shehadeh, his wife and young daughter, and sixteen others, of whom fifteen were civilians and nine were children under the age of eleven, including a two-month old baby.[48] Two neighboring homes were also destroyed and thirty-two others damaged.

Asked later by an interviewer from *Haaretz* newspaper whether he felt any remorse about the incident, which was condemned around the world, Halutz answered: "If you insist on wanting to know what I feel when I release a bomb, I will tell you. I feel a slight bump to the plane when the bomb releases. A second later it passes. That is what I *feel*."[49] Israelis celebrated Halutz as a hero, while Prime Minister Ariel Sharon roundly praised the killing of Shehadeh as an unqualified and complete success. Sharon then promoted Halutz to chief of staff.

For Israelis, the problem is that they are not fighting another state with an army, but terrorists who embed themselves among civilians. The terrorists place their children in harm's way by using civilians as human shields. They attack Israel anticipating that it will respond violently. The Israeli military response kills even more civilians, especially children. The children's deaths increase the Palestinian public's outrage against Israel and motivate people to join terrorist organizations and volunteer to be suicide bombers. The deliberate provocation not only ramps up support for the terrorist groups but also makes their propaganda against the enemy resonate in the hearts and minds of every Palestinian.

The Israelis consider the deaths of Palestinian children as "collateral damage." They have done little to limit the number of unintended victims of their counter-terror policies. Israel is unwilling to take the steps to ensure that children are not killed by accident, especially if this increases the danger posed to its soldiers on the ground. Officially, the country has implemented rules of engagement regarding the use of targeted assassination. The military is supposed to adhere to six iron-clad conditions: "that arrest is otherwise impossible; that targets are strictly combatants; that senior cabinet members approve each attack; that civilian casualties are minimized; that operations are limited to areas not under Israeli control; and that targets are identified as a future threat. Unlike prison sentences, targeted killing cannot be meted out as punishment for past behavior. In 2002, a military panel established that targeting cannot be for revenge, but only for deterrence."[50] The fact that such rules of engagement exist means nothing to the Palestinian civilians bearing the brunt of bombing campaigns. The Palestinian terrorist organizations' response appears to be to deliberately target Israeli women and children. This in turn outrages Israelis further and ramps up the next counter-terror measure, creating a bloody call-and-response cycle on both sides.

What both sides fail to grasp is how the cycles of violence persist and worsen over time. A demonstrable culture of martyrdom and a longing for death have evolved within Palestinian society. According to Eyad Serraj, a psychiatrist who treats Palestinians suffering from post-traumatic stress disorder, at least 25 percent of young people in Gaza aspire to a martyr's death. Some refuse to go to school because they fear not seeing their parents again because of the possibility that they will be arrested or killed, or will not find their house when they come home, because the Israelis have destroyed it. "In the First Intifada , the danger was limited to the places where soldiers and stone-throwers clashed. Now death comes from the skies and anyone anywhere can be hit. This has created a state of chronic panic."[51]

The pattern of violence makes the conflict multigenerational. Children who are brought up in this environment seek death and their parents will not dissuade them from following their dream. Palestinians live in the fear that they can die at any moment from aerial bombardment or a stray bullet. Becoming a bomber might in some ways be empowering, because at least a bomber chooses the time and place of his or her death. When failed female bomber Shefa'a Al Qudsi was asked whether she would discourage her daughter, Diana, from following in her footsteps and becoming a martyr, she said that she would teach Diana that education is the most important thing in life. But since children can be shot coming home from school, the best and the brightest Palestinian children become martyrs, whether or not they want to be. So if

Diana wanted to become a "living martyr," Shefa'a would not stop her.[52]

Suicide attacks have simultaneously radicalized Israeli viewpoints and hardened their political positions. Israel's heavy-handed military tactics, checkpoint abuses, targeted killings, and collective punishment are all justified in the name of security. Human rights abuses and the systematic humiliation of Palestinians are either ignored or tolerated by a population consumed by fear. In the end, it is the civilians on both sides of the conflict who pay the price. Within a month of Shehadeh's targeted assassination, the Izzedine Al Qassam Brigades he once headed perpetrated several more attacks against Israelis, in Safad at Meiroun's crossroads and near Damascus Gate in Jerusalem. This began yet another new cycle of violence with escalation on both sides.

THE WOMEN OF HASHARON PRISON

Ahlam at-Tamimi remains in HaSharon prison, a sprawling, multi-story concrete structure surrounded by tall palm trees, razor wire, guard dogs, and towers outside of Tel Aviv in the Plain of Sharon. The prison houses 106 other female security prisoners, 58 of them linked to Hamas, the Islamic Jihad, and other Islamist-inspired groups, and 48 from the secular movement Fatah. The women range in age from seventeen to thirty. Like Ahlam, many are serving life sentences with no chance of parole. According to Hamas's leadership, the Israelis are holding around 12,000 prisoners of both sexes, including 400 children (people under the age of eighteen). Other reports claim 360 children, including 200 awaiting trial and another 145 serving various prison terms.[53]

The women at HaSharon are kept in a virtual labyrinth, behind seven iron doors and gates at the ends of long corridors to which few people are allowed access. To reach the cells, one must climb and descend one flight of stairs after another, up, down, and around, like something out of an M.C. Escher drawing. Ahlam claims that the women of HaSharon have made the prison a beautiful place, an ersatz Garden of Eden. They have painted murals of roses and flowers and babies on the white walls and brought vibrant color to the gray and blue concrete jail.

Ahlam is located in Ward 11 with other Hamasawis (Hamas supporters) and several women from the Islamic Jihad. In some interviews, Ahlam refers to herself in the third person when she describes how "Ahlam brought jihad to the people" or says, "Since Ahlam entered prison, the Palestinians have become acquainted with the hidden aspect of Ahlam's personality. The idea of jihad and its agenda."[54] She can be extremely curt. When former *New York Times* reporter Judith Miller went to HaSharon prison in 2007 to talk with failed bombers, Ahlam brushed her aside: "We don't like America because of the war in Iraq and your support for the Zionists and Jews," she declared, and abruptly turned away.[55] She also monitors what all the other women say and feeds them pre-approved responses during interviews: "Say how many children you have, how they live, how they saw blood and murder," she tells Kahira Sa'adi, another inmate, during an interview, as she listens to ensure that Hamas propaganda is properly disseminated.

While in prison, Ahlam married her cousin Nizar, who is incarcerated at another secure facility for acts of terrorism. Ahlam herself has become a celebrity. She has starred in documentaries, been the subject of poems, and been heralded in the Palestinian press and international media. Mutawakil Taha, head of the Palestinian Writer's Union and a former deputy minister in the Palestinian Authority, wrote a book honoring her and her husband, Nizar, *Ahlam ibn al Nabi,* in which he describes the couple as heroes. Two years after publication of the book, on April 7, 2008, *al Quds* newspaper quoted Taha saying how proud he was of the two prisoners, Nizar and Ahlam at-Tamimi. In the *al Quds* interview,

Taha explained: "I feel that the prisoners are martyrs in potential, and that we should bond with them without question or accounting. We should bond to the prisoners unconditionally as we bond to the martyrs and the homeland."[56]

Avi Issacharoff, *Haaretz's* special correspondent for Arab affairs, claims that the lives of female suicide terrorists are no less tragic than those of male suicide bombers, yet the media accords these women more sympathy and treats them with kid gloves.[57] In fact, when women perpetrate acts of terrorism, they draw eight times the media attention given to men. Many of the terrorist organizations are aware of this and exploit women accordingly. Some of the Palestinian groups deliberately select more attractive and telegenic operatives precisely for this reason. Looking at a police lineup of female Palestinian suicide bombers (both successful and preempted) you would be struck by how attractive many of them are. The groups are seeking that reaction, followed by the obvious question, *What could make such a pretty girl do that? There must be something seriously wrong.*

Between 2002 and 2009, ninety-six Palestinian women attempted suicide attacks, though just eight were successful. Most of the women were preempted or caught before their attack could be completed, and a handful changed their minds at the last moment. Most of the attempts were conducted during the height of the Second Intifada, before the Israelis erected the security fence (known by some as the Apartheid Wall) to separate themselves from the Palestinians. According to Israeli counter-terrorism expert Anat Berko, Palestinian women are increasingly involved in all levels of terrorist activity, everything from scouting targets and smuggling guns and explosives to being suicide bombers. Berko claims that now that there is a sufficient number of successful and unsuccessful operatives, a profile of Palestinian female suicide bombers seems to be emerging. "The male suicide bombers tend to be introverts, the women less so. The women are older and better educated than their male counterparts. Whereas the men are usually in their late teens and early twenties with scant education, studies carried out by Shin Bet [the Israeli security agency] on sixty-seven women recruited to become suicide bombers from 2002 to 2005 found that 33 percent were college graduates and an additional 39 percent had finished high school."[58]

The terrorist organizations doubly exploit the women. They deliberately use women to avoid detection and catch the enemy off guard, knowing that the bombers will later become an issue for the Israelis with international human rights organizations. Several of the women, like Noor Al Hashlamoon, have given birth in the prison. The Israelis permit children up to two years old to stay with their mothers while incarcerated, and there are a half dozen babies and toddlers at HaSharon. Yusuf az-Zaqq, at one year and three months, is their youngest prisoner. The long-term imprisonment of children violates international law and puts Israel in an uncomfortable position when Hamas tries to negotiate for their release (for example, during prisoner exchanges). For critics, the women are mere pawns. The terrorist organizations consider the women strong and clever enough to coordinate and execute suicide attacks, but once convicted "they morph into delicate, fragile creatures deserving early release by dint of their femininity."[59]

In an interview with Al Jazeera television, the Shi'a cleric and spiritual head of Hezbollah, Grand Ayatollah Muhammed Hussein Fadlallah, who died on July 4, 2010, explained: "It is true that Islam has not asked women to carry out jihad, but it *permits them* to take part if the necessities of defensive war dictate that women should carry out any regular military operations, or suicide operations … We believe that the women who carry out suicide bombings are martyrs who are creating a new, glorious history for Arab and Muslim women [emphasis added]."[60]

The women in HaSharon prison tend to provide a laundry list of reasons for their involvement in terrorist activities. The death of family members is most often cited as the straw that broke the camel's back. To understand their motivations, it is important to differentiate between the structural conditions that affect the population as a whole (like the injustices of the Occupation) and the reasons specific to the individual bomber. One study suggests nationalism is the essential motivation. "There is no religious reason that in itself drives a man to carry out a suicide operation. Religion reinforces and helps the nationalist motivation. It is a political drive with religious backing."[61] This observation is congruent with the would-be martyrs' descriptions of their motivations for undertaking suicide missions.

WAFA AL BIS

In discussions with the journalist Judith Miller, one bomber confessed that two of her cousins had been killed and her brother jailed. The army invaded her city and demolished houses there. A war raged inside her: Shouldn't she do something? "The Israelis were killing us like rats and nobody was doing anything, not the Arabs, nobody. And I thought: No one will help us. I must make these dogs know how we feel. Even bullets that miss make noise."[62]

Miller discovered how difficult it is to assess the underlying motivations of female suicide bombers when she spoke with Wafa Al Bis, another inmate. Born into wretched poverty in Jabalya refugee camp in Gaza, one of twelve children, Al Bis had much of her body and fingertips burned in a freak cooking accident at home the year before her failed mission. She did not like the feel of the suicide pack or the outfit she was expected to wear. She told her handlers that the pants were too tight and the explosive pack too heavy. She felt uncomfortable. Her handlers assured her that they could get her other clothes. Wafa hedged and wondered to herself why she was doing this. Why was she at the checkpoint? She claimed that she was there because she had been coaxed—no, coerced—into becoming a martyr by Abul Khair, an older man from the Abu Riesh Brigade[63] (an offshoot of the Al Aqsa Martyrs' Brigade). She wished that she had never met him. During her interview, her eyes welled up with tears and she explained that when she looked into the mirror she did not recognize the reflection that stared back at her.[64] Al Bis claimed that she had no choice in the matter and had been coerced, but then she was forced to recant her story when the Al Aqsa Martyrs' Brigade aired her pre-attack last-will-and-testament video.

The issue of coercion is often neglected in discussions about terrorism. There is an assumption that most suicide bombers want to perpetrate the act. This is complicated by journalistic accounts after the fact, when the operative has become a hero in the community. Many interviews with the families and friends of the bombers can be misleading because there is a great deal of community pressure to support what their son or daughter or friend has just done. Because there is such a disconnect between the families' public and private faces, the grieving process is largely misunderstood and statements such as "I wish I had more than one daughter to give to the cause" create the impression that life is cheap for Palestinians and that the parents do not care whether their children become martyrs. This pressure explains the seemingly contradictory statements given to reporters by Al Masri's family as well as Al Bis's changing story.

The twenty-one-year-old Al Bis had used a special medical entry visa at the heavily fortified Erez Crossing (the main transit point between Israel and Gaza) on her way to blow up Soroka Hospital in Beersheba, where she had been treated for her second- and third-degree burns. It is difficult to fathom why she would attack the very doctors and nurses who had cared for her for six months. At one point, she told foreign journalists that the explosives had been planted on her without her knowledge and that she never really wanted to become a suicide bomber. Her father, Samir, agreed that his daughter had to have been coerced to carry out the mission. Although he remained in a state of shock after her arrest on June 6, 2005, he refused to believe that his daughter would blow herself up willingly. Al Bis's cousin, Wael, acts as the family spokesperson. He claims that Samir still believes that Al Bis was exploited by someone because of her injuries and fragile mental state. Samir says that it is not fair "that the whole Palestinian population should be punished for what she has tried to do. The Palestinians don't have to pay for her actions."[65]

All of these protestations of innocence, however, contradict what Al Bis herself said after she was arrested. In a press conference organized by the Israeli authorities on June 21, Al Bis, looking casual in flowery red flip-flops, a gray tracksuit, and a white cotton shirt, announced to the world that she did not regret what she had done and stressed that her decision to become a martyr had had nothing to do with her burns. She screamed at the reporters:

> My dream was to be a martyr. I believe in death. I wanted to blow myself up in a hospital, maybe even in the one in which I was treated … I wanted to kill 20, 50 Jews … yes, even babies! You, too, kill our babies. Do you remember the Doura child?[66]

However, at the same press conference Al Bis begged for mercy because she did not actually kill anyone. The claim she sometimes makes, that she was forced to become a suicide bomber, is contradicted by videotapes from Israeli security cameras, which show her trying to penetrate two sets of metal barriers at the Erez checkpoint. As she waddled toward the metal turnstiles, the Israeli guards commanded her to stop. There was something wrong with the way she carried herself and her bulky clothing did not suit the hot June afternoon. Through the loudspeaker, the guards demanded that Al Bis take off her outer garments. While the surveillance cameras recorded her every move, she began to slowly disrobe, removing her black headscarf, gown, black button-down shirt, and various other pieces of clothing until she was left with only beige chinos and a white T-shirt. Al Bis visibly flinched as she tried to detonate the twenty-pound explosive device hidden inside her pants. When there was no explosion, she repeatedly pushed the plunger in her pocket. She started to pace and scream in frustration like a caged animal and pulled out the detonator to check the wiring. The surveillance cameras record her screams and her hands clawing at her face and neck. The images capture her horror at the realization that the mission has failed.

It was extremely difficult for Al Bis's mother to watch the surveillance tapes of her daughter's failed operation. However, she agrees with the statements Al Bis made after her arrest, in which she claimed that it had been her dream since she was a little girl to be a martyr.[67]

Leftist Israeli journalist Amira Hass was highly critical of what she saw as the financial and material incentives for dispatchers to exploit weak and vulnerable women such as Wafa Al Bis. Many of the Palestinian old guard in Israeli jails were also horrified by the terrorist organizations' indecent exploitation of vulnerable people, including women, who are considered defective by societal norms. Because of her physical deformity, Al Bis was not going to fetch a good bride price and had no value on the marriage market. It was thus easy to incite her to join the terrorists. She might also have been persuaded that by becoming a martyr she could enter paradise a new woman, without all her scars and burns. The bastardized message they gave her was that she would be miraculously transformed in heaven into a beautiful girl. Her burns would be healed and she would be more attractive in death than she had ever been in life. The recruiters often tell women that in paradise they will be queens. No matter how old or grotesque they may be in this world, they will become the fairest of the seventy-two virgins that await each jihad warrior in the next.[68] For Al Bis, this might have seemed like her best chance of feeling normal again.

In most cases, it is difficult to ascertain whether there has been real coercion or whether such pleas are part of a bid for merciful treatment. There is a huge incentive for failed bombers to lie and declare that they were coerced, hoping that the justice system will moderate their sentences accordingly. Israel's judicial policy does not factor in regret, even for bombers who change their minds at the last minute and refuse to carry out their mission. As a matter of policy, most bombers get at least one life sentence, even if they were preempted and no one died. If there is "blood on their hands," a term that the Israelis use for bombers or those who aided them in a successful bombing in which Israelis have died, they will often get multiple life sentences with years added on for good measure.

AHLAM

If misconceptions about Palestinian female bombers have proliferated, this is in part due to Barbara Victor's depictions of them in her 2003 book *Army of Roses: Inside the World of Palestinian Women Suicide Bombers*. According to Victor, Ahlam at-Tamimi (whom she refers to as Zina in the book) had a history of problems at home and at school. Victor writes: "Beginning when she was an adolescent Zina rebelled. She refused to wear the hijab and the *jilbab* (traditional modest Islamic clothing) and told her family of her intentions to become an international journalist and live far from home ."[69] Victor writes that the relationship with her family was irreparably damaged when she refused to marry the man whom her family had chosen for her.[70] Zina (Ahlam) was pressured by her family to become a suicide bomber to redeem the family's honor after becoming pregnant out of wedlock by an Egyptian boyfriend she met at school in Jordan. They beat her to discover the identity of the father, and she had a baby in April 2001 in Jordan.

But this was not the case. Ahlam was politically mobilized to engage in violence against the Israeli occupation, not because she had had a child out of wedlock but because she had been radicalized and politicized by her activism in school. She certainly did not have a child four months before the attack (and two months prior to placing the explosive beer can in the market). It is clear from her newsreel that this was not a woman who had just given birth. Besides the fact that it is highly unlikely that a devout Muslim woman would admit such personal things to a foreign journalist, Victor's version implies that Ahlam was in two places (Jordan and Palestine) at the same time. Ahlam left Jordan for Ramallah back in 1998, three years before the alleged pregnancy, although Victor claims she arrived in Ramallah only one month before placing the explosive beer can at the co-op supermarket.[71] But Ahlam was a media personality on TV at that time, so there is a public record showing that she was actually in Palestine.

Like some researchers, Victor argues that all the Palestinian women involved in terrorism are attempting to right a previous wrong. The families of the first four Palestinian female bombers Victor interviewed claimed that their daughters had some personal secret or shame that becoming a martyr would fix. For Victor, women terrorists all require an act to clean the slate and allow them to reinvent themselves from a dishonorable existence to one that will be lauded by their community. While this set of conditions might apply to some bombers, not every female terrorist was mobilized because of a shameful event in her past, just as not every woman with a shameful event in her past is mobilized to become a terrorist.

In a 2006 interview with Israeli journalist Raanan Ben Zur, Ahlam explained that she would never recognize Israel's existence. She would only consider discussion after Israel recognized that Palestine was Islamic land. She offers no personal reasons for her political engagement. After two years of trials, she was sentenced in October 2003 to 16 life sentences with an additional 15 years, for a total of 320 years. In HaSharon prison, where she sat for the interview, Ahlam displayed little emotion or regret. Does she feel remorse? Ahlam says, no, of course not. She does not regret her actions and no Palestinian prisoner would because they are defending themselves, so they have no regrets. "And why should we?" she asks. "Should we regret defending ourselves? Should we feel regret that Israel murdered one of ours and we murdered one of theirs?"[72] Ahlam does not regret the deaths of all the children and feels that Israelis "should have returned to Poland, Russia, or the United States, to the countries their parents came from."[73]

Talking to Ahlam is chilling. Her case provides a classic example of Hamas's moral bankruptcy. When asked whether she was aware of the presence of women and children at the pizzeria, Ahlam says yes, she knew. Did she know how many children were killed? She says, "I think there were … three, maybe. I think three children were killed in this action." She is told simply, eight. "Eight," she repeats thoughtfully, "Eight." A smile spreads across her lovely face; she shrugs and her eyes gleam. But this scene is to be repeated over and over again as Ahlam, in every interview, pretends to not actually know the number of people she helped kill. It's an act, a show for the media. Terrorism would be nothing without the media attention and Ahlam relishes her fame.

Ahlam claims to have planned and orchestrated the Sbarro pizzeria attack. If she is correct, she is the exception to the rule. Most women involved in terrorist organizations are not leaders. Even when they are given a high profile in an organization's publicity, the women rarely play more than a marginal role, either numerically or in organizational terms. Women are sacrificial lambs in places like Turkey, where women comprised 40 percent of all suicide bombers in the Kurdish Workers Party (PKK), Sri Lanka, where women exceeded 25 percent of bombers in the LTTE, Chechnya, where they constitute 43 percent. They do not plan the operations they take part in. Often they have little say as to their targets, the timing, or the way in which the operations are conducted. Most are not even given thorough training. The mission itself requires little to no expertise or investment of either time or money. As one observer has noted: "Indeed, for many of the women, the contribution of a suicide mission to their national or religious struggle is precisely that: employment in the male-dominated domain of suicide bombing."[74]

Palestinian organizations present a different picture. Palestinian women are acknowledged as the equal of men in the steadfastness of their opposition to the Occupation. This form of resistance, called *Sumud*, is a way for Palestinians to convey to their enemies that their opposition is not ephemeral. *Sumud* means outlasting the Israelis and eventually prevailing. The importance of women has become especially notable since Al 'Aqsa Intifada. The increasing number of female bombers shows how proactive Palestinian women really are. Ahlam at-Tamimi is just one of a number of women who have become symbols of the new Palestinian woman and role models for other women and girls.

Women like suicide bomber Shefa'a Al Qudsi believe Palestinian women can do something more significant in the struggle. "Till Wafa, women had just helped jihad by making food. I thought: We can do more ... My body would be a bridge to a better future that my daughter would walk over. Yes, I would die, but I would help give her a better life, a future without occupation. I was placing her fate in Allah's hands."[75]

Palestinian political prisoners are occasionally made to mix with HaSharon prison's general population. When they do, Israeli criminals hurl insults at the political prisoners and beat them if they can. The guards do nothing to intervene. The women suffer from psychological problems, but are denied access to a psychiatrist. In addition, most women prisoners have skin diseases and other conditions because of the presence of vermin in the prison and neglect by the authorities. Ahlam at-Tamimi suffers from kidney stones and pain in her joints but Israeli authorities and the prison guards refuse to allow her medical treatment.[76] She resorted to a hunger strike in order to return to HaSharon after she was transferred to the Moscobiya prison. The strike made her medical condition worse, though Israeli authorities finally allowed her access to care.

Human rights groups have lodged multiple complaints with the World Organization Against Torture (WOAT), saying that the female prisoners in Israel are being abused and sexually humiliated while in custody. According to the complaint, prison conditions do not meet the minimum required standards and the women are allegedly subjected to humiliating body searches in front of male guards. In a society in which modesty is highly prized and immodesty can be punished by death as part of the honor code, forcing Palestinian women to take off all of their clothes is the ultimate humiliation.

The report to the WOAT describes a typical search of a female prisoner, who happens to be one of Ahlam at-Tamimi's prison mates. As Amneh reached her cell, she was asked to undress in front of Sireet and Asher and two other male guards behind the door. Because of the presence of men, she refused. She was then taken into a cell with five male and female guards. The guards beat her and sprayed her with large quantities of tear gas. She fell to the ground and the guards continued to beat her, inflicting injuries to her head and nose. They tied her feet and hands behind her back. Sireet strip-searched Amneh in the presence of the men, lifting her blouse and releasing her trouser buttons and inspecting her while she was lying on the ground. Amneh shouted and yelled all the while. After the episode, Amneh was put in solitary confinement for three weeks.[77] In Palestine, under the strict Islamic honor code, this type of sexual humiliation would ruin a woman's reputation and chances of getting married. While in this instance the Israelis apparently stopped short of actually raping their prisoner, this kind of attack easily inspires the women who are victimized to seek revenge against their tormentors.

Although the Israelis will never release her, Ahlam has become increasingly popular while incarcerated. She is a symbol of the resistance both in her role as the leader of the female prisoners at HaSharon and by the mere fact that Israeli prison officials have targeted her for especially harsh treatment and limited her contact with the outside world. Ahlam is one of several Hamas prisoners to have been subjected to a new policy of limiting communication between Hamas representatives and the international media. Perhaps this is a result of her newfound fame in films, magazines, poems, and literature and of the fact that she received the Al Quds Mark of Honor from Mahmoud Abbas, president of the Palestinian National Authority, in April 2008. In July 2009 she won general elections for Hamas's prison leadership.

5

THE FUTURE BOMBERS

With the name of Black Tigers—Would you see?
With a bomb which did blast the strong enemy
We march without a battalion army. We die by routing our adversary.
Our deaths become exceptional history. In them are written hundreds
*   of victories.*
There is nothing like this bravery
The gift of Life—the greatest philanthropy of all.
Marching with thoughts of not missing our aim
With prideful anger we kill the enemy. We die now for our families to
*   enjoy their lives*
In Tamil hearts—in death we still live.
Greeting the Leader's feet like thunder we blast. Drooping like a flag
*   for Tamil Eelam to stand*
The Tiger flag will flutter strong in the Motherland
And glory will engulf the global bands.
—Black Tigers' marching song, translated by Sachi Sri Kantha[1]

There was an election campaign under way in the state of Tamil
Nadu, India. On May 21, 1991, Thenmuli Rajaratnam stood
with many others waiting for the arrival of Rajiv Gandhi in the

industrial town of Sriperumbudur, near Chennai, where the former Indian prime minister was due to speak. Thenmuli wore horn-rimmed glasses that obscured her face and in her hands she held tightly to a garland. A pronounced bulge beneath her orange *salwar kameez* (the traditional Hindu tunic worn over baggy pants) suggested that she was pregnant. The appearance was deceptive: in fact, Thenmuli, whose code name was Dhanu, had been fitted with a denim vest containing an improvised explosive device. A large cylinder positioned under her breasts was filled with hundreds of three-millimeter steel balls. Underneath it, next to her skin, the vest held a quantity of C-4 plastic explosive. Two detonators, one on either side of her body, required only a gentle tug to be ignited.

Gandhi strode toward the podium, pausing at intervals to greet supporters. As he passed Dhanu, he clasped her hand. According to plan, she knelt before him and with her right hand activated the bomb.[2] The explosion had a lethal range of roughly a hundred feet. Gandhi, Dhanu, and sixteen others were killed instantly by the blast.

Investigations into the assassination later revealed that a policewoman had tried to prevent the assassin from reaching the former prime minister. But Gandhi had intervened, saying something like "Relax, baby"—quite possibly the last words he ever spoke.[3] Gandhi, like so many men, was blinded by Thenmuli's gender. He was not the first, nor would he be the last, to underestimate the lethality of a woman. Thenmuli's attack changed not just how counter-terrorism officials in Sri Lanka looked at Tamil women, but also how the women look at themselves.

It was widely assumed that Gandhi was assassinated on orders of the Liberation Tigers of Tamil Eelam (LTTE), often called simply the Tamil Tigers, in retaliation for Gandhi's "betrayal" when Indian troops sent to Sri Lanka as peacekeepers under the 1987 Indo–Sri Lankan Accord set about forcibly suppressing the rebel organization. The way Indian forces that were meant to end a crisis only made it worse forms just one strand in the knotty history of relations between the Sinhalese and Tamil peoples in Sri Lanka.

Dhanu's assassination of Gandhi was not the first occasion on which a woman used a suicide bomb, but it was the first of many targeted assassinations by women associated with the Tamil cause.[4] Her sacrifice ushered in a new era of violent activism for women in the LTTE. The organization created its own division of women bombers (the Suthanthirap Paravaikal or Freedom Birds),[5] and cadres of women were trained for martyrdom. The degree to which the Indian "peacekeepers" had abused the Tamil population would have a long-lasting impact on Indo–Tamil relations.[6] Allegations abound that Dhanu had been raped by Indian soldiers. During the course of my interviews, members of the organization stated that they   doubted this to be the case; nevertheless, the allegation provided great fodder for propaganda.[7]

CEYLON'S CIVIL WAR

In ancient times, Arab traders called Sri Lanka's lush, tropical shores Serendib, the root for the word *serendipity*. However, the tear-shaped island in the Indian Ocean, formerly called Ceylon, has experienced some of the deadliest ethnic conflict in the world. During twenty-six years of civil war, in excess of 80,000 people have been killed, more than have died in all the Arab–Israeli wars and the war in Afghanistan put together. The conflict in Sri Lanka is a prime example of how ethnic differences can be constructed and manipulated by ethnic entrepreneurs and of how a state's oppressive policies can give rise to one of the deadliest terror groups that has ever existed.

Historically, the ethnic boundaries between Tamils and Sinhalese were indistinct and permeable. Both peoples originated in India. In the third century BC, the Sinhalese Kandyan kings married women from southern India, mixing the two communities and making ethnic distinctions arbitrary.[8] Portugal and the Netherlands, attracted by the island's wealth in spices, coffee, and tea, colonized Ceylon in 1505. As in so many other parts of the globe, ethnic cleavages were codified and made permanent by the colonizers. Prior to the arrival of the Europeans, identity on the island could change depending on the situation. The social and economic developments under the Portuguese and the Dutch, in particular the bureaucratic requirements of colonial administration, solidified previously flexible ethnic boundaries. By requiring the inhabitants to register births and deaths, the colonizers forced people to choose whether they were Tamil or Sinhalese, a designation that became sticky and permanent.

In addition to fixing how people identified themselves, the Portuguese and Dutch colonizers fomented intense rivalries between the groups by favoring some and disadvantaging others— alternating their preferences from time to time. Competition over scarce resources or over access to the benefits offered by the Europeans drove the communities apart. A Sinhalese community evolved in the central and southwestern parts of the island while the Tamil community developed in the north and on the eastern shore during colonial rule.

Relations were further complicated when the British occupied the country beginning in 1815. The British focused the economic and agricultural development of Ceylon in the central and western parts of the island, a pattern of settlement that disadvantaged the Tamils vis-à-vis the Sinhalese. With few agricultural opportunities available to them, Tamils opted instead to take advantage of the schooling offered by missionaries and colonial officials. As a result, more Tamils than Sinhalese entered the civil service and other relatively high-paying jobs. Many Tamils converted to Christianity and sent their children to Britain to be educated. These émigrés returned and filled the expanding needs of the state services as well as staffed the hospitals, law firms, and engineering companies. The availability of employment and opportunities for upward mobility also meant that Tamils migrated from the north to the southern and central regions.[9] The demographic balance between the two communities was further altered when the British began to import indentured labor. The coffee and tea plantations brought more than one million Tamil workers from southern India to the island. At first, most were just seasonal migrants, but with the expansion of the tea plantations, the majority became permanent residents.[10] The addition of the Indian Tamils practically doubled the minority population.

The indigenous middle class spoke English and was genuinely multiethnic. However, Tamils and Burghers (the offspring of Portuguese, Dutch, or German/Sri Lankan mixed marriages) entered white-collar professions and the civil service in greater proportions than their population size warranted. This fed anti-Tamil rhetoric. Sinhalese leaders committed to their people's revival resented Tamil successes and manipulated the island's "origin" mythology to alienate the ethnic minority. According to the myth, Sri Lanka was the land of Dharma and Buddha. The religion, the people, and the island were all bound together in an indissoluble unity. Stories from the Buddhist text the *Mahavamasa* ("Great Chronicle") included accounts of repeated invasions and conquests of the island by Tamils from southern India. The revivalist leaders used these texts to feed nationalist fears as Tamils were increasingly portrayed as hostile outsiders. When British colonial rule gave way peacefully to independence on February 4, 1948, discrimination against the Tamils began immediately. The new xenophobic nationalist ideology denied the multiethnic and multireligious character of Sri Lankan society and refused to accept the collective rights of minority groups.[11]

In the 1950s, Sinhalese nationalism dominated the island's politics, as the majority people sought to redress the perceived imbalances created by colonialism and to diminish the advantages Tamils had enjoyed under British rule. In 1956, Solomon West Ridgeway Dias Bandaranaike, leader of the Sri Lanka Freedom Party (SFLP), was elected to power on a "Sinhala only" platform called *swabasha*.[12] The Sinhalese language became the only official language, replacing English as the language of administration, employment, and higher education. The immediate (and intended) consequence of these changes was to force Tamils who worked in the civil service, and who could not speak Sinhala, to resign.[13] Discrimination against Tamils continued throughout the 1960s, when the government granted Buddhism primacy as the only recognized state religion in the constitution, even though the country had many Hindus, Christians, and Muslims. In the new constitution, Srimavo Bandaranaike, the first female prime minister in the world who succeeded her husband after his death, disenfranchised Tamils from government and other positions of authority. The number of Tamils employed in the state sector dwindled. For example, in 1949, the year after independence, 41 percent of government employees were Tamil and 54 percent Sinhalese; by 1963, 92 percent were Sinhalese.[14] To redress the high numbers of Tamils in white-collar professions, a quota system was imposed to limit the number of Tamils attending university.

During this period, Tamils mostly responded politically, through the Federal Party (FP) and a nonviolent protest movement. However, the 1970s gave rise to increasing calls for separation and militancy. In 1977, the leader of the United National Party (UNP), Junius Richard Jayewardene, assumed power. The party's manifesto finally acknowledged some Tamil rights. Tamils had supported Jayewardene's campaign and his promise of improved ethnic relations, but his election led to an outbreak of ferocious communal violence throughout the island.[15] More racially inspired riots occurred in 1981 in what turned out to be a dress rehearsal for much worse violence in 1983.[16]

Separatist agitation went through several phases. In the 1950s, Tamil political mobilization was peaceful, moving to civil disobedience in the 1960s, to individual violence in the 1970s, and becoming a dangerous threat in the 1980s and 1990s.[17] A plethora of Tamil political organizations emerged to represent the community. In 1972, the Tamil Federal Party (TFP), the All Ceylon Tamil Congress (ACTC), the Tamil Progressive Front, and the Ceylon Worker's Congress joined forces to form the Tamil United Front (TUF), to campaign for equal rights and uniform status for the Tamil language. In May 1973, the TUF opted to work for an independent Tamil Eelam, or Tamil homeland. Not all the groups endorsed this position and those that did varied in the strategies they adopted to achieve their ultimate goal, oscillating between using the electoral process and resorting to violence.

The result of the debate about how best to achieve the Tamil homeland was the emergence of the Tamil Five—five organizations founded between 1973 and 1980 and all later designated as terrorist organizations. The Tamil Five was comprised of the Tamil Eelam Liberation Organization (TELO), the Eelam Revolutionary Organisation of Students (EROS), the People's Liberation Organisation for Tamil Eelam (PLOTE), the Eelam People's Revolutionary Liberation Front (EPRLF), and the radical Tamil National Tigers (TNT). The last one emerged in 1973 under Velupillai Prabhakaran and was renamed the Liberation Tigers of Tamil Eelam (LTTE) in May 1976, with calls for secession and violent action.[18] Prabhakaran sought to "refashion the old TNT/ new LTTE into an elite, ruthlessly efficient, and highly professional fighting force."[19]

In response to these developments (as well as to violence from the right-wing Sinhalese group, the People's Liberation Front or

Janatha Vimukthi Peramuna [JVP]), the government promulgated the Prevention of Terrorism Act (PTA) in 1979. The PTA permitted the army and police to hold prisoners incommunicado for up to eighteen months without trial. It made illegal any acts that resulted in "social, religious, or communal disharmony," essentially revoking the freedom of speech. It also annulled elements of existing British law similar to our Miranda rights, which limit what the police can and cannot do to people held in custody. Under British law, confessions obtained in police custody were admissible in court only if made in the presence of a magistrate. The new act admitted confessions made under duress or even torture. It was made retroactive, and the police and army interpreted the law as a license to arrest without warrant, search individuals at random, seize their possessions, and detain them long-term without trial or communication with their families. Over the years, increasing numbers of Tamil civilians were rounded up and detained for prolonged periods of time without access to lawyers or family.[20] According to the international human rights community, the government of Sri Lanka became one of the worst violators of human rights and executed the most disappearances (abductions, illegal arrests and detentions, kidnappings, extrajudicial killings, and enforced disappearances—many politically motivated or committed in the context of antiterror operations) of any country in the world.[21]

The PTA led to an increase rather than a reduction of Tamil violence. The government's repressive measures created a spiral of brutality. By the early 1980s, a younger, more radical generation prevailed over the older parliamentarians. The LTTE started out as the foot soldiers of the Tamil United Front but soon chose terror over ballots.[22] The communal violence escalated.

In July 1983, the government declared martial law in the Tamil areas of Jaffna, Vavuniya, and Mannar. Between July 24 and August 5, widespread and destructive riots broke out in these areas.

This marked the beginning of a prolonged civil war.[23] Some say that the violence erupted in retaliation for the murder of Charles Anthony, Prabhakaran's right-hand man, earlier that month by Sri Lankan forces. Others claim the trigger for the riots was the ambush of thirteen Sinhalese soldiers at Tinneveli in Jaffna.[24] The city of Colombo's population was incensed when the military returned the bodies of the slain soldiers, who had been mutilated after their deaths. The government, hoping to provoke public outrage and instigate communal violence, displayed the bodies publicly in Colombo's Kanatte Cemetery in Borella and invited the people to see what the Tamils had done. This led to a three-day wave of anti-Tamil violence, during which roaming bands of Sinhalese burned homes, destroyed Tamil-owned factories and businesses, and engaged in widespread looting, pillaging, and rape. The degree of state involvement was unclear. It appeared to be disorganized mob violence, and yet the "mobs were armed with voters' lists, and detailed addresses of every Tamil-owned shop, house or factory, and their attacks were very precise."[25] They also allegedly had detailed lists of personal belongings and knew what to look for in every home. The government admitted to 360 to 400 deaths; Tamils alleged that the number of casualties and displaced people was actually in the thousands.[26]

This was just the beginning of anti-Tamil violence. The army ran rampant in the Jaffna area, torturing and killing hundreds of civilians. Once the soldiers were unleashed, no civilians were safe. The government introduced Emergency Regulation 15A, which allowed the security forces to bury and/or cremate people they shot without revealing their identities or carrying out inquests.[27] As graphically detailed in Michael Ondaatje's 2000 novel *Anil's Ghost*, the army could kill anyone without trial or just cause and destroy the evidence. Bearing such provocation in mind, Tamil radicals felt justified in their use of any means necessary to combat the state.

President Jayewardene admitted that some of the armed forces had participated in the riots, and that some Sinhalese people may have taken part, but he ultimately blamed the riots on a joint Communist and Naxalite conspiracy,[28] implying Indian involvement.[29] His government's subsequent actions did not help alleviate the crisis. The president accused the victims of bringing the violence upon themselves, claiming that "Sri Lanka is inherently and rightfully a Sinhalese state ... and it must be accepted as such, not a matter of opinion to be debated. For attempting to challenge this premise, Tamils have brought the wrath of Sinhalese on their own heads; they have themselves to blame."[30]

Before 1983, the appeal of the Tamil Tigers was limited to a small segment of disaffected young men. The rural poor were ambivalent; few supported the LTTE even though they might have been sympathetic to its goals.[31] After the 1983 attacks, however, support for the LTTE increased dramatically. One observer estimated the pre-1983 membership at a maximum of 600. By March 1983, after the pogrom, LTTE support exceeded 10,000.[32] The Tigers drew support from marginalized Tamils who resented their second-class-citizen status and from the growing number of internally displaced people.

The government ramped up its emergency powers when it passed the Sixth Amendment to the Constitution, which effectively banned the Tamil United Liberation Front (TULF) from parliament. The amendment outlawed any political party from advocating secession within Sri Lanka. Violating the law could have dire consequences including the forfeiture of property, loss of passport, and the loss of any professional license. All members of parliament were required to take an oath to uphold the constitution and all of its amendments. The TULF 's commitment to creating a separate state thus meant that it was now illegal. With no political parties allowed to represent the aspirations of Tamils, violence became their sole means of political action.

Significant support for the terrorists came from expatriate Tamils who had fled the country for Britain, Malaysia, India, France, Germany, Canada, Italy, Australia, and the United States. The LTTE and international terrorist groups such as the Baader-Meinhof Gang, the PLO, the ANC, and the Provisional IRA cooperated and occasionally shared tactics and technology.[33] However, as the LTTE became the preeminent terrorist organization in the world by virtue of its reach and effectiveness—for a time, its forces were a match for those of the government of Sri Lanka—it increasingly resisted offers to share its lethal technology with other groups. The Tamil Tigers came to see themselves as legitimate insurgents rather than terrorists.[34]

Following the 1983 pogrom, more than 150,000 refugees from the northern regions of Sri Lanka fled to Tamil Nadu in southern India. Many Tamils who had previously lived among the Sinhalese in the central and southern parts of the country also migrated to the north and east of the island. This demographic shift strengthened the Tamil belief in a homeland of their own. It also established a close link between the Tamils of Sri Lanka and the Tamils of India.[35]

A car bomb exploded at a bus station in Colombo at the end of April 1987, killing 113 people. The government, faced with popular outrage, launched an "all-out offensive" on the Jaffna Peninsula and, by the end of May, captured it at great cost in life and property. Thousands of the area's inhabitants were displaced. As the violence escalated, India decided to send in humanitarian relief. When a flotilla of boats carrying supplies to the Tamils was turned back by the Sri Lankan navy, India dropped humanitarian relief supplies by air—in violation of Sri Lankan airspace.

Sri Lanka came under great international pressure to solve the conflict. There had been intermittent but short-lived efforts at negotiating peace over the years. The Indian government strong-armed both the Sri Lankan government and the LTTE into supporting an Indian intervention. On July 29, 1987, Indian prime minister Rajiv Gandhi and Sri Lankan president J.R. Jayewardene signed the Indo–Sri Lankan Accord.[36] The Indian Peace Keeping Force (IPKF) arrived on the island with ten thousand troops on July 30 to help protect the Tamil population. However, they eventually turned their forces loose on the civilian population. At the peak of the intervention, India deployed four divisions (almost 80,000 men), including three infantry divisions as well as paramilitary and special forces.[37]

The accord was intended to provide a conceptual framework to resolve the conflict and to outline arrangements to share power between the warring communities. It declared that Sri Lanka was "a multiethnic and multilingual plural society" consisting of four ethnic groups: Sinhalese, Tamils, Muslims, and Burghers. The accord recognized that the northern and eastern provinces had been "areas of historical habitation" of the Tamil-speaking population. "Thus without conceding the claim that the northeast constituted part of the traditional homelands of the Tamils, the accord provided cautious acknowledgement of the distinct character of the region."[38] This wording was significant because it framed a policy of bilingualism and a provincial council scheme, and called for the temporary merger of the northern and eastern provinces as a partially separate authority.

In Tamil Nadu, the Tamil stronghold in India, the IPKF came to be considered an invading and oppressive military force. At the same time the Indian government became alarmed at the implications of its support for a secessionist movement in Sri Lanka when there was similar agitation (for Sikhs in Khalistan) within its own borders and the possibility of a spillover effect as Sri Lankan Tamils influenced Tamils on the mainland. When the LTTE resisted the presence of the Indian troops (Prabhakaran was unhappy with this arrangement from the get-go) there were massive Indian casualties—more than a thousand. The Indian soldiers turned against the Tamils and started killing not just LTTE supporters but also Tamil civilians. More than seven thousand Tamil Tigers and thousands more civilians died in the ensuing confrontations. The Indians became guilty of all the abuses, including rape and extrajudicial killing, that they had been sent to stop. In the final analysis, India moved from being a mediator in the conflict to becoming a direct participant.[39]

The Indian intervention sparked reactions from both Tamils and right-wing Sinhalese groups. Both the LTTE and the JVP repudiated the accord and briefly coordinated their efforts to get Indian forces out of the country.[40] Prabhakaran wrote to Gandhi several times,[41] asking him to reconsider India's course of action. He told Gandhi that he was prepared to disarm in exchange for a ceasefire agreement. According to Tamil sources, "Rajiv Gandhi wanted to kill Prabhakaran and completely exterminate the entire LTTE fighting force, thus putting an end to the goal of an independent Tamil Eelam. So, far from halting the war, he inducted 150,000 more Indian soldiers into Tamil areas to execute his plan. As a result the war continued unabated."[42]

The struggle continued bloodily and without a decisive result until 1989, when the Sri Lankan government together with the LTTE requested the IPKF's withdrawal. In the years that followed, the Sri Lankan government took up the offensive, mounting successive and increasingly violent campaigns of its own against the Tigers. These took the form not only of open military engagements, but also of harassment and abuse of the civilian population. This is corroborated by several studies that showed, among other things, that the sexual nature of the government troops' harassment helped to mobilize young women into the LTTE and was one of the organization's best recruiting tools. Entire villages were razed in remote areas of the island. The government organized a systematic campaign of "disappearances," while turning a blind eye toward the use of rape by its own military forces. In particular, sexual abuse of Tamil women during checkpoint searches, intended to dehumanize them, was common.[43]

In response to these tactics, civilians joined the Tigers in droves. During a 1990 offensive, for example, the Sri Lankan army arbitrarily arrested 183 people from the village of Kokkurill, including many women and children. In the years that followed, the village sacrificed more lives for the cause than any other in Sri Lanka: one hundred of the five hundred men in the village left to fight for the rebels, never to return.[44]

EQUAL OPPORTUNITY MARTYRDOM

In a region where women's rights were few, the LTTE had the highest number of female suicide bombers in the world (and a significant percentage of female frontline fighters) because of its verbal support of gender equality. Military roles were gender-neutral, and the glory of martyrdom was bestowed equally upon men and women. But unlike the men, who usually sought to become martyrs for the glory of the community, some of the female bombers took on the role out of desperation or as a last resort.[45]

Not only did women constitute an important part of the LTTE's military leadership, but they also had their own combat divisions and participated at almost every level of fighting. They died in battle just like the men, and the Sri Lankan government targeted them for assassination regardless of their gender. From the point of view of the LTTE, there was even a psychological advantage to be gained by using women to defeat the Sri Lankan military in a country where women were seen as second-class citizens.

The organization trained the women in karate, hand-to-hand combat, the use of automatic weapons, and the techniques of suicide bombing. They even showed the women how to walk and sit as if they were pregnant, while carrying explosives around their waists. Once the female operatives were trained, the LTTE held them in reserve, to release whenever they wanted to flex their muscles. The organization enforced a strict code of personal conduct. Cadres were forbidden to drink alcohol, take drugs, or engage in premarital sex. They were all issued a glass vial of cyanide to wear around their necks and instructed to bite down on the cylinder in the event of capture. The cadres followed these strictures willingly and esteemed Prabhakaran with an almost cult-like devotion.

Prabhakaran was personally credited with establishing the separate unit for female cadres. He was confident that women had the potential for military training and combat. Prabhakaran was determined that women should have equal opportunity for participation in all aspects of armed struggle and issued a statement of equal rights on International Women's Day, March 8, 1992:

> Today young women have taken up arms to liberate our
> land. They have made supreme sacrifices to this cause, to the
> amazement of the world. I am proud to say that the birth,
> growth, and expansion of the women's military wing is a
> remarkable achievement, which marked a historical turning
> point in our struggle.[46]

Four years later, Prabhakaran further empowered Tamil women, saying, "For the awakening of a nation and the salvation of womanhood, the Tamil Eelam revolutionary woman has transformed herself into a tigress! Fierce and fiery, she has taken up arms to fight injustice."[47] The LTTE was adept at contextualizing the notions of martyrdom and selflessness into Tamil society. Peter Schalk, a professor of religion at Uppsala University, described the ideology of self-sacrifice employed by the LTTE as *tiyäkam* or "abandon-ment (of life)," a rather specifically Indian form of martyrdom cultivated in both male and female fighters. The abandonment of life (*tiyäkam*), for the Black Tiger is not suicide, but a gift of self-sacrifice that has Christian nuances. "A martyr of the LTTE has not chosen like the Christian martyr to suffer. The concept of *tiyäkam* that has its roots in the last section of the Bhagavad-Gita was revived in the struggle for independence of India."[48] Peter Schalk considers that the LTTE "martyr" is ready to get killed so that some others may be liberated.

Using these precedents for the concept of self-sacrifice, Prabhakaran established a special unit of the LTTE composed of specially selected individuals trained for suicide bombing opera-tions.[49] "Tiger leader Velupillai Prabhakaran's real genius was to build a culture of sacrifice and martyrdom around his guerrilla force, with himself as demi-god leader."[50] Prabhakaran stressed that he had "groomed his weak brethren into a strong weapon called the Black Tigers. They possessed an iron will, yet their hearts were still soft. They could perceive their interests to prevent their own annihilation. Yet they did not fear death. They eagerly awaited the day they would die. This was the era of the Black Tigers. No force on earth could suppress the uprising of Tamils who would seek freedom."[51]

According to critics of the LTTE, Prabhakaran used women as cannon fodder. The women were segregated and had no real power. Detractors further allege that it was the practice of the LTTE leader-ship to use women cadres on the most vulnerable frontiers. Not so, according to Tiger supporter Adele Ann Wilby (who was married to LTTE leader Anton Balasingham): "Women such as these belong to a totally new world, a world outside a normal woman's life ... They have taken up a life that bears little resemblance at all to the ordinary existence of women. Training and carrying weapons, confronting battle conditions, enduring the constant emotional strain of losing close associates, facing death almost every day, are situations that most women not only wish to avoid, but feel ill-at-ease with. But not the women fighters of the LTTE. They have literally flourished under such conditions and created for them not only a new women's military structure but also a legend of fighting capability and bravery."[52]

While the women fighters were exalted by their supporters, it remains the case that many of them had been the victims of abuse, assault, or rape. The LTTE explicitly used this fact as leverage, telling the women that they could either be victims of the state or join the organization and fight the aggressors. Large billboards that lined the dirt roads throughout the northern part of the island showed clearly that Sri Lankan soldiers were likely to rape Tamil women, whose only chance of maintaining their chastity was to become Tigers and fight back. Still other women, as we shall see, were not merely pressured to join but were actually kidnapped or sold into the organization.

Those who had not been coerced found other reasons to become Tigers. Peer pressure was a factor: young women and girls who were friends tended to join the Tigers in groups. Others were influenced by personal experience. Tamil sources recounted to me how one woman joined after her boyfriend was arrested, killed, and his corpse left in the village market for all to see. Another told me that one night she was alone at home thinking and listening to LTTE songs; the next day she and a few of her friends left their school to sign up. Once one girl in a village joined, there was a snowball effect of others wanting to join the organization too.[53]

Once in, members were in for keeps. Few ever betrayed the movement and escape was exceedingly difficult—and more than likely to result in death. It appears that it was also much more difficult for women to escape than it was for men. Two women on the east coast who had been kidnapped by the LTTE ran away from the LTTE base camp and sought refuge at the United Nations High Commissioner for Refugess (UNHCR); they were found dead days later, en route to an interview with this author. These women faced an impossible dilemma. Their initial disappearance from their village could mean only one thing: that they had joined the LTTE. If they escaped and returned to the village, they had to report immediately to the police station where, as members of an outlawed organization, they were subject to detention and the abuse that was sure to follow. If they returned (or were forced to return) to the LTTE camp, they would be branded as traitors, which would carry an immediate death sentence. For women, escape from the organization was dangerous at best.

IN TAMIL TERRITORY

Among the first things I noticed when I traveled in the Tamil regions of Sri Lanka in 2002 were the ubiquitous barbed wire and the signs, with images of smiling skulls and crossbones, that warned succinctly of the presence of land mines. Barbed-wire fences crisscrossed the lush green countryside. Corrugated-metal shacks riddled with bullet holes were visible evidence of the long civil war and the intense fighting that had scarred this place. The roads in Tamil Eelam were not paved. There was no running water or electricity and raw sewage ran freely in the gutters. The Sri Lankan government neglected the infrastructure in the Tamil areas, a fact that became even more obvious in the aftermath of the December 2004 tsunami, when international aid was distributed strictly along ethnic lines. The majority of the Tamils reside in the most basic rural settings.

As I traveled through the Vanni region, pictures of suicide bombers and martyrs were displayed everywhere. Everyone knew the bombers' names. Their images, printed up in slick pamphlets and distributed at Heroes' Day celebrations, were collector's items. Glossy booklets listed the name, date of birth, and age at death of every martyr, along with the time of the attack, where the attack occurred, and a photograph of the bomber's face. Young Tamils knew their names the way American children know the names of sports stars. The organization had actually toyed with the idea of issuing trading cards of the martyrs. Young people looked up to them and wanted to emulate their heroic acts of courage.

Among the people I spoke with, most were inspired by an extreme ethnic nationalism and complete dedication to Velupillai Prabhakaran. Others told reporter Francis Harrison, "We are given moral support by our leader and we have reached this position only because of him."[54] Prabhakaran was well aware of his charisma and his superstar impact. One of the highlights of a suicide bomber's preparation for his or her mission was the last meal he or she enjoyed with LTTE leaders. In some cases, the would-be bomber had dinner with Prabhakaran himself, who at the end of the meal offered to do the dishes, a symbolic act of great significance in a society where men rarely perform menial chores.

The question remains: Were the women in the movement brainwashed or did they join willingly? The answer is, likely a bit of both. In the pages that follow, I introduce three female combatants, Darshika, Puhalchudar, and Menake, all of whom were groomed to follow in Dhanu's infamous footsteps. All three were members of the Tamil Tigers' elite suicide bombing squad, the Freedom Birds division of the Black Tigers. Darshika and Puhalchudar awaited their final orders for a suicide mission, while Menake languished in prison after a failed suicide bomb attempt.

DARSHIKA

Ultimately, the women of the LTTE were motivated to join the organization and to fight the Sri Lankan state for a mixture of political and personal reasons. One suicide bomber defined the combination of factors that drove her to act succinctly: "The harassment that I and my parents have suffered at the hands of the army makes me want to take revenge … It is a question of Tamil pride, especially after so much sacrifice. There is no escape."[55]

Darshika joined the movement as a result of personal loss and from a firm belief that the Tamil Tigers was the only group that could provide her with security. She was twenty-four when she was interviewed by Norwegian filmmaker Beate Arnestad, but had left home to join the Malathi regiment of the LTTE when she was twelve. She was eventually promoted to the Black Tigers.

Darshika's father was killed in the center of Jaffna, at the junction close to the bus station. According to Darshika's mother, he had not been a man of influence, was not politically involved, and never discussed politics at home. He was a minor official at the post office who just minded his own business. One morning after he had left for work the Sri Lankan air force began bombing and strafing the town. A bomb fell near the bus station and Darshika's father was one of twenty-six people who were killed. He was simply in the wrong place at the wrong time.

Darshika was devastated by the loss. According to her mother, she ceased to have any feelings whatsoever. She became numb. Darshika made up her mind then to join the Tigers and aspire for a place in the suicide squad. Darshika's account agreed with her mother's. Since the enemy took her father, she said, she had witnessed murder with her own eyes. She said that the government routinely killed civilians in the Tamil areas. They even attacked areas that would be considered sanctuaries elsewhere. People ran to the churches for safety, even people who were not Christians, assuming that the government would never violate the sanctity of the house of God. But they bombed the churches too. Even when it was well known that villagers were taking shelter in the churches, the churches became a target of choice. The blood flowed freely in the churches, Dharshika said.[56]

Darshika remembered being harassed by the Sri Lankan military when she was very young. The army would turn up suddenly in their vehicles when the children went off to school. The girls were singled out for special attention, and not the kind that made them feel safe. They were afraid. Even the ten-year-old girls were scared of what the soldiers might do to them. Darshika and the others felt defenseless.[57] Her mother said that the military regularly targeted women. When they mounted house-to-house searches, the soldiers would touch them unnecessarily. Even when the women tried to hide, the soldiers would find them. In the end, Darshika could not go to school or church. She felt like a prisoner in her own home.[58]

While Darshika was prompted by the loss of her father to join the organization, this was not necessarily what made her stay or what made her willing to kill others.[59] She also had a political motivation of her own. Darshika explained that she and her friends were fighting for their homeland: "A country where people can freely live. That is why our leader is carrying on this struggle, and we are proud to be part of it. Outsiders have not seen our true face. That is why they call us terrorists. To be a terrorist we fight for true justice."[60]

Darshika did not seek to kill the man who had killed her father—which would be a normal vengeful response. Rather, she joined an organization that sought to bring down the corrupt and evil government that was responsible for Tamil oppression.

As a fully committed member of the Black Tigers, Darshika was thoroughly imbued with the notions of death and sacrifice that were part and parcel of the organization. Darshika said that neither she nor the other girls cared about death. That's just how it was. As Black Tigers, they would be told how and when they would die.[61] In a perverse way, the women saw this as a form of empowerment. Their certainty gave them a kind of inner strength. Darshika's fatalism was reinforced by her intense loyalty to the LTTE's cause and specifically to Prabhakaran. She was raised a Catholic and initially aspired to join a religious order and devote herself to God, but after her father's death, her passion and devotion switched to the "cult of Prabhakaran." Her faith may come as a surprise to those who saw the conflict as one between Hindus and Buddhists; many Tamil Tigers were Christian and the organization reflected the ethnic and religious demographics of the Tamil population as a whole. Most Tigers were Hindu, but the LTTE's ideology was secular and nationalist. Yet the worship of Prabhakaran matched the religious dedication of any jihadi to Islam.

Time magazine's Alex Perry understood this dynamic. For him, there was no doubt that that the Tigers genuinely loved Prabhakaran and never questioned anything he did or said. His name was so revered and inspired such awe that Tigers would not actually use it. Instead they referred to him as "the Leader." In every Tiger's home, Prabhakaran's picture sat on a desk where you might expect family photographs. Daya Somasundaram, a Jaffna psychiatrist, alleged that the faithful made pilgrimages to Prabhakaran's former home in Valveddithurai to fill little boxes of soil "like a holy ritual, as though they [were] collecting water from the Ganges." For many of Somasundaram's patients, Prabhakaran was higher than their own god.[62]

Perry's depiction is spot-on. In every Tamil home I visited there was a large portrait of Prabhakaran, garlanded, surrounded by incense, and set in a place of honor. Having one's photo taken with the Leader was a great source of pride. Darshika and her friend Puhalchudar venerated Prabhakaran like a deity. Before he was slain, S.P. Tamilselvan, the second-in-command of the LTTE, told me, "They love him and adore him as mother, father, brother or god." The organization encouraged and fostered Prabhakaran's cult-like status through imagery, poetry, and songs. Prabhakaran was like a sun. Nobody could even think of eclipsing him.[63]

PUHALCHUDAR

For best friends Darshika and Puhalchudar, membership in the movement was a huge honor. The girls embraced every challenge together and looked forward to the day when they would be called upon to conduct their final mission. Darshika said that they went often to the cemetery to remember and celebrate fallen LTTE war heroes. They left garlands and burned incense at the grave sites. They did not fear death for themselves.

In conversation, they were almost cavalier about the inevitability of their deaths. In describing a possible suicide attack, they waxed poetic about what would happen to their remains. They knew that when they blew themselves up they would likely be reduced to hundreds of pieces scattered all around, a piece here, a body part there. There would be nothing left for either their families or the authorities to identify. But if the battle was won, the organization would build a tomb at the site to honor them; if not, the LTTE would build a small memorial elsewhere, or the girls would be commemorated by a picture during the Heroes' Day celebrations every November.[64]

The LTTE International Secretariat issued a glossy booklet, the *Sooriya Puthalvargal Memorial Souvenir*, every few years with the photos and details of the fallen martyrs. The booklets were distributed at events around the Tamil diaspora and listed the Tigers' noms de guerre and their stats (including how many of the enemy they had killed). The 2003 edition of the *Sooriya Puthalvargal Memorial Souvenir* contained ninety-six pages in which the most "daring military maneuvers in contemporary warfare" performed by 240 Black Tigers were described. Some were shown smiling, some were stern-looking, and some even appeared aloof. For average Tamils, the fighters on the pages of the *Sooriya Puthalvargal* were superheroes of the highest order. Tamils regarded them as part of their extended family.[65]

Darshika and Puhalchudar were consumed by thoughts of battle against their enemy. Whenever they closed their eyes, they said, they dreamed of battles. In their dreams, they shot at the enemy but their bullets had no effect. Darshika explained it this way:

> In our dreams, the bullets never come. The soldiers don't die. The more we shoot, the more they keep coming. In reality, when we have no bullets left, we can't do anything … we have our cyanide capsules. If we bite it in our sleep, we won't wake up. Once you put the cyanide capsule in your mouth and bite it, the glass breaks and cuts your tongue. The poison seeps into your blood. This way, even if the girls are injured, and they cannot bite down onto the capsule, they can still break it and pour it directly into their wounds. The poison in the glass cylinder mixes with your blood, that's it.[66]

Puhalchudar was thirteen years old when her family was permanently displaced. The army had kicked them out of their house in Jaffna and they lost everything. They wandered around for weeks, staying with family or distant relatives to escape the violence. Puhalchudar had to quit school and stop studying. She remembered how upset she was not to be able to go to school. During the day it was too dangerous for the girls to leave the house. During the evenings there was heavy fighting all around them. The family lived in a simple shelter built by her parents adjacent to a big army base. Her parents would sit outside all night, watching and waiting to see whether this was the night they would have to pack up the kids and make a run for it. When the twenty-millimeter shells started falling in front of their house, they decided that the war was too close for comfort. They, along with thousands of other refugees, fled for their lives.

Puhalchudar and her brother got separated from the rest of the family when they found themselves on one side of a rickety bridge, their parents on the opposite. As a result of nearly constant shelling by the Sri Lankan military, the bridge had huge holes in it. The two children could not safely get across. For a time, they just stood facing the approach to the bridge while the shelling and gunfire moved closer and closer. Finally some Tigers defending the bridge offered to help the two children reach the other side. Puhalchudar was too young to understand much about the war, but she believes that they survived only because the guerrillas came to their rescue. She owed the Tigers her life. As soon as her brother was safe in her mother's arms, Puhalchudar left the family to become a Black Tiger.[67]

The women of the LTTE formed very intense friendships. Darshika and Puhalchudar had spent every day together for the seven years before their interview. They exercised together, practiced martial arts together, ate together, slept in the same room, and confided all of their secrets in one another. "Our friendship means that we share each other's happiness and sorrow. We help each other whenever help is needed. Of course we are prepared to separate, but as long as we are in the same unit, we do everything for one another." Puhalchudar said that of everyone, Darshika was closest to her. "Also our Leader [Prabhakaran], who takes care of everything."[68]

Their complete and utter devotion to Prabhakaran overrode their personal relationships. The women in the movement had invented a new family, one that was based not on blood or kinship but on a new identity—one of nationalism and camaraderie. Darshika and Puhalchudar prioritize loyalty to the Leader over all else. They discuss what would happen in the event of a betrayal. "Our Leader started the movement for the good of the people," said Darshika, "but if one person betrays us, we accept losing that person with no regret." Puhalchudar echoed this sentiment: "Instead of losing many people, it is better to just shoot the one traitor."[69]

The young women's comments dovetail with observations made by some outside observers. For example, *New York Times* journalist John Burns once likened Prabhakaran's firm control over the organization to a rule of terror in the city of Jaffna. "According to scores of accounts from defectors and others who have escaped Tiger tyranny, many of his own lieutenants have been murdered; Tamils who have criticized him, even mildly or in jest have been picked up and placed for years in dungeons, half starved, hauled out periodically for a beating by their guards."[70]

Asked how they would react if one of them betrayed the cause, Darshika replied, "I would not do anything if someone said Puhalchudar was a traitor, but if it was proved, I would not hesitate to shoot her." Puhalchudar agreed: "Everything, good or bad, goes right up to the Leader. So if we betray the movement, the Leader will be the final judge. He would probably tell someone else to do it. But if he tells me to shoot Darshika, I'll shoot her."[71]

Even for those women who survived government assassination attempts and hours-long pitched battles, life in the LTTE was difficult. They wore shapeless fatigues. They braided their hair and tucked it tightly under a military cap. Rarely were they able to wear perfume or makeup. The LTTE enforced a strict code of conduct that Darshika and Puhalchudar abided by scrupulously. Prabhakaran set the example that they and other cadres were required to follow. Like the LTTE cadres, Prabhakaran did not drink liquor or smoke tobacco. Even tea, coffee, and carbonated drinks were considered taboo. Sex outside marriage was forbidden and those cadres who violated the code were executed irrespective of seniority or personal loyalty. Gambling and financial dishonesty were also punishable by death. Homosexuality, interestingly, was not a capital offence; however, it was dealt with by public humiliation.[72] Prabhakaran initially outlawed marriage, but after he fell in love with Madhivadhani Erambu, an agricultural student kidnapped by his guerrillas, he changed his mind. They married on October 1, 1984, and had two sons and a daughter. He subsequently altered the rules to allow other senior cadres to wed.

Following Prabhakaran's example, the LTTE decreed that members could marry when women turned thirty-five and men turned forty.[73] By the time a woman attained the marrying age, only another LTTE cadre would consider marrying such a battle-hardened female. And when they did get married, off came the trousers: they were expected to wear traditional female garb—colorful saris or the *salwar kameez*—grow their hair long, and look feminine again. All their efforts and accomplishments within the movement had no effect on the ways in which the women were expected to behave. The former female cadres were just like any other Tamil girl: demure, obedient, and second-class. Their sole function in Tamil society, like generations of women before them, was to give birth to future fighters.

MENAKE

Many young Tamils found the idea of joining the organization glamorous and an expression of dedication to the cause and the Leader. But their attitude hardly reflected the whole story. After April 1995, 60 percent of Tamil casualties in the civil war were under the age of eighteen. This number was driven in part by the LTTE's policy of forced conscription of child soldiers, and in part by the deliberate targeting of civilians (especially in schools and orphanages) by government forces. The young people in Sri Lanka bore the brunt of the violence and inhabited a world in which brutality and death were the norm. The LTTE kidnapped many young girls, giving them no option other than the life of a child soldier.

Menake did not grow up with the dream of becoming a Black Tiger. She was handed over to the organization against her will by uncaring relatives. Her home was an impoverished fishing village in the northeast of the island. Her father drank heavily and regularly beat his wife. When Menake was three her mother died from one of her father's assaults. When she was seven, her father raped her repeatedly over the course of a four-day drunken binge. Finally her grandfather rescued her from her father's abusive care; she never saw the man again. When she was fifteen, her grandparents died and her uncle and aunt took her in. They were reluctant guardians, however, and in 2000 they sacrificed her for the cause. The LTTE had levied a human tax on its constituents: every Tamil family was ordered to donate a family member, male or female, to the organization to be trained for combat.[74] So Menake's uncle and aunt gave her up to the LTTE.[75]

Menake had cried and begged them not to take her. "I told them I didn't want to die so young. But a woman officer told me, 'Sorry, we can't help you. Your relatives said you came here of your own volition.'"[76] The LTTE has been cited by international observers for coercive recruitment by kidnapping, forced mobilization, and extortion. They fended off such attacks by claiming that the government had created so many orphans, and they alone were willing and able to provide for them.

Menake was forced to become a fighter, but she chose to become a would-be martyr. "I had nerve damage to my spine after falling from an LTTE tractor. The doctor said I might become paralyzed when I got older. I thought, why continue to live?" Menake felt that her life was over because she was physically damaged. Her only option was the life of a martyr. "A lot of girls were volunteering to be suicide bombers, so I thought I would, too … I felt I had no other choice. The LTTE calls its suicide missions *thatkodai*, Tamil for "gift of self." It made me feel that life still had a purpose."[77]

Menake, like other women in the organization, believed that death was sanctified in some way. For her, the main difference between Black Tigers and regular Tamil Tigers was that the regular Tigers didn't know when they would be killed. Black Tigers knew precisely when they would achieve their ultimate destiny.

Menake's experience contrasted with that of Darshika and Puhalchudar in significant ways. She lacked the comfort provided by friendship and definitely did not share their total devotion to the cause. Menake recalled that in her first weapons class, her group was handed sticks at first. After they had practiced with the sticks, they graduated to small arms. When they gave her a Kalashnikov, she realized that she might actually have to kill someone.

She had never really thought about whether the Sinhalese people were good or bad. She was, however, subjected to the same indoctrination—a constantly reiterated refrain that the Sri Lankan government is the enemy—that every LTTE member experienced. The terrorist organization told the cadres over and over that the government had perpetrated the worst human rights violations and that they had murdered innocent civilians. In order to take back what was rightfully theirs, the leaders told the girls, they would have to kill enemy soldiers.

Every evening, Menake and the other recruits watched military films, many of them in Chinese, along with some produced specially by the LTTE itself. The films showed the young recruits how to fight, how to use weapons, how to kill. The movies carried a consistent message, that when Tamil girls die in the service of the organization, they become heroes.[78] But despite the training, the movies, and the constantly repeated message, for Menake, the prospect of becoming a suicide bomber remained bleak. She was consumed by sadness. She was miserable that she would never have a family of her own. She would never hold a child in her arms and have a normal life. That was her biggest sorrow.[79]

In September 2006, Menake was given orders to blow up the Sri Lankan prime minister, Ratnasiri Wickremanayake. In spite of her reluctant recruitment to the cause, she enjoyed the notoriety and star treatment she received prior to going on her mission. On the eve of the attack, like all suicide bombers, Menake was given her last meal with an LTTE leader, in her case Pottu Amman, second-in-command and head of intelligence. She was offered the meal of her choice, which included chicken, fried rice, vegetable curry, and vanilla ice cream. "Amman said I would be known as a *mahaveera*, or great warrior, and venerated in a way I'd never been in life. Only then would I be given a military rank, based on the importance of my target."[80] Menake recalled that Amman was tall and handsome. For her, he seemed like a movie star.[81] Also according to standard procedure, a photographer took one last photo of Menake and Pottu Amman, so that after she was dead, it could be decorated with garlands and incense and placed on display at the center of her village.

For several days, Menake stalked the ritzy quarter where the prime minister lived. However, in a neighborhood where jeans and miniskirts were the norm, Menake's *salwar kameez* made her look like she did not belong. On the third day of her reconnaissance, the authorities stopped her outside the prime minister's mansion. They demanded her ID card. When it showed that she was from Jaffna, a Tamil and LTTE stronghold, she was taken in for questioning. The cyanide vial around her neck meant only one thing: that she was an LTTE operative. At the Boosa detention center, Menake revealed her plan and, eventually, informed on her handlers.

THE END OF THE REBELLION

From 1983 until 2009, the LTTE fought the Sri Lankan government for a separate state for the Tamil minority. In that time, more than 70,000 Sri Lankans were killed, tens of thousands fled abroad, and some 600,000 were displaced internally. Children on the way to school were routinely abducted and forced to become child soldiers—by both sides. Sri Lanka became infamous for its number of disappeared. More than 60,000 people were abducted by government militias, never to be seen again. Before its decimation in May 2009, the LTTE was considered one of the most ruthless terrorist organizations in the world. By using persuasion and extortion throughout the Tamil diaspora (notably in Canada, the UK, Australia, and the U.S.), in what the Tigers referred to as the Nandavanan system, they also become one of the world's most successful and prosperous.

Although a promising peace process was launched in 2002 under the auspices of the Norwegian government, politics and personalities ultimately intervened. The process was annulled in 2006, not by spoilers within the terrorist organization, as one might expect, but by the Sri Lankan government's extremist wing. While denying that a military solution was the best solution, the government launched major offensives against the LTTE throughout 2007 and 2008 and finally destroyed the organization in 2009.

After army commander Lieutenant General Sarath Fonseka barely survived an assassination attempt by LTTE in May 2006, government forces actively sought to assassinate as many of the organization's leaders as they could. That same year they killed the LTTE's political chief, its military intelligence leader, and the head of its naval unit, known as the Sea Tigers. In May 2007, they killed the leader of the Charles Anthony Regiment, Lieutenant Colonel Nakulan (whose nom de guerre was Nagulan), a personal friend and comrade of Prabhakaran. Brigadier S.P. Tamilselvan, the LTTE political chief, was assassinated on in November 2007 in a targeted aerial bombardment by the Sri Lankan air force. Tamilselvan had been one of the chief negotiators between the Norwegian SLMM

(Sri Lankan Monitoring Mission), the Sri Lankan government, and the Tigers.

From 2006 until 2009 the government targeted the women of the LTTE specifically. In September 2006, an alleged government death squad killed V. Thangaratnam, a female leader who had organized protests against the Sri Lankan Army's occupation of private land.[82] In May 2007, government troops killed "Mala," the leader of the Sothiya regiment.[83] In January, an LTTE area leader, Sudarmalar, and eighteen others were killed by government troops during clashes in Mannar. On May 25, 2008, government troops killed Lieutenant Colonel Selvy, deputy leader of the Sothiya regiment, during a battle at the Mannar "forward defense line."[84]

In May 2009, everything changed for the female Tigers and for the organization as a whole. During a pitched two-hour gun battle with Sri Lankan special forces in which a rocket was launched into his armor-plated ambulance, Velupillai Prabhakaran was killed. Several of the LTTE's highest-ranking lieutenants; Prabhakaran's son and heir apparent, Charles Anthony; and as many as three hundred cadres also perished in the battle.

The battle followed several months of intense fighting, targeted assassinations, and attacks against the civilian population in areas where the LTTE were most popular. Among the dead were both militants and peacemakers. The Sri Lankan army did not discriminate between those with "blood on their hands" and those members of the organization who were working toward reconciliation to end the twenty-six year civil war.

Although the organization has been decapitated and hostilities have officially ceased, Tamil calls for separation have not come to an end. According to the public opinion surveys that I conducted, both Indian and Sri Lankan Tamils want regional autonomy and devolution of central power. The Tamil diaspora in Canada, the United States, the UK, and Australia remains steadfast in its demand for autonomy and freedom.

While the LTTE is gone, its legacy lives on. Irish expatriates in the diaspora became radicalized in the 1920s after British atrocities (the term for human rights abuses at the time) in Ireland. The Palestinian movement was directed from abroad for forty years until they inspired a second generation of Palestinians to rise up against the Israeli occupation. If the underlying grievances that first led the Tamil groups to abandon parliamentary opposition and turn to violence are not addressed, the conflict will become multigenerational, as was the conflict in Northern Ireland and as is the conflict in Palestine. Although the West (outside of Canada and the UK) paid little attention to the conflict in Sri Lanka, there is much to learn from the ways in which the Liberation Tigers of Tamil Eelam integrated women into nearly all the echelons of the struggle.

Although some women willingly gave their lives for the cause, they were only represented within the military leadership, especially at the lieutenant-colonel level. There were few, if any, female political leaders at the very top. Women provided more than support: they had their own tank battalions; they were snipers, trackers, and spies; they planted claymore mines; they engaged in hand-to-hand combat; and they killed on demand, just like the men. The female tank unit of the LTTE successfully routed the Sri Lankan Army several times and won great battles. But off the battlefield, the women did not experience the same level of equality one would expect from an organization that depended on their fighting spirit and that regularly paid lip service to the principle of gender equality.

6

THE CRUCIAL LINKS

An Islamic state must be the goal of all people ... Once that has been achieved, we will live together in peace.
—Paridah binti Abas, 2005

Our family is not afraid of execution. Because life and death [are] only in the hands of God.
—Paridah binti Abas, 2008[1]

PARIDAH

Paridah binti Abas is a classic example of a female member of the terror group Jemaah Islamiya (JI). Born in Singapore on September 30, 1970, into a middle-class family, Paridah was one of six children of Abas bin Yusuf. She attended a secular high school and grew up planning to become a kindergarten teacher. Her father, Abas, had participated in the study groups established by two radical clerics, Abu Bakar Ba'asyir and Abdullah Sungkar, in Malaysia. He was so inspired by Sungkar's teaching that he promised Paridah in marriage to one of Sungkar's most ardent students, Ali Ghufron bin Nurhasyim, infamously known as Mukhlas. In her autobiography, Paridah writes that this marriage was arranged without her consent and was the occasion of intense parental pressure.[2]

Paridah found out that she was getting married one night when she was out for a drive with her father. Abas informed her that he had chosen an Indonesian preacher named Ali Ghufron to be her husband. "Mukhlas" was devout and Abas told his daughter that he respected the young man's dedication to Islam and the cause. Paridah met Ghufron only once before the wedding, and only for five minutes, when she served him tea at her parents' house. On their wedding night, Paridah warned Ghufron that she was not like other girls. He supposedly replied that this was music to his ears: "Thank God," he said. "You are the one I am looking for."[3]

Ali Ghufron had trained at bin Laden's camp in Afghanistan between 1986 and 1989. He regaled anyone who would listen with stories of the two mujahideen (meaning himself and bin Laden) fighting side by side. Paridah eventually grew to love him. She writes in her autobiography that she wants to thank her father for forcing her to marry Ali Ghufron. She never regretted the marriage. "Being the faithful wife of a man who is an earnest example of His Messenger is beautiful … I thank you, father."[4]

After the marriage, Paridah's brothers also became involved in JI's terror network. Hashim went to Afghanistan and eventually became mixed up with another radical cleric, Imam Samudra, and took part in terrorist attacks in Batam and Pekanbaru, Indonesia, in December 2000. Her other brother, Mohd Nasir bin Abas, became the head of JI's third division, Mantiqi 3. Her sister, Nurhayati, married a Malaysian preacher, Shamsul Bahri bin Hussein,[5] who also became involved in the network. Shamsul Bahri was eventually sentenced to three years in an Indonesian prison for helping plan the 2003 suicide bombing at the Marriott Hotel in Jakarta, which killed twelve people.

In 2003, Paridah herself was tried for falsifying immigration documents and faced a possible five-year prison sentence.[6] She was acquitted. Her more serious crime was likely aiding and abetting her husband's activities in Bali, where he organized the bombings that took 202 lives in October 2002. On the evening of the bombing, Paridah recalls hearing the blasts and the ambulance sirens, but suffering from nausea and being too pregnant to care. When her son was born, she named him Osama.[7]

Her children consider their father to have been a hero. Even her youngest children allegedly support what he did. Paridah called her autobiography *orang bilang ayah teroris*, (*People Say Father's a Terrorist*). In its pages, she explains that Mukhlas was not a terrorist but a mujahideen, a Muslim guerrilla warrior. She claims her children feel that Indonesia owes a debt of gratitude to their father and should say thank you rather than vilify him and blacken his name. Paridah admits that her husband might have wanted to teach the tourists in Bali a lesson but claims that he had not intended to kill as many people as he did. In fact, both Paridah and Ghufron's brothers propagate the theory that the CIA added explosives to the bombs to make them more powerful and kill more people. Shockingly, there are people in Indonesia who prefer to credit this proposition and see conspiracies everywhere, than admit that there is an Islamist problem in their nation.

Paridah now lives in Malaysia, in Ulu Tiram, three hundred kilometers south of Kuala Lumpur, with her six children. She has had to raise her family on her own: Ali Ghufron spent five years on death row, from 2003 to 2008, before exhausting the avenues for appeal. He was finally executed by a firing squad on November 9, 2008, for his responsibility in planning the Bali bombings.

SCHOOLS FOR JIHADIS

Jemaah Islamiya is practically the ideal model of jihadi terrorism, and yet few Westerners have even heard of it. A shadowy militant underground organization consisting of loosely assembled cells and individual militants spread across Southeast Asia, it originated in a radical Islamist group called Darul Islam, established just after Indonesia's independence. In the 1980s, the Egyptian Muslim Brotherhood (*al Ikhwan al Muslimun*) became influential throughout the region.[8] At the same time that radical Egyptian clerics and their ideas arrived from the east, similar religious teachings arrived from the Islamic Republic of Iran. Unlike many other societies, which were reshaped by the coming of Islam, most of Indonesia's existing social norms and values remained relatively unchanged. The Indonesian version of Muslim Brotherhood's Islamism was rendered almost completely local and retained a particularly regional flavor.[9] Society and gender relations did not change radically, and upper-class and high-caste Indonesian women were able to preserve their public roles.[10] Unlike other radical Islamist groups in the Arab world and South Asia, which tended to be male-centric, JI is consequently more "woman-friendly."

With no headquarters, no main office, no public outreach, and no official spokesmen to represent it, it is a wonder that the group flourished as it did. JI's success depended on strong kinship, marital, and familial bonds. The women of JI ensure its survival by forging critical links between disparate and geographically isolated groups. Marriage alliances, in particular, serve as the glue that holds the organization together. Women also make a crucial contribution to JI's solvency by engaging in cottage industries, making and selling Islamic headscarves, marketing Islamic herbal remedies, and undertaking a variety of piecework at home.[11] In many ways, JI operates like the Sicilian Mafia, using family connections and strategic marriages to make the organization cohere. It thus owes its success to the women, who form the links that reproduce both the ideology and the children for succeeding generations. JI is not a static terrorist organization but rather has evolved into a social organization that engages in economic activities, public relations, and social outreach. The International Crisis Group asserts that the women of JI are also critical to its ability to evade arrest.[12]

Al Qaeda is said to have commenced operations in Indonesia as early as 1988, when Osama bin Laden dispatched his brother-in-law, Muhammed Jamal Khalifa, to the Philippines to establish contacts with local militant groups throughout Southeast Asia. Unlike other affiliates all over the world that were directly controlled by Al Qaeda, however, JI functioned semiautonomously, pursuing its own local agenda. In addition to Al Qaeda, it associated with several other terrorist groups, including the Filipino organizations the Moro Islamic Liberation Front (MILF) and Abu Sayyaf, with whom JI members trained and shared tactics and safe houses.

The 9/11 Commission Report linked JI to the 1993 World Trade Center bombers and to mastermind Khalid Sheikh Muhammed (popularly known by his initials, KSM), who spent some of his formative years as a terrorist in the region before he was even a member of Al Qaeda. KSM hatched the preliminary plot for 9/11 in the Philippines with a plan, Operation Bojinka, to ram commercial airplanes into buildings.[13] In 1994, several key members of Operation Bojinka formed a front corporation called Konsonjaya, a trading company that supposedly exported Malaysian palm oil to Afghanistan and traded in Sudanese and Yemeni honey. All these countries were important nodes in Al Qaeda's global network. (Bin Laden actually resided in Sudan at the time, and ran several companies that exported these products.) As late as 1998, KSM still used Konsonjaya as a cover for his international travels. The names on its board of directors read like a who's who of the Al Qaeda network, with jihadis from Saudi Arabia, Afghanistan, and Indonesia.[14]

Over time, JI developed a closer association with Al Qaeda, sharing members and jointly planning operations. Riduan

Isamuddin, a.k.a. Hambali, was a member of both Al Qaeda and JI and provided the key link between KSM and the terrorist-cell leaders in Southeast Asia.[15] JI's leaders circulated bin Laden's speeches and writings. Many JI operatives were trained in Afghanistan and worked closely with the Afghan Arabs as part of the international brigade during their nine-year fight against the Soviets.[16] In the training camps, the new recruits pledged a *bay'ah*, a formal oath of loyalty, to bin Laden and to Al Qaeda.[17] As many as three hundred Indonesians "graduated" from the jihadi camps in Afghanistan.[18] The two groups shared tactics and expertise and created a jointly operated training camp in Poso, on the coast of the Indonesian island of Sulawesi.

JI can also be linked to 9/11 more concretely. Yazid Sufaat, a former Malaysian army captain and microbiologist, was instrumental in aiding the 9/11 plotters. He hosted Zacarias Moussaoui (the so-called twentieth hijacker) on his way to flight school in the United States. *Time* reported that Sufaat was a member of Jemaah Islamiya and that Moussaoui stayed at the Sufaat house several times, where they discussed Moussaoui's dream of crashing a plane into the White House.[19] Sufaat and his wife, Dursina, had both attended California State University in Sacramento in the 1980s and understood the ins and outs of entering the country with a foreign visa. When Moussaoui was arrested in the month before the attacks, he carried with him a letter of employment on letterhead from Sufaat's company, InFocus Tech, to legally sponsor his entry to the United States.[20] The letters of introduction named Moussaoui as InFocus Tech's "marketing consultant" for the United States, Britain, and Europe. Sufaat had signed the letters as the company's managing director and provided Moussaoui with a $2,500 monthly stipend during his stay in the United States, along with a lump sum of $35,000 to get him started at the flight school.

FBI chief Robert Mueller singled out JI as Al Qaeda's principal

Southeast Asian partner. The organization received more than 1.35 billion rupiahs ($140,000) over three years from Al Qaeda, and still it remained off the radar screen until the Bali and Jakarta bombings. Even though several of JI's leaders were arrested in Singapore in 2002, many Americans only really became aware of Indonesia after it was struck by the tsunami in December 2004, and few understood anything about the terrorist movement there until it was too late.[21]

By the beginning of the millennium, the group had bombed as many as thirty churches in Jakarta, West Java, North Sumatra, Riau, and Bandung, killing eighteen people in the process.[22] In 2000, it perpetrated terror attacks throughout Indonesia, including a car bomb at the Jakarta Stock Exchange and Christmas Eve bombings in East Java and Nusatenggara. At 11:05 P.M. on October 12, 2002, Paridah's husband, Ali Ghufron, masterminded the deadly explosions at Paddy's Irish Pub and the Sari Club across the street from Paddy's Pub in the Kuta district of Bali. "A Saturday night at two popular nightclubs ended with friends ripped to pieces and burned to death. Dozens, maybe hundreds, were dead, and an entire block of buildings was gone."[23] The carnage was "incomprehensible."[24] For terrorist leader Imam Samudra,[25] echoing comparable statements by Osama bin Laden, the Australians, who were the majority of the casualties of the nightclub attacks, were suitable targets due to their country's efforts to separate East Timor from Indonesia.[26] The attack comprised three separate blasts, a hallmark of Al Qaeda operations, intended to wreak the maximum carnage by killing people fleeing the scene as well as any first responders to the initial explosion. The same modus operandi was repeated in 2005 when Bali was bombed again.

Bali is an attractive target because it is a tourist destination that caters to Australian and American holidaymakers. It also has relatively lax security even though it has now been targeted repeatedly (before he was assassinated, another notorious Islamist militant, Noordin Top, had allegedly planned yet another Bali attack for 2009). According to journalist Kelly McEvers, the group wanted a target that would bring the greatest possible destruction to America and her allies. After considering an international school in Jakarta and an American-owned gold mine, the group settled on Bali, the island of indulgences—food, drink, sun, and sand.

The fact that the majority of the island's inhabitants are Hindu and that alcohol was offered at all the possible targets minimized the chance of killing fellow Muslims. The purpose of the attack was to send the unequivocal message that Westerners were neither safe nor welcome in Indonesia.[27] The $35,000 to fund the operation allegedly came from Al Qaeda via a wealthy businessman, one of JI's leaders in Malaysia.[28]

JI has also been credited with the 2003 attack against the Marriott Hotel in Jakarta, the bombing outside the Australian embassy in 2004, the second bombing in Bali in October 2005, and the attack against the Marriott and Ritz-Carlton hotels in Jakarta in July 2009, which followed three years of relative inactivity.[29] Al Qaeda allegedly footed the bill for these operations as well, and handed JI operative Hambali a $100,000 bonus for killing so many Westerners in them.

The geography of Indonesia plays a significant role in JI's success and in the government's failure to contain it. The country is the world's largest archipelago, made up of more than 17,500 islands covering an area of 1,919,440 square kilometers. The remote islands and dense jungles are an ideal environment for terrorist groups to operate in and hide from the authorities. Indonesia is home to more than two hundred million Muslims. The isolation of the islands affords JI the sort of autonomy and maneuverability that few other terror groups enjoy. Indonesia is a weak state with porous borders that is rife with corruption.[30] Its diverse population is also severely divided along religious and sectarian lines.

These internecine conflicts provide fertile recruiting grounds to the organization in areas like Maluku and Sulawesi.[31] JI played a critical role in the violence that killed more than 5,000 people in Maluku in 2004–05. Nevertheless, supporters of JI and many Islamists look upon the sectarian rioting as a conspiracy orchestrated by Western (and notably Israeli) powers.[32]

Many Indonesians do not believe that JI really exists.[33] Even the Indonesian government did not officially recognize it as a terrorist organization until April 2008—eight years after its first major attacks and six years after the United States added JI to its terrorist watch list.[34]

TOWARD THE CREATION OF AN ISLAMIC STATE

The former spiritual head of JI, Abu Bakar Ba'asyir, is a lanky, white-haired, wispy-bearded cleric who wears wire-rimmed glasses. His ancestry, like bin Laden's, reaches back to the Hadramawt region of Yemen. Ba'asyir began by fighting the rule of Indonesian dictator Suharto, who ruled the country from 1967 until 1998; Ba'asyir was designated an Amnesty International "prisoner of conscience." Ba'asyir brought together the university-based student movements that opposed Suharto and the Islamic opposition.[35] He founded several Islamic religious boarding schools, known as *pesantren*,[36] the Southeast-Asian equivalent of the madrassas of the Middle East. He modeled his principal seminary, the Pesantren Al Mukmin, on his own alma mater, the Gontor Pesantren in East Java, which had combined puritanical Islamic doctrine with a rigorous modern curriculum. The school itself was located on the outskirts of the city of Solo in Central Java, behind imposing wrought-iron gates and surrounded by green rice paddies. Together with Abdullah Sungkar (Paridah's father's mentor), Ba'asyir also founded the Pondok Pesantren in Ngruki, Solo, in 1972. This school has yielded more jihadis than any one madrassa in Pakistan or Saudi Arabia.

Arrested and jailed in 1980, both Sungkar and Ba'asyir were eventually released on appeal. They resumed teaching at Al Mukmin school and handpicked their most promising students to establish small, self-sustaining communities, *jemaah*, in their villages. These Islamic *jemaah* would be governed by Shari'ah law and avoid association with any of the state's secular institutions.[37] Forced into exile in neighboring Malaysia in 1985, Ba'asyir and Sungkar literally went door-to-door preaching, spreading their interpretation of the word of God and creating a parallel movement of students and study groups. Finally, after Suharto was deposed in 1998, the two men returned to Indonesia to teach at the schools they had founded decades earlier and formalize their movement, the Jemaah Islamiya.

Sungkar designated himself the group's first emir, or supreme leader. An imposing figure, in contrast to the rather bookish Ba'asyir, Sungkar required all members to swear a personal oath of allegiance, or *bay'ah*, in which they promised "to hear and obey to the best of my ability all things pertaining to the word of Allah and the way of the Prophet."[38]

Sungkar and Ba'asyir organized the group into four regional brigades or *mantiqi*: Mantiqi 1 for Singapore and Malaysia, whose focus was fund-raising and religious indoctrination; Mantiqi 2 in Indonesia, for the promotion of jihad; Mantiqi 3 in the southern Philippines, Sulawesi, and Brunei, created in 1997 for training; and Mantiqi 4 in Australia and Papua, although it was never fully established as a separate administrative unit.[39] When Sungkar died of a heart attack in 1999, Ba'asyir became the de facto head of the movement while Hambali became its operational chief.

In JI's founding document, *Pedoman Umum Perjuangan aj-Jama'ah Al Islamiyya* ("The General Guidebook for the Jemaah Islamiya Struggle"), Ba'asyir advocated the creation of a sovereign Islamic state to bring together Muslims from Indonesia, Malaysia, Brunei, Singapore, Philippines, Cambodia, and Thailand.[40] Since

1998 (or a bit later, according to some experts), JI has had the additional goal of cleansing the region of its non-Muslim elements, known as the *uhud* project; specifically, it aims to remove Christians and Hindus from those regions where they are demographically significant.

Ba'asyir was in and out of jail for treason, immigration violations, and providing false statements to the police as a result of his involvement in the Christmas Eve bomb attacks and the Bali bombings. In 2004 he was arrested again; the following year he was found guilty of conspiracy and served twenty-six months in prison on that charge. In 2008, after a dispute with Muhammed Iqbal Rahman (known as Abu Jibril), a rival and the leader of Majlis Mujahideen Indonesia (MMI), over whether the JI organization was really being run Islamically, Ba'asyir "left" both MMI and JI and founded Jemaah Anshorut Tauhid (JAT), "Partisans of the Oneness of God."Although he officially severed his ties to the MMI and to JI's core, Ba'asyir retained his affiliation with the Pesantren Al Mukmin. Several of the hard-liners followed him to JAT.

Even hard-core Islamists regard JI with a modicum of suspicion. They object to the clandestine nature of the organization and its practice of swearing oaths to the emir; for pure Salafists, it is appropriate to swear allegiance to the commander of the faithful but not to the head of a covert group. Most Muslims reject JI's interpretation of jihad because its extremist wing sanctions suicide bombs and killing civilians.[41]

JI is similar to the Muslim Brotherhood, in the sense that it contains many divisions, some of which are involved in purely legal activities, while others engage in violent deeds and terrorism. The divisions that provide benevolent and humanitarian efforts bestow upon the organization a veneer of legitimacy. Nonetheless, JI is split between its mainstream and its extremists. Extremists like Hambali and Top are responsible for the suicide bombings, whereas the majority of the mainstream pursue the goal of an Islamic state but do not support the killing of civilians, especially other Indonesians or other Muslims.

For many hard-line Islamists (including some Salafists), suicide bombers and terrorists are considered *muharibeen*—people who cause harm and death—and their acts are punishable by death. Furthermore, JI's goal of toppling the regime is highly problematic because, according to Islamic tradition, the faithful are forbidden to rebel against elected Muslims leaders. In the Hadith (the words and deeds of the Prophet Muhammed [PBUH]), the Prophet addresses the idea of consensus among his people and in several Hadith he is quoted as saying "My community will never agree in error."[42] If a rebellion against a Muslim leader has little chance of succeeding, or will lead to more bloodshed and tyranny than under the current leader, the theologians advise against it. Even Muhammed 'Abd al Wahhab (the founder of the fundamentalist Wahhabi movement) argued against rebelling against Muslim governments.

He told the people of Al Qaseem, "It is obligatory to hear and obey the leaders of the Muslims, whether they are righteous or immoral, so long as they do not enjoin disobedience toward Allah. Whoever has become Caliph and the people have given him their support and accepted him, even if he has gained the position by force, is to be obeyed and it is *haram* [forbidden] to rebel against him."[43]

Indonesian Muslims are not being ruled by nonbelievers or by foreign occupiers but by their own democratically elected Muslim representatives.

When Ba'asyir left MMI to start JAT, several JI members migrated with him, virtually dissolving the MMI organization in the process. The suicide bombings and attacks against Westerners are a manifestation of Noordin Top's offshoot organization rather than of the mainstream of JI.[44] This issue has caused division within

JI and led to several members leaving the group and even working with counter-terrorism officials.[45] While Top maintained close contacts with JAT and MMI through an operative, it is unclear whether Ba'asyir condoned or supported the suicide operations against Westerners in 2005 and 2009.

According to a Western convert to the movement, Rabiah (Robyn) Hutchison, Ba'asyir is a mild-mannered and patient man who is much less dogmatic than several of his students. He disapproved of the freedom with which many of his students accused others of being *takfir*, meaning that they had strayed from the faith and become nonbelievers, just because they disagreed with JI's mission and tactics. Al Qaeda has used the same term to justify its attacks against Muslims who work with American occupiers or even those who participate in democratic elections. Hutchison quotes Ba'asyir as saying: "If someone believes in Allah, even though they may be ignorant of many things in Islam, it is not the basis to say they are outside of Islam."[46] Hardly a moderate, Ba'asyir is also quoted as saying: "There is no nobler life than to die as a martyr for jihad. None. The highest deed in Islam is jihad. If we commit to jihad, we can neglect other deeds, even fasting and prayer."[47] Of bin Laden, Ba'asyir says that he supports his struggle because it is the true struggle to uphold Islam. Ba'asyir denies having any direct connection to bin Laden, but dreams of one day meeting him.[48] For Ba'asyir, the real terrorists are America and Israel, and he advocates sending Indonesian mujahideen to Palestine to drive out the Israeli occupiers and demonstrate the Islamic nations' resolute stance against Israel's persecution of the Palestinian people.[49]

In 2003, JI faced disintegration as an organization when more than ninety of its leaders were arrested and a quarter of its leadership killed as part of the counter-terrorism campaign in the aftermath of the Bali attacks. So many Muslim civilians had been killed by JI attacks that a serious rift developed among the extremists, between those (like Imam Samudra) who advocated the killing of civilians and others (like Nasir bin Abas, Paridah's older brother) who rejected it. Group members expressed serious opposition to the fratricidal nature of the attacks and were concerned that a handful of radicals had diluted JI's core purpose—to combat corruption and address the socioeconomic needs of Indonesian Muslims.[50] The Mantiqi 3 leader Nasir bin Abas broke with the organization and started working with government agencies to help deradicalize or at least demobilize his former colleagues.[51]

JI attracts its recruits from within four key societal institutions: kinship or family groups, mosques, *pesantrens*, and friendship networks. The mosques and *pesantrens* appear to be closely connected and highly effective in recruiting cadres. While the number of *pesantrens* in Indonesia has risen over the past few years, it should be emphasized that of the eighteen thousand schools teaching three million students, no more than one hundred and fifty are radicalized and only four have been directly linked with terrorist training and operations.[52]

Of the four recruitment mechanisms, kinship and friendship groups are the key for radical mobilization. Among their virtues, from the point of view of the jihadis, is that both methods are resistant to government infiltration. In addition, siblings working together can offer each other support during an operation. This increases operational efficacy and improves security.[53] JI understood what the Chechen jihadis eventually learned: that brothers (and sisters) would be more loyal to each other and less likely to defect, change their mind, or disappoint one another than people who are not related. During the 2002 Bali bombing, Ali Ghufron[54] involved both his younger and his older brother in the operation. Attacks involving teams of brothers or relatives are fairly common in JI.

Once people join JI, the group becomes an all-encompassing force that regulates every aspect of their social lives.[55] Members socialize and marry within the group, and rarely associate with people outside it. In this context, kinship and friendship are two sides to the same coin, in the sense that when an individual is brought into JI by means of friendship, these ties are likely to be reinforced through marriage.[56] Senior members of JI offer their sisters or sisters-in-law to new and promising recruits, so the individual is drawn both into the organization and into a family.[57] The daughters and sisters of terror-cell leaders also intermarry with the leaders of other cells, creating bonds that ensure that no operative or leader defects or "walks away."

Marriages have been arranged deliberately to forge links between Malaysian and Indonesian JI members. This network of marriages makes JI like an extended family.[58] Sungkar himself married off his stepdaughters to Ferial Muchlis bin Abdul Halim, a head of the Selangor JI cell, and Syawal Yassin, a prominent South Sulawesi figure and former military trainer in Afghanistan.[59] Ali Ghufron was married to Paridah, the younger sister of Nasir bin Abas, the head of JI's Malaysian wing.[60] Haris Fadillah, a Muslim militia leader, arranged for his daughter, Mira Augustina, to marry Omar Al Faruq, the Al Qaeda representative in Southeast Asia, in the course of one day. In many cases, senior JI figures arrange the marriages of their subordinates to their own sisters and sisters-in-law to keep the network secure.

EXTREME MARRIAGE

Noralwizah Lee Binti Abdullah[61] is the Sabahan Chinese wife of JI's former operational commander, Hambali.[62] Noralwizah's father was Malay and her mother a Chinese convert to Islam. Born in 1970, Noralwizah grew up poor and her youth was plagued by her father's alcoholism and philandering. To escape the pressures of home, she converted from Buddhism to Islam and headed to Lukmanul Hakiem Pesantren in Ulu Tiram, in the southern Malaysian state of Johor. The boarding school was a hotbed of radicalization and a hub of JI activity. All the major JI players crossed paths in the school in the early 1990s, including the organization's founders, Ba'asyir and Sungkar, and Ali Ghufron and Noordin Top. Top became the school's principal in 1994.

In 1990 Noralwizah joined Sungkar's female corps, which the JI leader used to spread his radical message. The girls networked among Sungkar's wives and offered lectures on the role of women in jihad to other women. When Noralwizah met Hambali at the school, he immediately proposed marriage, and they were wed in a simple ceremony in 1991.

Noralwizah wasn't just Hambali's wife: she was a full-fledged JI member. She shared his conservative religious outlook and agreed with him that jihad was a necessity rather than an option. She is believed to be a member of JI's central command and one of its chief financial accountants.[63] Noralwizah held the purse strings while also organizing activities for JI women members. She actively recruited women to form her network of friends and to provide potential wives for new male JI recruits.

Hambali used Noralwizah's girlfriends to enlist and reward his best people. As men marry women within the network, the men become more fervent in their support, and less likely to disappoint their new families. In many cases, their in-laws provide the core link to the jihadis. In many cases, the women seem to be more radical than the men.[64] Yazid Sufaat, for example, became more religious as a result of the influence of his wife, Sejarahtul Dursina.

At a monthly discussion at the Khadijah Mosque, one of the most active mosques in Singapore, half of the audience is made up of female religious teachers who counsel and help rehabilitate the families of JI detainees. One woman expressed concern that so little attention had been paid to understanding the role of women in the terrorist group. But some of the women know of and support their husbands' activities through fund-raising, or by hiding their husbands or their husbands' colleagues from the authorities. Several of the women (like Noralwizah) play a role in managing finances.

Women in the region have always been politically active, and have made great strides toward female emancipation, education, and political empowerment. Because JI is an Islamic group, people assume that the women take a backseat to the men, but this is hardly the case. The women form the strategic nexus that allows the organization to function throughout the Philippines, Indonesia, Malaysia, and Southeast Asia generally. There are no Islamist movements in Southeast Asia today, be they moderate, progressive, fundamentalist, or militant, from which women are excluded.[65] From the 1930s to the 1960s, many of Indonesia's political parties recruited, trained, and armed women as active party members. Every single major Islamic political party in Indonesia and Malaysia, including Indonesia's Prosperous Justice Party (the Partai Keadilan Sejahtera or PKS) and the Pan-Malaysian Islamic Party (PAS), has a women's wing with thousands of active members.[66]

For the most part, the women of JI remain behind the scenes; they are organizers, not fighters. Their primary role is to ensure that the organization remains solid. The difference between the women of JI and their sisters in the Palestinian, Chechen, or Tamil conflicts is that they are not fighting an occupation and do not have to endure the repressive measures taken by a treacherous and brutal state. Their role as supporters and believers, however, is crucial in ensuring the longevity of the movement so that future generations may carry on the fight.

Women may be courted by JI and even encouraged by the movement's leaders to contribute to the jihad against the West, but there will never be a female leader of the movement. It would be difficult to classify the women of JI as "Muslim feminists." The likes of Noralwizah Lee binti Abdulla, Munfiatun al Fitri, and Mira

Agustina may be seen as pioneers, but in their commitment to help their men tear down the secular Indonesian nation-state, they are actually helping to corrode, downplay, and marginalize Indonesian women.

Sidney Jones, the project director for International Crisis Group (ICG) in Jakarta and the world's leading expert on the Jemaah Islamiya, argues that while the women might not participate directly in violence, they do egg the men on and do not deter the men from participating in terrorism. Some of the women's fathers promise them in marriage to jihadis while others deliberately seek out JI men as a matter of course. When Ali Ghufron (Mukhlas) was on death row, he reportedly received written offers of marriage from women who wanted to be the wife of a martyr.[67] The women create a radical ideological atmosphere for their children and not only support the men's insurgent activities, but also encourage their children to follow in their fathers' footsteps.

Among the most fervent supporters of the assassinated Malaysian jihadi leader Noordin Top were several of his wives. Top led a break-away faction of JI. He attained legendary status because of his ability to evade capture and perpetrate acts of suicide terror directed against Western targets. Top met his first wife, Siti Rahmah, at the Lukmanul Hakim Pesantren, where they were both teachers. The couple married in the late 1990s. Siti's brother, Muhammed Rais, partici-pated in Top's operation against the Marriott Hotel in 2004, and her father, Rusdi Hamid, was also a member of JI. Thus Siti provided an extremely important link between Top and different parts of the organization. Top eventually deserted Siti, leaving her with two small children while she was pregnant with her third child.[68]

In June 2004, Noordin Top married again, this time to Munfiatun al Fitri. Munfiatun claims that at the time she did not realize she was marrying a JI leader. She met him through mutual friends, who were JI members, in 2004, and thought Top's name was Abdurrahman Auf. Their mutual friend Hassan then told her that Top was a jihadi. Munfiatun was a teacher who worked at a *pesantren* in West Java and had always expressed the wish to marry a jihadi.[69] She was not opposed to her husband's activities, even after she found out that he was wanted by the police. In 2004, when Top was being investigated for his involvement in the first Marriott bombing, Munfiatun claimed that she knew everything about her husband's activities and had known in advance about the attack. However, she did not report any of this to the police because she loved her husband very much.[70]

In 2005, Top married once again, this time in an arranged wedding to a young woman named Arina, whose father, Barhudin Latif, had orchestrated the match. Arina told police that she was unaware of her husband's true identity when she married him, even though her father certainly would have known. She thought his name was Abdul Ade Halim, and that he was a teacher from Sulawesi.

All these marriages to local women produced a number of benefits for the terror-cell leader. First, in the cases of Siti and Arina, Top's marriages cemented a connection to sympathetic families in the broader jihadi movement. According to police sources, Top married Arina to secure the loyalty and protection of her father, Barhudin. The marriages also allowed Top to blend in with the local population. As Arina's husband, he assumed the identity of a religious man who traveled often, kept strange hours, and avoided social contact with the neighbors. Journalists have presented Arina as a victim, suggesting that she knew practically nothing about Top when she married him and was unaware that their marriage was intended to cement network connections. If these accounts are accurate, it still seems likely that Arina did know he had at least two other wives. She may have believed that his long absences were for visits to his other family back in Sulawesi.[71]

Ba'asyir's views on the role of women, gender equality, sexual relations, and social harmony correspond to the Salafi tradition. He opposes women's direct involvement in operations while encouraging them to study Islam and the Hadith. In his *pesantren* women occupied a separate compound, where only female students and teachers were housed. Although the school enforced the strict separation of the sexes, both leaders (Ba'asyir and Sungkar) had an open-door policy for any student, male or female, to ask questions of law or interpretation. One of their most famous female graduates was Rabiah (Robyn) Hutchison, an Australian convert to Islam who spent time with the mujahideen in Afghanistan. Hutchison began her jihadi career in Pesantren Al Mukmin in the 1980s. She grew close to both clerics: Sungkar presided at her wedding in 1984 and Ba'asyir signed the *akad nikah*, or wedding contract, when Hutchison married Abdul Rahim Ayub, who became the head of JI's Mantiqi 4 operations in Australia.[72] Hutchison spent four years working as a doctor in a mujahideen hospital and orphanage on the Pakistan–Afghanistan border during the Afghan jihad in the 1990s. After several years of marriage, the couple divorced and Hutchison returned to Afghanistan in 2000. There, she consulted with bin Laden to ask him where she could be most useful to the cause.

As there were no midwives or gynecologists in Kandahar and Hutchison had years of medical training, bin Laden sent her to Kabul, where she established a women's clinic and set up schools for girls. (Bin Laden had been largely responsible for opening girls' schools in Kabul, even though the Taliban opposed the education of women, and he was very interested in women's health.)[73] Hutchison became famous among the Afghan Arabs for her good deeds and dedication to Islam. She eventually married one of the leading ideologues in Afghanistan, Mustafa Hamid (known as Abu Walid al Misri), a journalist for Al Jazeera.

Hutchison demonstrates yet another way in which women play a strategic role among jihadi groups. In her case, her citizenship combined with marriage gave Ayub access to a foreign passport. This was useful both for carrying out operations outside the region and for traveling in general. Her own passport was confiscated by Australia's counter-terror squad, ASIO (the Australian Security Intelligence Organisation). Several of Hutchison's children went on to join Islamist groups. Two of her sons (Muhammed and Abdullah) were arrested in Yemen; they were allegedly connected to Jack Roche, who was arrested for plotting to blow up the Israeli embassy in Canberra. Her daughter Rahma is married to Khaled Cheikho, a veteran of Lashkar e Toiba, Pakistan's most infamous terrorist organization, and one of nine men charged with conspiring to make explosives in preparation for bombings in Sydney and Melbourne.[74] Cheikho was sentenced to life imprisonment in October 2009 after a trial that took almost two years, making it the longest in Australia's history.

All of JI's suicide bombings to date have been carried out by men. A small number of JI women have been caught smuggling bomb detonators and explosive materials from Malaysia into Indonesia, although this would still be considered a support rather than an operational role. However, in 2007 Superintendent Edwin Corvera, the deputy director for the police in Central Mindanao, received reports that the local chapter of JI planned to use women for terrorist operations. Apparently the organization was recruiting women to carry out suicide bomb missions against infrastructure targets and public transportation terminals in the region. Whether the reports were true or not, authorities prepared themselves for a worst-case scenario: more bombings by previously unsuspected operatives. Corvera ordered the police to deploy policewomen in public bus and train terminals to search female passengers.[75]

Sidney Jones is not convinced that women in Indonesia will

become fully operational. Instead, they spread the message of jihad and contribute to the cause financially. Many JI women are involved in selling Islamic products, from headscarves to home remedies. They often do piecework jobs that at times require them to travel from place to place selling their wares. As they travel, they spread JI's message and brand of Islam. Overall, these women are not facing the same kinds of pressures as their sisters in Chechnya, Palestine, and Iraq, but are just as fervent in their dedication to the terrorist movements.

Not only does JI employ women strategically to cement the organization's bonds but it also uses them to guarantee the survival of the group, ensuring generational continuity by sending the children of JI operatives for militant training to mold them into the next generation of JI. The women, rather than transforming from support roles to operational ones, are instead preparing the way for their children.

THE FUTURE OF THE MOVEMENT

During periods of heightened security and counter-terror activity, JI goes underground to focus on rebuilding and to ensure the future of the group. A source within the organization contends that four pairs of young suicide bombers swore oaths in April 2005, followed by another six pairs in July. The prospective suicide bombers underwent training in *pesantrens* in Central Java and in the Ciamis and Garut areas of West Java. Following training, they were deployed for periods of one to two months in areas of conflict such as West Seram, Maluku, and Poso.

The activists appear to be getting younger and younger. One of the most notorious of JI's new generation of operatives was Fathur Rohman al Ghozi, a product of one of Ba'asyir's boarding schools, the Al Mukmin Pesantren in Ngruki, Solo, three hours from his village in East Java. At the ripe old age of thirteen, al Ghozi was arrested in the Philippines for planning a bombing spree in Manila that killed twenty-two people and injured eighty.[76] One observer reported, "Fathers send their children to the city of Karachi in Pakistan to further their education. These children form the al Ghuraba (foreign) cell. During the spring vacations they undergo military training in Afghanistan."[77] Even in its highly weakened state, JI continues to renew itself and is likely to reemerge from the flames, like a phoenix born again.

By recruiting children, JI has created cadres that are almost impervious to government crackdowns: it is virtually impossible for any government agency to target operatives who are so young. At the same time, the children form extremely strong bonds with other youthful jihadis that will likely last a lifetime. More to the point, should the adult organization be at risk of complete eradication due to failing public support, crackdowns by the police, or the imprisonment of leaders, JI can reconstitute itself with the next generation.

Aware of the potential generational shift, the Indonesian government is mass-producing materials to inoculate children from joining the jihad, such as a comic book aimed at children and teenagers, entitled *When the Conscience Speaks*, in which Bali bomber Ali Imron regrets his actions. In the book, Imron reveals what the recruitment process is like and how to avoid becoming a jihadi.[78]

Jemaah Islamiya was originally founded with the goal of toppling Suharto's corrupt regime. Once Suharto's dictatorship ended in 1998, JI's new mission became to depose the Indonesian government and fight the evil influence of Western secular culture. However, Indonesia is also the most vibrant democracy in the Islamic world; its democratic institutions provide a moderate response to the radical Islamic messages emanating from the Wahhabis, the Salafis, and the jihadi terror networks. Moderate

Muslims promote a pluralistic and democratic version of Islam in Indonesia and throughout the region.

Unlike in the Middle East, the Islamic political parties advocate and actively participate in free and fair elections. As a result, most Indonesians view JI as a fringe movement. The likelihood that it will depose the Indonesian government through either democratic or other means is low. JI's political ally, Hizb ut Tahrir, performed miserably in the 2009 elections. In fact, the July 2009 attacks against the Ritz-Carlton and the Marriott in Jakarta came only ten days after the reelection (by an overwhelming majority) of President Susilo Bambang Yudhoyono, who had ordered the antiterror attacks that nearly ended JI.[79]

In the aftermath of the 2002 crackdown, women were able to rejuvenate and reproduce JI's support, operational setup, and cellular structure with the next generation of fighters. They are having to do this again as most of the organization's new leaders have been arrested and killed. Samudra was executed—along with Ali Ghufron (Mukhlas) and his brother Amrozi—by a firing squad in November 2008, for complicity in the Bali attacks. The arrest of the second generation of leaders and the assassination of Noordin Top in 2009 have also weakened the organization and will likely force it underground once again. Such setbacks would leave most other terror groups in tatters, yet because of the family links within JI, and because of the significant role played by women, it is likely to survive this current onslaught.

7

THE RECRUITERS
AND PROPAGANDISTS

*We will stand, covered by our veils and wrapped in our robes,
weapons in hand, our children in our laps, with the Qur'an and the
Sunna [sayings] of the Prophet of Allah directing and guiding us.*
—Al Khansa'a jihadi website, August 2004[1]

*I use my pen and words, my honest emotions … Jihad is not
exclusive to men.*
—Umm Farouq[2]

MALIKA

In May 2010, a Brussels court sentenced fifty-year-old Malika el
Aroud to eight years in prison and a 5,000 euro fine for establishing,
leading, and financing a terrorist group. According to the judges,
Malika used her website to attract the most vulnerable Web surfers
and to indoctrinate and then recruit them to the global jihad. Her
website got 1,500 users a day and showed reckless disregard for the
deaths of young European Muslim men who went to Afghanistan
on jihad. After years of house arrests and scrutiny by the police,
Malika was finally caught by Belgian officials, on a technicality.
In private they told me, "We knew she would make a mistake and

this time, *this time*, we have her."[3] During the almost three years in which she lived under house arrest in a three-bedroom apartment in the Brussels neighborhood of St. Gilles, the police monitored her every move. On trial, she was no longer covered from head to toe in traditional black Islamic garb. Instead she donned Western clothing and let her thick wild hair fall to her shoulders—something she claims her defense attorney and the judge made her do even though it violated the spirit and the letter of Islamic law. Malika had lived in Brussels all her adult life. She speaks fluent French and is extremely articulate. She is also an Al Qaeda legend known to most European intelligence agencies.[4] Malika occupies a place at the forefront of the women's movement in the global jihad and is considered extremely dangerous.

Malika el Aroud was five years old when she moved with her parents from Morocco to Belgium. They were part of a wave of Muslim immigrants that helped rebuild Europe after the devastation of World War II. Initially men came to work temporarily and sent remittances home, but with time, their families joined them. Many European countries saw Muslim ghettos grow on the outskirts of their cities and towns. As a young immigrant, Malika grew up like other children, playing, going out, and having "an average life" according to her sister, Saida.

As she grew older, she indulged in the various vices Belgium had to offer: sex, drugs, alcohol, parties, discos, and lots of boys. Her sisters recalled that she was a wild child who became pregnant by her first cousin and had a baby out of wedlock. By her own account, Malika claims that, after a while, she became so disgusted with herself that she wanted to die. She even attempted suicide.[5]

In high school, she attacked a teacher for making racist remarks, and was promptly expelled. She recalls being treated like a "dirty foreigner" wherever she went. She claims her radicalization was a reaction to the right-wing racist xenophobia she encountered as an outsider in Belgium. Like many children of Muslim immigrants, Malika faced the identity crisis associated with being neither European nor fully Moroccan. She did not fit in either society.

Malika wanted to give her daughter a better future than she had. But she could not find work, had serious financial problems, and fell into a deep depression. As, one by one, the doors around her closed, she gravitated toward the Centre Islamique Belge (CIB) in Sint-Jans-Molenbeek, a mosque and community center founded in 1997 by a radical Syrian cleric named Ayachi Bassam. There, Malika found a new identity in political Islam. It opened a door that offered money, work, psychological support, and, best of all, a husband.[6] At the center she quickly married and quickly divorced twice before meeting the love of her life, Abdessater Dahmane.

Abdessater had heard about Malika. One day, he approached her outside the center while she waited for the tram. He apologized for being so forward, gave her his phone number, and asked if he could talk to her again. Malika, impressed by the dark prayer callus on his forehead, which indicated he was truly a man of faith, readily agreed. The two of them enjoyed a chaste courtship consisting of long walks in the park and discussions about politics and the evils of America. When Malika contracted tuberculosis she feared Abdessater's reaction to the news would be to abandon their courtship. But instead of spurning her, he asked her to marry him so that he could take care of her.[7] That April they wed. Sheikh Bassam himself performed the ceremony.[8]

Bassam indoctrinated his followers with a puritanical interpretation of Islam, making the center a breeding ground for extremism.[9] There was enormous pressure on students in the study groups to conform. Many girls walked in bareheaded, but within a week or two they were almost certain to be sporting a headscarf. Surrounded by Muslims who embraced a "pure" form of Islam, Malika donned the hijab and began her metamorphosis, first reading the *Qur'an* in French, then abstaining from drugs and alcohol. The rigid environment and strict code of conduct provided her with a welcome sense of purpose.[10]

Abdessater shared Malika's worldview and politics. They both regarded Shi'a and secular Muslims with contempt. They considered Moroccan Islam overly traditional, superstitious, and sexist. In their view, colonial influence had poisoned the country, whereas the Salafi interpretation of Islam represented a true form, much closer to the ideals of the Umma, the Islamic Community of Believers. The most dynamic interpretation of Islam, in their view, was Osama bin Laden's. The couple greatly admired bin Laden and followed his charitable deeds in Afghanistan while he fought the Russians. Bin Laden spent his own money, which in itself was worthy of their respect and love. Malika recalled the day bin Laden appeared on the news and Abdessater was deeply impressed. He said, "Look at his face, don't you think it is beautiful?" Malika enthusiastically agreed. Bin Laden was combating injustice in Afghanistan and Abdessater was scared of dying without having done anything important for God or in the name of jihad. He felt that Osama was talking directly to him.[11]

Bin Laden's example inspired the couple to travel to Afghanistan in 2000, to Al Qaeda's ad-Darunta training camp in Jalalabad. Abdessater hoped to fight the Russians in Chechnya, but instead was recruited into bin Laden's terror network. Within a few months, the couple was housed in the enclave reserved for bin Laden's most trusted lieutenants.[12] It was in Afghanistan that Malika was launched into jihadi stardom. Housed separately in the camp for foreign women, she had hoped to open an orphanage but was unprepared for the poverty and devastation she saw around her. The ravages of war shocked her and she blamed American sanctions against the Taliban for the destitution of the Afghan people. As a good jihadi wife, she supported her husband's decision to accept bin Laden's leadership and to do his bidding.

On bin Laden's instructions, Abdessater assassinated the Taliban's chief rival, Ahmad Shah Massoud, on September 9, 2001. Together with a partner, Abdessater posed as a Moroccan journalist sent to interview Massoud. It was the partner, Rachid Bouraoui El Ouaer, who detonated an improvised device disguised as a camera in Massoud's presence. Abdessater was shot and killed by Massoud's bodyguards as he tried to flee the scene.[13] Massoud's death was bin Laden's gift to the Taliban since Massoud, the so-called Lion of Panjshir, had been the only obstacle preventing their complete dominance of Afghanistan. More important, Massoud's death paved the way for the 9/11 attacks, which took place just two days later, by giving the Taliban free rein in Afghanistan and guaranteeing that the Taliban would protect bin Laden from any retaliation that might follow.[14]

Malika was tried for complicity in Massoud's death but, by playing the part of the grieving widow, she persuaded the court that she knew nothing of her husband's plan. Belgian human rights organizations secured her release from the NATO prison in which she was held, and the government entertained the hope that they might turn Malika into a double agent.

But Malika really had aided in the attack on Massoud. She had returned to Belgium from Afghanistan, picked up Abdessater's laptop computer, and delivered medicine and two envelopes full of cash to cover the costs of the operation. Once she was acquitted, her husband's death propelled her to fame as the widow of a martyr—the pinnacle of achievement for a devout Muslim woman.

Malika soon found new love in a jihadi chat room and married Moaz Garsallaoui, a Moroccan man several years her junior. Moaz shared Malika's fervent devotion to radical Islam. They moved to a small Swiss village where they ran four French-language pro-

Al Qaeda websites that carried the unabridged speeches of Osama bin Laden and snuff videos of hostage beheadings in Iraq. Moaz, a radical since 1985, was under almost constant police surveillance. He was linked to Muriel Degauque—a Belgian woman who became the first Western female suicide bomber in 2005—through his friendships with Tunisian soccer star Nizar Trabelsi and Belgian jihadi Bilal Soughir. Malika greatly admired Muriel (whom she called Maryam), saying that she had a lot of courage to go to Iraq and kill Americans.

In 2005 Malika el Aroud was convicted for supporting a terrorist organization, distributing propaganda over the Internet, publishing images of executions and mutilations, and operating jihadi websites,[15] but received only a six-month suspended sentence. She was detained again in December 2008 for plotting domestic terror attacks against the EU summit meeting in Brussels and, specifically, against British prime minister Gordon Brown.[16] Belgian law required that she be released within twenty-four hours if no charges were filed against her. When police searches failed to turn up weapons, explosives, or any incriminating evidence, she was freed once again. However, that arrest and the follow-up operations, which included the May 2009 arrest of two members of her so-called kamikaze network for smuggling suicide bombers to Italy, struck a major blow to Malika's fund-raising and recruitment efforts.[17] She was arrested several more times for her alleged involvement in terrorism, but until 2010 had always been able to evade jail.

At her 2010 trial, the government took no chances and instituted extreme security measures, including masked agents, metal detectors, and roadblocks on the streets to and from the courthouse. Malika faced an eight-year sentence for advocating terror and for indirect responsibility for the deaths of several European Muslims killed in Afghanistan. Her husband, Moaz, was sentenced in absentia, having rejoined the jihad in Afghanistan and claimed to have personally killed at least five Americans.[18] To Malika's website he posted a chilling message in May 2009: "If you thought you could pressure me to slow down by arresting my wife, you were wrong. It will not stop me from fulfilling my objectives. My wife's place is in my heart and the heart of all mujahideen and it is stronger than ever. There are surprises in store in the days ahead. Those who laugh last, laugh more."[19]

A MARTYR'S WIFE

Malika, often known by her nom de guerre, Oum Obeyda, is one of the new women of Al Qaeda. Unlike the women of JI, these women comprise a group that includes supporters, propagandists, recruiters, and suicide bombers, and that reflects the diversity of the organization itself. Unlike the women of JI, their agenda is not specifically local, but encompasses a view in which the House of Islam (*Dar al Islam*) opposes the House of War (*Dar al Harb*).

Malika has claimed in interviews that she did not know about Abdessater's mission. He had told her that he was being sent to film the jihadis on the northern front. In fact, bin Laden had selected Abdessater for a top-secret suicide mission. Malika learned of her husband's death when she stepped out of her house and someone congratulated her on being the wife of a martyr. She told CNN's Paul Cruickshank that her heart jumped. Over the next few days several visitors came to see her and congratulate her, although she claims that she was grief-stricken. Eventually, a courier from bin Laden arrived with a check and a video that Abdessater had made for her, breaking the news about his mission. Abdessater had hoped that the video would arrive before she found out from anybody else.[20]

After Abdessater's death, the "Voice of the Oppressed" website described Malika as a female holy warrior for the twenty-first century. Malika was transformed into a role model for jihadi women all over the world. For Malika, it is not a woman's place to set off bombs. It would also be out of the question for her to personally participate in an attack. Yet she has a potent weapon at her disposal: her pen, or rather her laptop, was mightier than any sword. Her mission is "to write, to speak out. That's my jihad. You can do many things with words. Writing is also a bomb."[21]

Malika acknowledges that if the act of disseminating information about the massacres of her Muslim brothers and sisters in Iraq and Afghanistan means that people label her a terrorist, then yes, she is a terrorist.[22] However, she does more than report on the events of the war; she also urges men to go there on jihad and encourages women to support them. Her website is a place where she can express her own convictions and a personal platform calling for Islamic resistance. "There is a war going on, and it is necessary for each one of us to chase the occupier out of our land. Those countries that have invaded Muslim lands are pigs and dogs and their presence in Afghanistan, Iraq, Chechnya, or in Palestine is only a matter of time."[23] For Malika, resistance against the occupation is an obligation. Remaining silent is cowardice, if not complicity. She knows people call her radical, and she embraces the term. God willing, she waits for Afghanistan to be purified of those "pigs' stains" (the soldiers of the Coalition and the current government of Hamid Karzai) so that she may someday return again and join Moaz in jihad.

In Malika's 2003 autobiography, *Les Soldats de la Lumière*, she likened the mujahideen fighters in Afghanistan to "soldiers of light" fighting the Western soldiers of darkness. She writes that she was on the battlefield with her brothers and can vouch that they were proud and brave. She pays tribute to the warriors who died defending the honor of their sisters, and to those who are imprisoned in Guantánamo. She writes: "My ancestors' blood flows in my veins ... which boils in me, I want to say today: Today I am proud to be the granddaughter of the mujahideen ... the wife of a muja-hid ... the sister of the mujahideen!" She triumphantly concludes: "The criminal President George Bush spent billions of dollars to extinguish the light, but could never extinguish the light of Allah."[24]

As a self-proclaimed mujahid, Malika boasts that she is a woman of Al Qaeda.[25] Her propaganda efforts have promoted suicide terrorism in Iraq and supported domestic terror cells in Europe. According to a counter-terror official in Europe, "Malika is a role model, an icon who is bold. She plays a very important strategic role as a source of inspiration. She's very clever—and extremely dangerous."[26] For jihadi women, Malika is a source of inspiration because she is telling women to stop sleeping and open their eyes. Wherever she goes she inspires other jihadis with her charismatic personality.

Malika balked at wearing a burqa while at the women's training camp in Afghanistan. In principle, she understands that men are stronger than women, but her resistance and activism are a personal testimony to Allah. Her mantra is: "People resist, people fight, and people should be ready to die ... It is better to die than to live in humiliation."[27] It is important that Muslim women participate in the struggle. As is the case with so many other terrorist groups, part of the logic for women's participation is to shame men into joining the struggle. Malika acknowledges that there are men who don't speak out because they are afraid. She speaks out for them. In doing so, she has been at the center of every major attack or terrorist plot in Belgium in the past ten years.

Malika managed to avoid long-term incarceration for so long because she played the European legal systems. She knew the rules and just how far she could go before actually being convicted for committing a crime. She once told a Swiss court: "I know what I'm doing. I'm Belgian. I know the system."[28] While she hosted Internet chat groups and encouraged European Muslims to go to Iraq, she also claimed unemployment benefits from the Belgian government, which paid her $1,100 a month. For counter-terrorism officials and police, the situation was galling. It was only when she convinced a young French Muslim, Hamza el Alami, to go on jihad to Waziristan, on the Afghan border, and kill NATO troops that Malika made a crucial error. Belgium is a NATO member, so her recruitment of Muslims to fight against NATO troops in Afghanistan was considered an act of treason. Furthermore, el Alami was not completely sure that he wanted to go. Malika pressured him and when he died, she became an accessory after the fact. For the judges, she bore sweeping responsibility for the young man's death.[29] Head judge Pierre Hendrix said she had been "trapped in a sickening logic of a conflict that did not concern her in any way" and even wondered whether she was sane.[30]

THE NEW GLOBAL JIHAD

Malika el Aroud is a representative of the new global jihad. A Muslim expatriate living in Europe, she communicates her messages of resistance over the Internet to a worldwide audience of true believers. Her words inspire men to travel thousands of miles to become suicide bombers in Iraq and Afghanistan. This new Al Qaeda has no return address—it is everywhere and nowhere at the same time. Al Qaeda is unlike traditional terrorist groups. Rather than being formally linked, many Al Qaeda terrorists find themselves in a loose network of affiliated groups. For the most part, Al Qaeda is a source of inspiration rather than a formal organization with a hierarchical structure and clearly identified leaders. Its amorphous structure helps to explain why it is so difficult to defeat and why it seems to be spreading throughout the world.

The majority of Al Qaeda's members are men, and its power base is decidedly masculine. At present, there are no women in the

core leadership of Al Qaeda al Sulba, the main core of the organization and the heart and soul of the global jihad. Beyond this core is a
nebulous movement with loosely connected offshoot organizations
in countries all over the world and sympathizers who do not always
engage in violence. Women are among its most fervent supporters,
and some participate in the affiliated organizations, but it is rare
for them to be on the front lines.[31] Instead, they form an army
of organizers, proselytizers, teachers, translators, and fund-raisers,
who either enlist with their husbands or take the place of those who
are jailed or killed.

They have found an especially significant outlet for the dissemi-
nation of radical ideologies online. The Internet has afforded jihadi
women like Malika the opportunity to participate in jihad without
affecting their inferior status in society. In Italy, Umm Yahya
Aysha (Barbara) Farina directs the website and blog, *Al Muhajidah
Magazine*. The October 2001 edition (posted immediately after
9/11) featured an editorial entitled "I Support the Taliban" and
featured a picture of President George Bush with the caption
"Wanted dead or alive, commander of crusade."[32] Farina regularly
posts her blogs to Malika el Aroud's websites. American Colleen
Renee LaRose, more commonly known as Jihad Jane, showed
how infectious the use of the Internet and YouTube has become.
Arrested in October 2009, LaRose was indicted in March 2010
for conspiring to commit murder and providing material support
to terrorists. She boasted on the Internet of her readiness to help
terrorists, recruit men and women for jihad, and raise money for
operations in the United States, Europe, and Asia, according to
her indictment.[33] LaRose was arrested specifically for encouraging
jihadis in Ireland to kill cartoonist Lars Vilks in Sweden after a series
of insulting drawings in 2007 made Vilks public enemy number
one in many Islamic circles and Al Qaeda offered $100,000 for
his death.[34] The arrest and investigation into Jihad Jane (and her

accomplice Jihad Jamie) demonstrated that the Internet, combined with women's ability to mobilize new recruits, has become a force to be reckoned with in the globalized jihad.

Back in 2004 Al Qaeda created a Web-based women's magazine, *Al Khansa'a*—named for the pre-Islamic female poet and convert who wrote lamentations for her brothers killed in battle. When Al Khansa'a received the news of her sons' deaths, she did not grieve, but exclaimed, "Praise be to Allah who honored me with their martyrdom. I pray for Allah to let me join them in heaven."[35] The webzine is published by the Women's Information Office in the Arab Peninsula, and its contents include articles on women's appropriate behavior, exercises for getting physically fit, how to support male jihadi relatives, terrorist training camps, and even the occasional recipe. Its first issue, with a bright pink cover and gold lettering, appeared in August 2004. Its lead article was "Biography of the Female Mujahid." Though some of its articles discussed military training for women, the magazine's authors did not call on women to take part in combat. However, they did admonish women to watch their weight and advised them to stay physically fit (including the occasional fast) to be ready for jihad. The lead editorial promises, "We will stand up, veiled and in abayas, arms in hand, our children on our laps and the Book of Allah and Sunnah of the Prophet as our guide. The blood of our husbands and the bodies of our children are an offering to God."[36]

The use of women in terrorist attacks carried out by Islamist organizations remains rare. It is, however, on the rise. Militant jihadi women have emerged in groups affiliated with Al Qaeda rather than in the core organization, because the core ideologues continue to oppose women's participation. The affiliated groups have been more practical and flexible with respect to this issue. In instances where women are more likely to succeed than men, conservative ideologies go by the wayside. Hence the increased use of women bombers in Palestine, Chechnya, North Africa, and Somalia, which contradicts traditional Islamic ideology.

Al Qaeda has merged on a number of occasions with other like-minded groups. Bin Laden established the Maktab al Khidmat, commonly known as the Afghan Services Bureau, in 1984. In 1988 he established a new organization called Al Qaeda, and in late 1990, he merged with Zawahiri's Egyptian Islamic Jihad and Al Takfir Wal Hijra to create a new organization. Different attitudes about women can be an unintended consequence of these mergers.

In 2004, after years of competition and rivalry, bin Laden combined with Abu Musab al Zarqawi's al Tawhid wal Jihad insurgent group to create what later became Al Qaeda in Iraq (AQI). At the time of the merger, Zarqawi was conferred the title "Emir of Al Qaeda in the Country of Two Rivers." It has been suggested that Zarqawi achieved prominence only because American officials exaggerated his importance. Whether or not this is the case, the brief collaboration between Zarqawi and Al Qaeda allowed the introduction of female suicide bombers into the Iraqi theater of operations—something that neither bin Laden nor Al Zawahiri (Al Qaeda's main ideologue and number-two leader) enthusiastically supported. The merger also expanded al Qaeda's links in Europe: Zarqawi had operatives throughout the continent and in the United Kingdom providing funds and recruits. The alliance ultimately proved fragile because Zarqawi acted independently of directives and irritated the leadership by instigating outrageous acts of violence and focusing on Iraqi Shi'as rather than the forces of occupation.

We know very little about the first female suicide bomber for Al Qaeda in Iraq, except that she was dressed as a man. The attack occurred on September 28, 2005, at a United States military recruiting center in Talafa, northern Iraq. The bomber took five lives and injured thirty. Her name has never been published and

Zarqawi filmed no last-will-and-testament video to mark the attack as his own. In fact, Zarqawi used an alias "ghost group," the Malik Suicidal Brigades, to claim responsibility. Zarqawi may have been hesitant to claim the operation: never before had any branch of Al Qaeda sent a woman on a suicide mission and no affiliated group had yet dared to break the taboo of using women as front-line fighters. The only acknowledgment of the unnamed woman's sacrifice posted on Zarqawi's website said: "A blessed sister carried out a heroic attack defending her faith … May God accept our sister among the martyrs."[37]

The Talafa bomber's loose-fitting clothes concealed the explosives strapped around her waist. Because she was dressed as a man, the fact that she was a woman played no part in her reaching her target. The revelation of her gender secured for the organization a psychological rather than a tactical advantage; it was meant to prompt more Iraqi men to carry out martyrdom operations at a time when there were plenty of foreign fighters but few Iraqis willing to volunteer. Zarqawi found it useful to exploit the image of a desperate Iraqi woman throwing herself into battle because there were not enough brave men to step up.

Zarqawi was quick to appreciate the fact that using female operatives provided his organization with a competitive advantage when new insurgent groups were popping up all over the country. He understood that women were effective stealth weapons in an environment where it was indiscreet and inappropriate for a man to talk to a woman without a male relative present, let alone frisk her for weapons at a military checkpoint. Iraqi culture forbids men from searching women or even making eye contact with them. A former U.S. Marine officer who fought in the Battle of Falluja said, "If we are not allowed to look at Iraqi women, then how can we search for the bomb under the abaya?"[38] Women could bypass the checkpoints across the country, which were normally manned by male members of the Coalition forces or Iraqi police. The traditional and modest Islamic robes could easily conceal a vest packed with explosives. If anything, an IED strapped around a woman's waist gave her the appearance of late-term pregnancy and discouraged invasive body searches and frisking even more.

Because of the nature of Al Qaeda's conservative Islamic ideology and bin Laden and Al Zawahiri's vocal opposition to female operatives, American and British troops were not anticipating the introduction of female bombers. Although loath to admit it, they were also hesitant to shoot women, not least because they had been instructed, repeatedly, to avoid civilian casualties.[39] They were certainly aware that, if they did frisk women at checkpoints, there would be hell to pay from the locals for humiliating their women.

Iraqi women have a history of protecting their homes and honor in the absence of their husbands or male family members. In Iraq's two previous wars (against Iran and during the first Gulf War), women took up arms to protect their children and communities from danger. It was only a small psychological leap from playing this role to participating in suicide bombings. Less than two months after the attack at Talafa, Zarqawi dispatched two more women as part of a coordinated operation in Iraq and Jordan. One of the women, Muriel Degauque, was the Belgian convert to Islam so admired by Malika el Aroud.

Muriel, code-named Oum Abderrahmane, rammed her explosive-laden Kia car into a U.S. military convoy in Baquba (the capital of Diyala province in Iraq) on November 9, 2005. She was the first Western woman to become a suicide bomber. Her suicide attracted widespread attention. Newspaper stories stressed the worrying notion that Caucasian converts were increasingly committed to radical Islam. Some of the converts could not distinguish between Islam and Islamism. (For many, Islam is a religion of peace, of complete submission to God, whereas Islamism is a distinct and radical interpretation of the faith.) It has been suggested that many late converts may have an inferiority complex and feel they have to prove themselves by being more radical and extreme than those who are born into the faith. The phenomenon has other implications. European women who marry Muslim men are now the largest source of religious conversions in Europe. As early as May 2003, France's famed antiterrorist judge, Jean-Louis Bruguière, warned that European terrorist networks were trying to recruit white European women to handle terrorist logistics because they would be less likely to raise suspicion.[40]

Detailed psychological autopsies of Muriel appeared in the news. Pundits, after noting her place of birth, talked to her family and friends and attempted to identify her various influences. Like Malika, as an adolescent, Muriel had dabbled in drugs, smoked cigarettes, drunk alcohol, and run away from home. She was allegedly more interested in boys than school until she converted to Islam. For her parents, her descent into radicalization was reflected in her changing clothing styles. At first when she converted to Islam, she wore the hijab, but soon she switched to the head-to-toe chador. Her radicalization was complete when, after living in Morocco with her husband, Issam Goris, she adopted the all-covering burqa. From Sweden, a Bosnian named Mirsad Bektasevic recruited both Muriel and Issam via the Internet into Abu Musab al Zarqawi's organization. The couple left Belgium and drove across Turkey and Syria into Iraq, determined to kill themselves and as many American soldiers as possible.[41] Issam was wearing a bulletproof vest packed with fifteen pounds of explosives. Muriel's mission was successful, but American troops shot Issam and five of his "brothers in arms" the following day before they could detonate their IEDs.

On the day of Muriel's suicide, Zarqawi also coordinated attacks against three Western hotels in Amman: the Grand Hyatt, the Radisson SAS, and the Days Inn. The agent sent to blow up one of these hotels was another of Zarqawi's female operatives, the sister of his Western field commander, Mubarak Atrous al Rishawi. Sajida became politically active when three of her brothers were killed by Coalition forces in Iraq. She penetrated a wedding reception at the Radisson SAS Hotel but her device failed to detonate and she was eventually caught. She sits on death row in Jordan awaiting her sentence.

In September 2005—even before the suicide missions in Baquba and Amman—Ayman Al Zawahiri warned Zarqawi that Muslim public opinion was turning against his organization. Too many Sunni Muslims were being killed by his bombs. According to terrorism expert Paul Wilkinson, "Al Qaeda figures were uncomfortable with the tactics he was using in Iraq. With Zarqawi, the core leadership could not control the way he operated."[42] The merger began to show signs of collapse.

Zarqawi was finally killed by the American forces on June 7, 2006. Senior leaders within Zarqawi's own network tipped off the Americans about his whereabouts and the United States Air Force dropped a 500-pound bomb on his safe house. Military sources suggest off the record that they were only able to assassinate Zarqawi after Al Qaeda cut their ties with his organization and left him vulnerable.[43] Zarqawi's wife, Umm Muhammed, posted a letter in July 2006 on the Mujahideen Shura Council's website, calling on Muslims everywhere to defend the honor of her husband. She appealed to Muslim men to avenge his death, but it was the women who really stepped up to the plate.

Zarqawi's imprimatur on the conflict has lasted well beyond his death. By 2007, female suicide bombers had become the weapon of choice for AQI and the tactic had spread to several of the other Iraqi insurgent organizations fighting the Coalition—of which there were many, and more emerging every month. Women account for almost a third of the suicide bombings in Iraq and as many as 60 percent in Diyala province. We do not know whether all of these women are local or what percentage are foreigners. Iraqi sources claim that, other than Muriel, all the female bombers have been Iraqi. As the tactic has become more commonplace, the Iraqi terrorist groups have altered the profile to include both older and younger women. A civil affairs officer in Baghdad, Steven Ernesto, notes an even more sinister development: he claims that not only women but also children are the new weapons for insurgent groups. Both have the ability to penetrate civilian targets easily because they look like the "normal" people Al Qaeda is targeting. Suicide bombings by women against Shi'a civilians have become the trademark of Al Qaeda in Iraq. These attacks are succeeding despite the massive security operations mounted by the Iraqi authorities to combat them.

DAUGHTERS OF IRAQ

Beginning in 2006, the U.S. military devised a new strategy to combat female suicide bombers without eliciting the negative reaction caused by invasive body searches. In 2007, American and Iraqi officials established the Female Awakening Councils, also known as the Daughters of Iraq. As part of the new security plan, the councils set out to curb female suicide bombers and prevent extremist radicalization of women and children in the areas at risk, especially in and around Diyala province, where so many of the attacks have been concentrated. The female volunteers get weapons and self-defense training as well as instruction on how to investigate and inspect for IEDs. One hundred women have volunteered to be trained by female American soldiers in detecting and combating female suicide bombers.

The use of women bombers can be seen as a clever tactical adaptation to the changing security environment, in which targets have been hardened against traditional attacks and men are routinely searched for IEDs. Coalition forces have established standard operating procedures for detecting and preventing car bombs, which almost invariably are driven by men. They monitor everything from the behavior of the driver to the load distribution on their vehicles to gauge whether the trunk contains explosives. But these measures are of no use in guarding against women suicide bombers, so their deployment seems smart.

An alternative view argues that using women bombers is actually a sign of Al Qaeda's weakness. As Coalition forces push the militants from their strongholds, the pool of potential recruits is shrinking. According to Diaa Rashwan, an expert on Islamic militancy at Egypt's Al Ahram Center for Political and Strategic Studies, it is the tightening noose that has prompted the insurgent groups to employ more female operatives. Extremist Muslim organizations use women only when they see no alternative. "Women should be in the last rows of fighting … So to see women [suicide bombers] shows an abnormal situation—the absence of men."[44] Al Qaeda has resorted to female bombers due to the "decrease in funding, the decrease of foreign fighters who could cross the border, and the change in society's attitude that previously embraced them."[45] The fact that the women are often cajoled and coerced (or physically forced) makes Al Qaeda's weakness all the more apparent.

Al Qaeda in Iraq and the other Iraqi insurgent organizations do not ordinarily record the women's names or details as they do with male suicide bombers, which makes identifying and researching women all the more challenging.[46] With no martyrdom videos, last wills, or recorded messages, it is difficult to determine the perpetrators' motivations. Insurgents who take credit for suicide attacks by female bombers usually refer only to their "blessed sister." A rare exception was Nour Qaddour ash-Shammari. In the martyrdom video released in 2003, she said "I have devoted myself to jihad for the sake of God and against the American, British, and Israeli infidels and to defend the soil of our precious and dear country."[47] What set Nour and her female colleague, Wadad Jamil Jassem, apart was that they were not operatives for AQI but rather suicide bombers sent by Saddam Hussein. In their video they bless and congratulate Saddam: "We say to our leader and holy war comrade, the hero commander Saddam Hussein, that you have sisters that you and history will boast about."[48]

The martyred women of Al Qaeda are rarely identified and reports about their frequency vary wildly between Western and local sources. U.S. Army officials have drawn attention to the rising number of female detainees at the secure detention facility in Baghdad. While the military places the total number of women bombers in Iraq at around forty to date, Arab and Iraqi media claim more than seventy bombers in 2008 alone. Adnan Al Asadi, under-secretary for the Iraqi interior minister, claims that security forces have recorded seventy-nine attacks by women suicide bombers between the arrival of American forces in Iraq in April 2003 and August 2008.[49] Part of the discrepancy might be explained by the criteria used in counting. Iraqi sources include preempted bombers—those who were caught prior to detonation—as well as bombers who killed only themselves, an approach which places the number of female bombers in Iraq closer to 174 in 2009.

Despite the stealth of the insurgents, the identities of a handful of women suicide bombers have been discovered, although long after the operations, and as part of other investigations. These bombers share some common features. Iraqi women, like their sisters in Chechnya, appear to be motivated by proximity to the conflict and the loss of loved ones. Many of the women who turned to violence have had relatives, either civilians or militants, killed in the fighting. Many of the Iraqi female bombers were recruited by Itisam Adwan, a thirty-eight-year-old woman more commonly known by her nom de guerre, Umm Fatima. Adwan warned U.S. troops that scores of widowed Iraqi women and their young relatives and friends were being groomed to perpetrate deadly attacks. According to the police in Baquba, Adwan was one of several mothers who tell their daughters that they will go to heaven, sit in comfort by rivers of honey, and lunch with the prophet Muhammed (PBUH) if they perpetrate an act of martyrdom. The girls are married off to Al Qaeda members and their husbands tell them that martyrdom will be glorious and that their willingness to kill in the name of Islam will automatically get them into heaven.[50]

When Iraqi authorities arrested Adwan in September 2008, she was replaced by a high-ranking Al Qaeda wife. Umm Salamah, believed to be the wife of the slain AQI commander Abu Ubaydah al Rawi, is now commander of the Dhat an-Nitaqayn Martyrdom Brigade. She has vowed to unleash her army of female martyrs on the streets of Baghdad to combat disbelief and vice. She claims that scores of women in Falluja, Baghdad, Mosul, and Diyala are anxiously awaiting the opportunity to meet their loved ones in heaven after a martyrdom operation. "They are counting the hours for the moment to attack the infidels like bitter colocynth [a vine mentioned in the Bible]. They are close to the zero hour."[51] The Dhat an-Nitaqayn Martyrdom Brigade has successfully merged the Salafi interpretation of Islam with a woman's perspective and capitalized on women's emotional experiences under occupation. Among the female bombers thus far, fifty-five have been the wives or daughters of Al Qaeda leaders and most have lost loved ones during the war.

According to a report by the Iraqi Ministry of the Interior, more than a hundred women have been arrested for terrorist-related activities, seventy of whom have been tried by the government and are behind bars. Most if not all of the female suicide bombers are relatives of male terrorists. The filial connection is no accident. The terrorist organizations deliberately recruit women who have a brother, father, or son already affiliated with one of the groups. In part, this is a vetting process, a way of being assured that the person is not providing information to the other side and can be trusted to complete the mission tasked to them. The likelihood of a woman changing her mind, and so bringing shame to her entire family, is slim. Another significant motivating factor is the reinforcement of belief systems provided by family. According to a former U.S. military officer, "More women are being exposed to jihadi propaganda through the men who bring home videos to watch them. Women are also watching the same indoctrination videos."[52]

As is the case in other struggles, women are often coerced into taking action. Women who have lost loved ones find themselves marginalized in Iraqi society and especially vulnerable to predation. There are more than 100,000 widows in Iraq because of the war and the sectarian violence between the various communities. Al Qaeda has succeeded in deepening women's depression by using their personal tragedies to its advantage. Many of the women are poor and borderline illiterate. Al Qaeda recruiters make use of their poverty, despair, resentment, and eagerness to take revenge against the American troops to recruit them.[53] The women are exploited based on three factors: tribal affiliation, financial pressure, and revenge for the loss of family.

In traditional Islamic societies, women without close male relatives are subjected to economic and social hardship that may make them more susceptible to radicalization and recruitment by terrorist groups. The lack of government programs for widows and orphans leaves the women with severe psychological issues. According to Iraqi psychologist Dr. Sa'ad ad-Din, it is easy to recruit a person who is emotionally unstable or of mediocre intelligence.[54] However, a person with mental illness is not an ideal recruit.

Al Qaeda has also not used mentally handicapped women as suicide bombers in Iraq. It was reported by some agencies that two women who blew up the Baghdad bird markets had Down syndrome, but this was not, in fact, the case. They *were* under the care of a psychiatrist, who turned out to be the local recruiter for the terrorist organization, but they did not suffer from any birth defects, which would have made them far too conspicuous in public. Rather, the force of the blast distorted their facial features and the Iraqi police tried to discredit Al Qaeda by disseminating the false imputation with its implication of cowardice.

Iraqi terrorist groups do, however, target underage women who are living on the streets and have no men to protect them. Most of the female bombers have no religious background whatsoever and can be manipulated into thinking that such operations are Allah's will and are justified in the *Qur'an* and Hadith. At other times, the women are simply tricked. They are told that the packages they are transporting contain contraband, and then their minders detonate the IEDs by remote control before the duped women even know they have "volunteered" for a mission.

Among the more blatant forms of coercion brought to bear on susceptible women are drugging, kidnapping, and sexual assault. In October 2008, fifteen-year-old Raniya Ibrahim Mutlaq (Mutleg)[55] was caught before she could detonate her improvised explosive device outside a school in Baquba. Iraqi police officers spotted red wires dangling from beneath her clothing and deduced that she was carrying a bomb. When the officers approached her, Raniya did not resist, but rather acted as if she was in a drug-induced trance. One officer handcuffed her to a fence's metal railings and slowly began to remove the outer garments of her outfit. While he carefully defused the bomb wrapped around her waist, Raniya seemed to be in a daze. The police officer was able to remove the IED without injuring her or causing any casualties. (For his coolness under pressure, he received five million Iraqi dinars—around $4,250—for a job well done.)

During her initial interrogation, Raniya denied knowing that she was wearing an explosive vest, even though it weighed nearly thirty pounds. She claimed to have been a victim of circumstance. Raniya was from a poor family. She grew up in a mud hut in a small village near Abu Seida, eighty kilometers northeast of Baghdad. Although as a little girl she fantasized about someday becoming a doctor, poverty and the war meant that she would never realize her dreams. Raniya's father and brother were killed by sectarian violence after the American invasion in 2003. Instead of allowing her to stay in school, her family forced her to marry Muhammed Hassan al Dulaimi, a member of Al Qaeda in Iraq, when she was fourteen. Dulaimi went on the run, and Raniya felt all alone in the world. Her mother and aunt were the local recruiters for Al Qaeda, and both were prepared to sacrifice her for the cause. But according to Raniya, it was actually her husband's cousins who got her involved: they gave her some spiked juice to drink that made her feel dizzy and submissive. The cousins fastened the suicide belt around her waist and directed her to the marketplace to explode. Interrogators could not determine whether Raniya had been a willing participant or if she had been coerced. The Diyala juvenile court judge said she was young and naïve and took into consideration the fact that she had not resisted arrest. He sentenced her to seven and a half years in jail.

Raniya's capture provided valuable insight into the nature of Iraqi suicide bomber cells. Whether Raniya was drugged and coerced or willingly volunteered, after her case Iraqi officials posted warnings throughout Diyala province that Al Qaeda was kidnapping girls to use as suicide bombers.[56] Baquba police were able to dismantle and capture three of the terrorist cells that were recruiting female bombers and subsequently publicized the insidious practices used by Al Qaeda in its recruitment of women.

Several new reports detailing incidents of coercion have emerged since 2008, as the number of female suicide bombers in Iraq increased by 400 percent. A teacher named Sumaya was forced to undergo training and carry an explosive belt beneath her clothes against her will. Sumaya was allegedly "volunteered" by her husband, Amjad al Dulaymi, a former army officer in Saddam's Republican Guard who joined Al Qaeda in Iraq. She later claimed that Amjad, under financial pressure and with no opportunity for work, had no choice but to join the terrorist organization. He played many roles in the insurgency, planting explosives, transporting small rockets, and coordinating attacks against army and police convoys. After a year of working with AQI, his emir requested that he gather all the mujahideen's women and task them with operational and support activities. Amjad dutifully brought in his wife, whom he assumed would be tasked with information-gathering or assisting the jihadi fighters. Instead, and without his consent, Sumaya was selected to be a suicide bomber. According to Sumaya, when the AQI emir came to see her, she thought that he wanted to benefit from her work as a teacher to collect information on the area and its people. She was surprised to be chosen for a suicide attack. Sumaya protested and tried to resist, saying that as the mother of three young children she had responsibilities to her family. She certainly did not want to be a martyr!

The emir ignored her. He praised Allah and congratulated Amjad for having a wife who was a future martyr. The emir offered Amjad $5,000 compensation for his loss and to help him raise the children. However, Amjad's conscience troubled him. He recalled the years he had spent in the army away from his family and the sacrifices Sumaya had made to raise their children alone. The emir told him to recite the *Qur'an* and to prepare his wife for the operation. Just a few hours later, Amjad fled with his wife and family, leaving the Al Ghazaliyah area where he had lived for more than twenty years.[57] They moved quickly, fearing the consequences if their escape was discovered before they reached a safe haven. The family headed to Sadr City in Baghdad, beyond the reach of Amjad's former Al Qaeda comrades, and settled in a Shi'a neighborhood protected by their Shi'a friends.[58]

Not all Iraqi husbands make the same choice in favor of their wives. In March 2008 authorities arrested a male recruiter who was going to use his wife for a suicide attack. At the beginning of the war in Iraq, many families married off their daughters to local Al Qaeda leaders while the girls were still quite young. At the time, Al Qaeda cadres were fairly popular, as the group posed the sole challenge to American domination of the country. The early marriages were partly a precautionary measure, because women were being routinely sexually victimized at the time and girls who had been attacked sexually were considered damaged goods. One flaw in this strategy was that if a girl's husband died or was captured, the girl was obliged to marry his successor in the organization.[59] Another flaw was that some Al Qaeda leaders allegedly were recruiting their wives to carry out suicide operations. There are numerous reports that the women were manipulated in other ways. Some male militants, for example, reportedly married a woman and then allowed her to be raped and dishonored, making it easier to groom her as a bomber.

The idea that women who are sexually abused can be funneled into terrorist organizations is one thing. Another, more common phenomenon is the abuse perpetrated by soldiers of the other side. Chechen girls raped by Russian soldiers at checkpoints or Tamil women sexually abused by Sinhalese soldiers in Sri Lanka have been a recurring image of those conflicts. The formerly victimized women reinvent themselves as terrorists and redeem their honor by killing as many of the enemy's soldiers as possible.

While there has been a handful of high-profile cases of Iraqi women being raped by U.S. soldiers at Abu Ghraib, and the case of Abir al Janabi, a fourteen-year-old girl who was raped and killed by Americans, there have been surprisingly few cases of rape reported in the American or foreign media (and fewer military courts martial) compared to previous foreign wars. This is partly an issue of access. American soldiers simply do not encounter many Iraqi women on a daily basis. They are also inhibited by the powerful societal taboo against looking at, let alone talking with, local women. And the availability of American servicewomen and female contractors—who have been increasingly victimized during their tours of duty—has diverted the soldiers' attention away from the indigenous population as well. In effect, the level of violence perpetrated by the soldiers against women is about the same as in other foreign wars, but the targets have switched from foreign to domestic.[60]

So instead of being abused by foreign soldiers, increasing numbers of Iraqi women have been raped by members of their own community in order to create squads of suicide bombers.[61] Initially allegations to this effect by the Iraqi government were assumed to be propaganda, intended to undermine the popularity of the insurgent Sunni organizations. Then, in February 2009, a female recruiter named Samira Ahmed Jassim was arrested for arranging the rape of eighty girls over a period of two years and turning them into suicide bombers for Ansar Al Sunnah, an insurgent group in Diyala linked to Al Qaeda in Mesopotamia (one of the aliases for AQI). Of the eighty girls victimized, twenty-eight had successfully carried out operations by the time Jassim was arrested by the Iraqi police. Her confession offers some insight into the growing wave of suicide attacks by women in the past two years. She confirmed what several military and intelligence officials have contended: that the Iraqi insurgents prey on women who are in dire social and economic situations and who are often suffering from emotional or psychological problems or abuse.[62]

Samira Jassim worked as a recruiter for Shakir Hamid Malik, one of the lower-echelon leaders of Ansar Al Sunnah. She admitted that she routinely used rape to recruit female suicide bombers. She convinced the shamed victims that the only way to redeem themselves was through suicide attacks. According to Jassim, she identified vulnerable women and instructed men to attack them. Jassim would then approach the women as a friend and confidant. She would advise them how best to avoid bringing on their families the shame that could trigger the full wrath of society. After some cajoling, she told them that the only solution was to become a martyr or *shahida*. She then escorted them to a farm in Diyala province for bomber training and served as their minder, accompanying them to their final target.

Samira Jassim recounted the fate of one of her victims, Umm Huda. After she had been raped, Jassim said, Huda could barely make eye contact. She would not answer Jassim's questions, but instead stared straight ahead or looked at her feet while mumbling verses from the *Qur'an*.[63] Over time, Jassim was able to wear her down and convince her to become a bomber. Within weeks, dressed in a black abaya, Umm Huda walked into the crowd at the main gate of the Muqdadiyah police station and detonated her explosive belt in a crowd of about two hundred police recruits.[64] Sixteen people died and thirty-three others were wounded in the blast. The newspapers did not report Umm Huda's name until Jassim was arrested and authorities began tracking down and identifying her string of victimized female bombers.

Another would-be bomber, Amal, a former elementary school teacher, needed considerably more convincing to become a suicide bomber after her rape. According to Jassim, Amal had been living in fairly difficult conditions. Her husband and his family were having problems with her brothers and she found herself stuck between them. Amal was in bad psychological shape and Jassim had to meet with her several times to gain her confidence. Over a period of more than two weeks, Jassim convinced her that she had no choice. Amal eventually attacked the Sunni Awakening council in Diyala and killed fifteen people in December 2007.

On jihadi websites, like that of the Islamic Front for Iraqi Resistance (JAMI), Al Qaeda has denied all allegations that it employs coercion to recruit female bombers. The group says that their women, like their men and youths, are committed to resisting the occupation. They claim that Al Qaeda would never be involved in violence against the innocent Iraqi people.[65] Yet according to a memo from President Nuri al Maliki's office, the number of female bombers used to perpetrate violence against Iraqi civilians has increased dramatically. The success rate for female bombers varies. Several have changed their mind at the very last minute. As many as 40 percent of suicide operations were aborted and the female bombers killed before reaching their target. Often the female bomber detonates, but kills no one other than herself. However, the women bombers in Diyala are not always in control of their own suicide belts and men occasionally detonate them remotely.[66] In some cases, belts containing explosive materials have been given to women who believe that they are acting only as couriers, taking the belts from one place to another in return for a large sum of money. The belts are detonated by remote control. The women never know that they have "volunteered" to be martyrs.

It is wrong to assume that all women have been tricked. Some women are in fact participating in this violence willingly. The Dhat al Nitaqayn Martyrdom Brigade[67] is the newest commando unit composed exclusively of women and led by a radical woman, Umm Salamah. According to Al Qaeda in Iraq, it is the equivalent of one thousand fighting companies.[68] The women's brigade is linked to two important insurgent leaders, Shaykh Abu Hamza al Muhajir, current emir of AQI, and Abu Umar al Baghdadi of the Iraq Islamic State group. The brigade has announced plans to create a special Abir al Janabi unit named after the fourteen-year-old Iraqi rape victim.

While Al Qaeda in Iraq proudly recognizes its female bombers (although not always by name), Ayman Al Zawahiri, Al Qaeda's second-in-command, claims that there is no place for women in the global jihad. Islamist hard-liners have banned women from participating in jihad against the West. Al Zawahiri emphatically insists there are no women whatsoever in Al Qaeda's ranks. In Al Qaeda and Taliban military camps in Afghanistan, women are separated from their husbands and asked to care for their children while the men dedicate their lives to jihad. The women's role is to support their men, helping them endure the hardships associated with frequent moves, difficult terrain, and harsh living conditions. Osama bin Laden's first wife had severe difficulty acclimatizing to a Spartan existence in Afghanistan and eventually left him, taking the children with her.[69] Not every jihadi wife can stand by her man while he's on the run.

In an article entitled "This Is How Women Should Be," posted online by the Islamic Army in Iraq, Al Zawahiri said that a Muslim woman should "be ready for any service the mujahideen need from her," but advises against traveling to a war front like Afghanistan without a male guardian. Al Zawahiri acknowledges that women have played a role in other areas of the *Dar al Harb* (House of War) in the global jihad. In Algeria, he admitted, the Al Qaeda in the Maghreb makes use of women in bombing campaigns. But the women are largely responsible for support: the provision of medicine, food, and clothes. To a woman who asked Al Zawahiri whether she should participate in jihad in the Maghreb, he responded that while jihad is a universal obligation for both men and women, if by joining the jihad she has to abandon her children, she should not do it.

For some jihadi women, Al Zawahiri's answer is a disappointment because they feel that they can make an important contribution to the cause. More to the point, his comments do not reflect the reality of women's involvement in Iraq or in other conflicts in which they have played vital roles. Online, some women have pleaded for the right to get involved. "How many times have I wished I were a man … When Sheikh Ayman Al Zawahiri said there are no women in Al Qaeda, he saddened and hurt me," wrote one woman who claimed to have listened to the speech ten times. "I felt that my heart was about to explode in my chest … I am powerless."[70]

In December 2009, Ayman Al Zawahiri's wife, Umayma Hasan, released a letter identifying three kinds of Muslim women: female jihadis, sisters in Islam who have been imprisoned, and the rest. In the letter she calls on the female jihadis to remain steadfast in the path of jihad as "victory is near!" God, she assures them, is not about to forsake them, and they shall either be rewarded with victory or martyrdom, of which, she writes, "each is sweeter than the other." Like many of the emerging leaders of Al Qaeda, she too argues that "jihad is an individual duty incumbent upon every Muslim man and woman." She does acknowledge that the path of fighting is not easy for women because they are required to have a male companion or *mahram* to chaperone them at all times. But she lauds the many sisters who have carried out martyrdom operations in Palestine, Iraq, and Chechnya, and "caused the enemy high costs and caused the enemy a big defeat. We ask from Allah to accept them and connect us with them with goodness." She reminds her readers of the female Companions who fought alongside the Prophet Muhammed (PBUH) and showed more courage than many men at the time. She explains that there are many other ways women can fulfill their obligations: "Put yourselves in the service of the jihadis, carry out what they ask, whether in supporting them financially, serving their [practical] needs, supplying them with information, opinions, partaking in fighting or even [volunteering to carry out] a martyrdom operation." For the rest of the Muslim world, she urges women to observe Islamic law, wear the veil, and bring up their children to love jihad. For Umayma Hasan, women are critical for the jihad's success.[71]

In one of his addresses to the Islamic community of believers, bin Laden commented that women's role is just as valuable as that of men, for "you have spurred on and exhorted [men to join jihad], and you have raised all the men who fought in Palestine, Lebanon, Afghanistan and Chechnya, and you are the ones who produced the squadron of heroic [men who carried out] the raids in New York and Washington."[72] This is a far cry from Muhammed Atta's last-will-and-testament videotape recorded on January 18, 2000, in which he proclaimed that no women should attend his funeral or touch his body after death.[73]

The underlying fear of women's sexuality has driven much of Salafist ideology. Al Zawahiri's comments demonstrate that Al Qaeda is required to walk a fine line in its public-relations approach to, on the one hand, the modern Arab world and, on the other hand, its more conservative constituency. Dozens of the Internet responses to Ayman Al Zawahiri's earlier statement were signed by men who agreed that women should stick to supporting men and raising children.

Dr. Fadl, former mentor of Al Zawahiri, remarked in his book *Al 'Umda* that women can only partake in military activities to defend themselves against an enemy who has invaded Muslim territory and raided their homes. For this reason, women can receive basic training so that they can be prepared to repel their attackers.[74] The ideologues believe that the success of jihad depends on the support of women, but not as warriors.[75]

Still, the notion that women are equal to men in the execution of jihad is gaining ground among radical ideologues from both Sunni and Shi'a traditions. Grand Ayatollah Muhammed Hussein Fadlallah, the former leader of the Lebanese group Hezbollah, who died on July 4, 2010, emphasized that jihad is not obligatory for women, but expressed no reservations about martyrdom operations carried out by women. In his view, Islam permitted women to fight in the course of a defensive war, and he approved of martyrdom operations by women—if they are necessary.[76]

According to the leading Sunni religious authorities at Al Azhar University in Egypt, jihad is not obligatory for women, but may be imposed under three conditions: first, if the enemy invades Muslim lands; second, if Muslim leaders call upon the whole *umma*, or community of believers, to perform jihad; and third, if Muslim leaders appoint women to do certain tasks such as monitoring the enemy, burying land mines, and so on. Under such conditions women must carry out the duty entrusted to them.[77]

Jihadi women cling to the *fatwa* (religious ruling) of ideologist Yusuf al Qaradawi, dean of Islamic Studies at the University of Qatar, who declared that women's participation in jihad does not contradict the *Qur'an*.[78] According to Qaradawi, women as well as men can dedicate themselves to Allah, and serve as human bombs. He writes: "I do not think that this is impossible or even difficult. There are genius women just as there are genius men."[79] When jihad is a personal obligation and the enemy seizes Muslim territory, a woman is entitled to take part in jihad alongside men.

It is actually more common to find scholars who endorse female jihadis in the West than in the Middle East. A militant Islamist based in the UK, Hani al Siba'i, approves of women bombers. Siba'i says that Islamic holy law, the Shari'ah, allows women to take part in jihad and argues that even Al Qaeda does not disapprove of female jihadis. According to his interpretation of the *Qur'an*, men and women are equal in terms of their obligation (*fard*) and personal responsibility for holy war and are rewarded equally for their actions. It is only because of the practical limitations that restrict women's movements in Islamic societies that most of the women who carry out martyrdom operations are related to male jihadis.[80] Siba'i's justifications mirror the rulings of Qaradawi, who has endorsed female suicide bombers throughout the Islamic world.

However, Al Qaeda's leaders continue to resist the interpretations promulgated by Fadlallah, who, as a supreme Shi'a leader and Grand Ayatollah, was considered a greater Satan than George W. Bush. The others, like Al Qaradawi and Siba'i, who advocate a greater role for women, remain on the outer fringes of the organization. According to the strictest interpretation of Salafi ideology, a woman's place remains in the home and not on the battlefield. The ideological split within Al Qaeda over the issue of women jihadis is one of the really significant fault lines within the organization.

There is not even a consensus about the use of men as self-destroying agents. While attacks in Chechnya, Palestine, and other places are called *amaliyyat istishadiyya* (martyrdom operations), in Iraq, they are often referred to as *amaliyyat intihariyya* (suicide operations). In Islam, as in all major monotheistic faiths, suicide is a cardinal sin. So while Islamists throughout the region praise attacks against Israel, they are equally critical of attacks in Iraq aimed against Muslim Iraqis. Dr. Muhammed al Habash, a Syrian Islamist, praises martyrdom in defense of the homeland—for example, as part of the Palestinian intifada against the Israeli occupation—but criticizes its recent proliferation in Iraq by both men and women:

> The honorable sons of Palestine used to halt the advancing
> criminal tanks with their booby-trapped bodies, protecting

the lives of hundreds of people who could have been crushed by the invading tanks and their bombs. They planted martyrs on the land so that their children could enjoy the orange tree, the blessing of the school, and the smile of life ... But the mad work we see today in the sectarian strife that the occupation created in Iraq is the biggest distortion of martyrdom and martyrs, when the death industry became the best selling industry in Iraq, with male and female suicide bombers blowing themselves up in condolence houses, funeral processions, markets, or restaurants ... these have nothing to do with the culture of martyrdom.[81]

While most terrorist organizations provide some benefit to their constituents in the form of benevolent organizations, infra-structure, hospitals, or clinics in order to ingratiate themselves with the civilian population, Al Qaeda in Iraq makes no such effort. In fact, other than bin Laden's charitable works in Afghanistan in the 1980s, Al Qaeda does not build or create anything: it is merely an organization seeking to kill the maximum number of civilians, be they Western or Muslim. As time has gone on, Al Qaeda has focused as much of its violence against its own people—those who oppose its ideology or methods—as it has against foreigners. In this sense, the organization has become self-cannibalizing. While the "surge" of American military forces has undoubtedly helped decrease violence in Iraq, the plummeting popularity of Al Qaeda has also had a significant impact.

Al Qaeda's manipulation of Iraqi women will have negative effects on the Iraqi state that will continue to be felt long after the war is over. Involving women in preventing women from carrying out terrorist attacks by expanding the Daughters of Iraq is a useful step in the other direction. It is important to support women's civil society to provide alternative mechanisms for their political mobilization. It is also vital to highlight Al Qaeda's insidious tactics of raping and kidnapping Arab mothers and daughters, and to use any means available to help drive a wedge between Al Qaeda and its global supporters, who view it through rose-tinted glasses. They need to know that the organization they think is fighting evil is, in fact, the very embodiment of evil.

8

THE FOUR Rs PLUS ONE

The time is now. Arm your women and children against the infidel!
—Osama bin Laden, Tora Bora, 2001[1]

THE THREAT WOMEN POSE

Only a handful of countries have taken into consideration the danger posed by female terrorists. Even agencies that should know better are surprised and unprepared for the threat women pose. The common assumption that women are inherently nonviolent remains fixed in people's minds. Even when women are implicated in violence, there is a tendency to assume that they are merely the pawns of men, despite the fact that there have been plenty of cases of women's involvement in terrorist groups going as far back as the 1960s, and in spite of the emergence of female suicide bombers since 1985. Even in the super-security-conscious United States in the aftermath of 9/11, the Department of Homeland Security failed to include women on its list of potential attackers. The unofficial terrorist profile developed by the department to assist officials scrutinizing visa-seekers did not include women even after two women bombers attacked U.S. forces in Iraq.[2] The 2009 Transportation Security Administration training manual, which was leaked to the press, does not explain specifically how to handle female terrorists or those pretending to be pregnant in order to smuggle an explosive device through airport security.

Not until a Western woman attacked U.S. forces in Iraq did counter-terrorism officials begin to take notice of female suicide bombers. Muriel Degauque's detonation in November 2005 was supposed to change the way the American military looked at women. Yet on the ground, in 2006, U.S. forces were still unaware of the threat women bombers posed, and were never told what to do when faced with a suspected female operative.[3] The fact that Muriel was a European convert to Islam from a modern "egalitarian society" was highlighted in almost every analysis of the attack. Commentators seemed to think that a traditional Arab or Muslim woman could never do such a thing. Views have changed, finally, with the recent upsurge of Muslim bombers, but we need to understand the women better to fully understand the threat. This book has provided the reader with some preliminary ideas about what causes women to mobilize into terrorist groups and the variety of roles they play within such groups. This research is no more than a prologue to what will be an ongoing chronicle of women and violence.

THE FOUR Rs PLUS ONE

Part of the challenge in understanding a woman's motivations to kill depends on whether we consider that she joined the terrorist organization by coercion or by choice. As the detailed case studies in this book have shown, the distinction is not always clear-cut and shades of gray proliferate. The spectrum of coercion includes everything from subtle community pressure to brute force. Some women find themselves in impossible situations and in cultures that value them in death as they could never be valued alive. Some experience multiple motivations simultaneously or sequentially. At times, they might not even know themselves what has led them to act. Gender stereotypes provide part of the explanation; occupation provides another part; religion yet another. The reality is often a complicated mix of personal, political, and religious factors that are sparked at different times by different stimuli.

This book has shown that women across a number of conflicts and in several different terrorist groups tend to be motivated by one or several of the four Rs: *revenge, redemption, relationship,* and *respect. Revenge* for the death of a close family member is most often cited as the key factor that inspired a woman to get involved in the first place.

Some of the women appear to need *redemption* for past sins. There have been reports that recruiters approach their targets by making romantic advances, literally seducing them into joining the group and then involving them in suicide operations. A woman caught up in a romantic relationship might consider martyrdom an attractive option, particularly if the relationship is illicit (involving a family member, for example) or if it is considered in some way scandalous. Anat Berko, an Israeli criminologist and author of the book *The Path to Paradise*, claims that a woman's martyrdom wipes away all of her sins and stigmas.[4] A *shahida* is transformed from being an embarrassment to her family to a source of great pride with just one act of violence.

Relationship, the third R, is particularly crucial in understanding how women are mobilized. The best single predictor that a woman will engage in terrorist violence is her relationship with a known insurgent or jihadi. The relative provides the entrée to the organization and also vouches for her reliability, an important consideration for terrorist leaders who need to guard against government infiltration. In some groups, family and kinship ties are used deliberately to construct a cohesive network. At the same time, marriage into the organization allows it to "force" women to perpetrate acts of violence. In some cultures, men dictate women's actions and have the power of life or death over them.

Finally, although usually in conjunction with other motives, women often seek the *respect* of their community. By engaging in violence they can demonstrate that they are just as dedicated and committed to the cause as men. Women bombers are held up as role models. Little girls grow up wanting to be just like them. After their deaths, schools, parks, streets, even Girl Scout troops are named after particularly successful bombers. These women would never have achieved this kind of fame in life, and yet in death they become heroines and superstars. It is a powerful pull factor for a young woman to want to do something great with her life, especially if the life she leads is difficult or, worse, a source of pain and fear.

These factors may apply equally to men, although men's opportunities to achieve recognition in life are more numerous. Men can aspire to go to university and become doctors and engineers. Even those who reside in conflict areas are freer to pursue their dreams abroad than women, who are expected to stay close to home with whatever limits exist under an occupation or oppressive state. The desire to win the respect of their peers can lure women into violence and instill in them a sense of purpose. More often than not, some or all of these motives coexist simultaneously.

We can add another R to our list: R for *rape*. There has been an increase in the sexual exploitation of women in conflicts worldwide. This is especially evident in Iraq and Chechnya, where rape has been used to coerce women to participate in combat. Rape as a source of motivation bears some similarity to redemption. However, while women who have done something of their own free will of which they are ashamed might seek redemption, women who have been raped are essentially involuntary recruits. What is most shocking is that women have actually assisted in setting up attacks on other women. Either these women are unaware of who is ultimately to blame or they are suffering from such a deep sense of traumatic shock that they are willing to work for the organization that has victimized them. These women are victims of the conflict, victims of their attackers, and victims of the situation in which they find themselves. We cannot help but sympathize with women in this situation and yet they kill and maim hundreds of innocents.

TERRORISM AND OPPRESSION

Often there is something else at work that explains what propels women (and men) to violence. The structural conditions vary significantly between regions such as Northern Ireland, Chechnya, and the Palestinian Occupied Territories. In most areas, the people who join terrorist organizations are not necessarily the poorest or the least educated members of their society. In fact, among certain groups, the operatives are better educated and better off financially than the average person in their community. What is striking is how many people (including women) with university degrees and presumably a promising future become mobilized. In such cases, sending more money or resources or encouraging education and alleviating poverty may not lessen the violence.

The structural conditions, for example, of an occupation by a foreign military force certainly play a part in radicalizing the population, yet many women and men are engaged in terrorism in the absence of foreign troops. In essence, for there to be terrorism, both motive and opportunity are necessary. Though the presence of foreign troops provides opportunities (i.e., targets) that insurgents might not ordinarily have, the individual's motives remain complex. Occupation alone provides only a part of the story.

That said, if foreign troops are present in a conflict zone, it is crucial that they understand how their presence can alter the dynamic between men and women in that society. It is of the utmost importance that the soldiers do not target the women of the other side in sexualized ways. Abusing the population's women might have the desired effect of demoralizing the men in the short term, but in the long run, it will only increase the number of women joining the terrorist movement. Abusive behavior is also guaranteed to alienate huge swaths of the civilian population. To paraphrase the American general David Petraeus, in every conflict the population is the prize. Winning over any population is the best way to separate it from the terrorists embedded in its midst.

COUNTERING THE THREAT

In order to curtail women's involvement in terrorism, counter-terrorism authorities need to understand the relationship between their own agencies (police, intelligence services, the military) and the female half of the civilian population. It is important to comprehend the long-term ramifications of subjecting the local women—whether they are bystanders or prisoners who have been taken into custody—to humiliating treatment. The key is to offer the women some options other than joining the militants. Abusive or disrespectful treatment by government authorities or foreign forces provides a recruitment tool to the terrorists, allowing them to issue propaganda to the effect that the government or foreign occupiers are raping their wives, sisters, and daughters.

Sexual atrocities committed against women during wars and military occupations are increasingly common. These crimes take different forms and have various consequences. Often, women are raped during ethnic conflicts as a way to dilute the racial integrity of future generations of the opposing community. Women have been targeted for decades as part of ethnic cleansing campaigns; the violence in such cases is intended to force movement of a group from one desirable area to another less desirable one, or across borders. In counter-terror operations, women have been targeted to extract information, create collaborators, or as a form of torture against the men who might be forced to witness the abuse.

Some of the cases described in this book demonstrate that abusing women to demoralize men is a tactic that can come back and haunt the abusers. Kurdish, Chechen, and Tamil women, all of whom have been vulnerable to predation and sexual exploitation by enemy soldiers, transition easily into terrorist organizations as frontline operatives. Even when the other side stops engaging in sexual atrocities, the fact that they once did so remains a powerful motivator and source of propaganda for insurgent groups. Such abuse resonates with the target population as part of the terrorists' information and propaganda campaigns. Iraq provides a perfect example of this. Although the actual number of Iraqi women exploited by U.S. or British soldiers is small compared to most wartime situations, the mere fact that such abuses have occurred has whipped up jihadi sentiment in places far from the battlefield. In all events, respect and restraint on the part of the government or occupying forces is clearly essential if women are to be discouraged from throwing in their lot with the terrorists.

Another often-recommended approach to curtailing violence by women (and men) is the introduction of democracy. One of the justifications offered for the invasion of Iraq was to bring democracy to the region. Some authorities assume that this form of government is a panacea, the implication being that only people without a legitimate outlet to express grievances turn to violence. This is not the case. In fact, democratization has resulted in some fairly perverse unintended outcomes. In most instances when elections have been held in the Middle East, the first parties to be voted in were the very same Islamic fundamentalists who opposed a democratic system to begin with. This was the case, for example, in both Algeria and the Palestinian Territories. When people who have suffered for years under authoritarians finally get the vote, they don't necessarily vote for the good guys! And the victorious fundamentalists are rarely the strongest supporters of women's rights. The status of women in Iraq is worse now, by almost any measure, than it was under the authoritarian regime of Saddam Hussein. The imposition of democracy from above in Iraq led to voting that has congealed sectarian divides and made the emergence of a vibrant democracy unlikely in the future.

Almost anything Westerners do has the potential to backfire. If Western governments try to encourage the growth of domestic institutions and civil society in the Middle East, assuming that such organizations will provide women with an outlet to contribute with their lives and not their deaths, their footprint necessarily has to be imperceptible. If the indigenous population identifies these institutions with Western or American influence, civil society will be undermined from the get-go. The institutions will appear to be puppets of the imperialists and the people who participate in them will be at risk from terrorist groups for their perceived collaboration.

It has been proven that as women become more educated and have fewer children, their rate of development increases exponentially. Women in positions of leadership serve as role models, causing other women to aspire to something more positive than participating in violence. Women's participation in the political realm does not necessarily require a secular state in the Islamic world. In Indonesia, for example, women's participation is not at odds with Islamic institutions. This means that women are not forced to choose between their religious traditions and modern society when they campaign in elections or run for public office. Having more Islamic women in visible positions of leadership in a traditional context resonates in a way that forcing a Western template on all Muslim women does not. This more culturally sensitive approach to reform requires us to rethink modernity and feminism in a way that allows for the perpetuation of religious tradition and does not require a separation of religion and state in order to be successful.

RECOMMENDATIIONS FROM THE SIDELINES

It is important that scholars share their findings with policymakers, analysts, and members of the military to ensure that they learn the lessons of the past and do not make the same mistakes over and over again. Tel Aviv University psychologist Ariel Merari is often quoted as saying that the terrorism researcher has the obligation to make terrorism *known*. By this he means it is important that we show terrorism for what it is, and not for what people might imagine it to be. Actual terrorism and counter-terrorism are far removed from their depictions in movies and fiction. Terrorism is mostly dull; there is a lot of waiting around. It is not the thrilling, nonstop roller-coaster ride portrayed in books by writers such as Robert Ludlum or John le Carré or in films featuring imaginary heroes such as James Bond or Jason Bourne. We need to make known, for example, what terrorist organizations are doing to the women of their own community. When terrorists deliberately put women in harm's way, when they capitalize on women's victimization or, even worse, when they abuse women themselves, we have an obligation to advertise their crimes.

More and more examples have emerged of terrorists using coercive techniques to pressure or force operatives to commit heinous acts. We have seen cases of individuals who have been duped and of suicide car bombers (in Iraq, for example) who were unaware that they were on a deadly mission. In several cases, the drivers were told they were taking something, possibly illegal, through checkpoints, only to have the payload detonated from afar with a cell phone or a mobile device. In other cases, people's families have been held at gunpoint and threatened with death and dismemberment unless a family member goes through a checkpoint with a car bomb. Finally, there has been an increasing number of cases in which the operative could not possibly have made the decision to be a bomber because he or she was either too young or mentally incapacitated.

We need to do a much better job of showing what involvement in terrorism is really like. Even among those individuals who believe that suicide attacks (or martyrdom operations) are an appropriate response to occupation or oppression, few support the use of children or coerced women. There is no sacrifice to Allah when there is no choice. If people who truly believed in the Salafi message knew that this was how Al Qaeda–affiliated groups in Iraq operated, Al Qaeda's popularity would surely plummet further. The fact is that Al Qaeda is increasingly alienated from most Muslims and even from most Islamists, having lost the strategic initiative in Iraq, Indonesia, and elsewhere.[5] This is a trend that we need to encourage.

TERRORISTS AND THEIR CONSTITUENCIES

There is no single template that describes women who become involved in terrorism. Some women choose to get involved with terrorist organizations to help their community. Others have no choice. Facing the certainty of death at the hands of their own families, dismemberment by Wahhabites (the Chechen term for jihadis), or being sold to terrorist organizations, those with no choice are in a truly grim situation. The organizations that either attract willing commitment or obtain compliance by force seem to have a different relationship to the civilian population in which they operate. Where the insurgency is inspired by ethnicity or nationalism, the terrorist organizers may make great efforts to inculcate a sense of devotion from their people. They see themselves as the future leaders of the community and strive to protect their "constituents" to the best of their ability. For these groups, all politics is local and the core public is also local. JI's rhetorical support for the global movement has been useful for its local struggle. It affords the organization greater prestige as well as access to international financial support. At the end of the day, however, JI's focus will always be local first, and then maybe regional, rather than global. Similarly, groups such as Hezbollah and Hamas create infrastructure, provide social services, and make a significant effort to improve the lives of men and women in their communities, while also fighting the other side. These groups make an important distinction between *their* civilians and those who oppose them. And though they certainly do not respect the lives of their enemies, they do seem to care about their own people.

However, in the globalized terror networks, particularly Al Qaeda, the people doing the fighting often have no connection to the civilians around them. The leadership's goals extend beyond the parameters of one state or area, and so the local population is just one of several possible constituencies. Also, the people they mobilize may be far removed from the location of the conflict. These outside recruits may have little or no knowledge of the conditions in which the local population lives. This disconnect may lead them to be far more cavalier about the value of life and the extent to which they coerce the local population. This is equally true for both religious and secular terrorist organizations.

Palestinian terrorist groups know that whatever they do will be observed by the Palestinians upon whose support they rely. In contrast, many of the Sunni insurgent groups in Iraq do not care what happens to ordinary Iraqis. Both their goal and their audience lie outside the Iraqi state (jihadis do not even recognize Iraq as a state because it was "created" by the British during the colonial period). The Sunni insurgents have only a superficial connection to the local population. It follows that they have no qualms about subjecting Iraqi women to heinous treatment. In Chechnya, the situation is complicated by a culture in which kidnapping and rape have been institutionalized as a form of courtship. Selling one's daughter or sexually exploiting a woman to get her parents' permission for marriage are—shockingly—almost routine. The terrorists have been able to adapt existing customs for their own purposes.

Among the Tamils, Irish Republicans, and Palestinians, there has been little need to convince women to join the movement. The women themselves pressured the leadership of the terrorist movements to allow them to participate in violence. Eventually, the leaders agreed. Both the pressure and the agreement occurred within a supportive environment: a majority of Catholics in Northern Ireland expected, even demanded, that everyone step up and do something for the good of the community. Similar conditions applied among Tamils, Palestinians, and Chechens. Siobhan, Darshika, Puhalchudar, Zura, and Ahlam, were not coerced. And yet, the subtle pressures exerted by the culture of violence in their societies may have limited these women's options from the very beginning. Such a culture perpetuates more violence and the cycle may appear impossible to break.

WOMEN'S STATUS

Given the increasing prevalence of women on the terrorist front line, it is curious that so few women have achieved leadership positions within terrorist organizations, as they did in the 1970s. Both Astrid Proll and Ulrike Meinhof, for example, held crucial leadership positions in the Baader–Meinhof Group.[6] We have seen no comparable development in Palestinian organizations, for example, where patriarchy remains the rule.

Women's involvement in terrorist groups has not helped level the gender playing field after all. Even in groups where women comprise from 30 to 60 percent of the bombers, they are rarely in charge. Few organizations have female ideologues who might include something about women's equality in their manifestos. Even in the groups where women play a larger role, they are still the second string. Women tend to become necessary when men are incapacitated, but they are an expedient choice at best. Until women's lives are valued as much as their deaths, women's participation in violence will not create more opportunities for other women; it might actually hurt a society in ways we cannot fathom. If the only way intelligent and politically motivated women can participate in politics is through death, these societies are losing their most capable women. They will not be able to run for office, have satisfying careers, or contribute in other, more positive ways to building or enhancing their communities.

Almost all of the women whose stories have been examined in the course of my research for this book agreed on one thing: feminism was not the basis of their participation in the terrorist movement. Many of them were decidedly antifeminist. Several confided in me that they felt betrayed by the feminist movement in their respective countries, because the feminist agenda conflicted with nationalist agendas. Those committed to the terrorist cause tended to look upon women's issues as either irrelevant to the nationalist cause or as a lesser priority. When asked whether they felt any unique experiences as women terrorists *qua* women, they found the question to be puzzling, and eventually all answered no. They had no unique experiences of being women, just of being oppressed. When a terrorist movement treated women as equals, feminist motivation was not part of the calculus. Jihadi women like Umayma Hasan, the wife of Al Qaeda's second-in-command, do not consider themselves particularly oppressed, regardless of whether Westerners see them that way. Thus participating in violence is not intended to level the playing field in their societies—this is not one of their goals.

These findings contradict those of at least one observer, Anat Berko, who argued that Palestinian women bombers were seeking equality with men. Among the women with whom she spoke, several reported that they were fighting for their rights as women. "Whatever a man can do, a woman can also do,"[7] said one; another claimed: "There is no difference between a man and a woman in the Intifada. We all want to protect our land, there is no difference in the recruitment of a guy or a girl, but the percentage of women that are recruited is lower because there are women that have another role in society as homemakers."[8] The women with whom Berko spoke might reflect the specifics of Palestinian society and women's roles in it. Certainly, Ahlam at-Tamimi is a model of women's liberation and leadership. She does not consider herself unequal to men even though she works for a conservative religious organization with no female leaders. Yet with her fame or notoriety she is winning office for Hamas in local elections by becoming the face of Hamas's women. She chooses to do this while wearing traditional Islamic robes and the veil.

Western assumptions are not always helpful in this context. Not all women aspire to Western-style equality (where it exists!). The fact that many terrorist women are at loggerheads with the feminists in their society was, for me, completely unexpected. Apparently, the desire by some women to show a terrorist organization that women are just as dedicated to the cause as men does not mean that they want to be the same as men, or be treated as men.

MEETING THE TERRORIST THREAT

To avoid the impossible dilemma of either invasively checking women for explosives and causing popular outrage or of not checking women at all and getting bombed, Coalition forces in Iraq established the Daughters of Iraq—Iraqi women who conduct searches at checkpoints. In other parts of the world, security services are increasingly drafting women to prevent attacks by female terrorists. Indonesian police employ women to look out for JI militants; the Israeli Defence Forces makes sure that female recruits are stationed at border crossings; and Turkish police have hired a handful of women police officers in case they have to search potential Kurdish Worker's Party operatives. Women can no longer pass through checkpoints without scrutiny. Still, the number of female terrorists continues to rise. Innovations in security technologies and practices will be only short-term solutions at best.

We will also soon see new kinds of operatives emerge as terrorists adapt to changing security environments and as their targets become more difficult to penetrate. Already some terrorist groups have turned to young children, either coercing them into becoming bombers or "volunteering" them without their knowledge. In Iraq and Afghanistan, this manipulation of young operatives has already started. In Indonesia, the women of JI are preparing a new generation of child militants. In the West Bank and Gaza, Hamas has television shows that feature a fundamentalist Mickey Mouse–like cartoon character, Farfour, who tells children that the ultimate goal is to be a *shahid*. In Afghanistan in May 2006, the Taliban tried to dupe a six-year-old boy, Juma Gul, into becoming a suicide bomber. They forced him to wear a vest that they said would shower flowers when he pushed the plunger. They told him that as soon as he saw a group of American soldiers, he was to "throw [his] body at them."[9] In Iraq, terrorist organizations are recruiting girls as young as fourteen and may soon try to find even younger girls to carry out attacks.

While counter-terrorist units like the Daughters of Iraq may have some short-term effect, a more fundamental approach is needed for the longer term. I suggest responding to the four plus one Rs with three Ds: *delegitimize, deglamorize*, and *demobilize*. This entails showing what involvement in terrorism is actually like and, in the process, undermining the basis upon which women (and men) become involved. In order to combat the lure of terrorism, and the support and appreciation women martyrs receive from their communities, we need first to *delegitimize* violence by showing that violence is sanctioned neither by the *Qur'an* nor by the Hadith. We need to challenge involvement in terrorism at the level of image and undermine its attractiveness. Doing so might involve having former terrorists tell their stories, showing how they became disillusioned.

The media has all too often inadvertently glamorized terrorists, depicting them as very evil but also very powerful. Instead, they should be *deglamorized*, shown to be corrupt and hypocritical. According to John Horgan, director of the International Center for the Study of Terrorism, there is no shortage of celebrity ex-terrorists who can deglamorize and demythologize the terrorist lifestyle. Detailing how the women participate against their will is key. This can also be done by stressing the devastation caused by terrorist attacks against other women and children. Finally, we need to show the futility of terrorism. Terrorists rarely if ever succeed in achieving their primary political or religious goals, whereas negotiation and reconciliation have a significantly better track record.

Most of all, we need to provide pathways for women's exit from terrorist organizations. Few of the current deradicalization programs (whose effectiveness remains an open question) have facilities or programs specifically for women or children. Yet it is the women and children who will carry on the conflict in the future. We need to *demobilize* the women so that they are no longer involved in shooting, killing, and bombing. Given that often the women are more radical than the men and that some are true believers, it is too lofty a goal to try and change their minds, but we can certainly aim to change their actions. By eliminating the immediate source of violence from the community while simultaneously undermining its very legitimacy, we might finally break the cycle of violence.

Much of the groundwork needs to be laid by the local women themselves. An organization in Indonesia led by Lily Munir has the right idea: they have set up several Islamic schools for girls. The girls learn the *Qur'an*, but they also learn the positive things that the *Qur'an* has to say about women. At the same time as they are empowered by the curriculum, the girls learn practical skills like mathematics, computer science, and English.[10] They will have the resources to become future leaders of their communities. They are learning enough about Islam that, in the future, no charismatic leader can manipulate the text and convince them that Holy Scripture endorses the killing of other Muslims. At the same time, they are also learning the skills to be successful in the modern world. The women in these schools have a chance to do something great with their lives, not their deaths. Some of the women in this book, like the Irish operative Siobhan, have shown that a peaceful transition is possible and that they can make a positive contribution to the future instead of being the shells for the bombs that they carry for men.

NOTES

Prologue

1 Magomed Abdurashidov and Yuliya Rybina (Makhachkala), "They Found a Conductor for the Bombed Subway Trains," *Kommersant Online*, April 30, 2010, p. 5.

2 Irina Gordiyenko, "What Anvar Sharipov, Suspected of Organizing the Terrorist Acts, Had to Say," Moscow *Novaya Gazeta Online* (in Russian), April 12, 2010.

3 www.jamaatshariat.com/ru/content/view/406/29

4 momento24.com/en/2010/04/02/moscow-bombing-teens-widows-and-suicide-bombers

5 Reuters, "Suicide Bomber Spotlights Russia's Islamist Battle," May 18, 2010, www.politicalscandalnews.com/article/Suicide%20 bomber%20spotlights%20Russia%27s%20Islamist%20 battle/?k=j83s12y12h94s27k02

6 www.cnn.com/2010/WORLD/europe/04/06/moscow.subway. bombings/index.html

7 http://english.aljazeera.net/news/europe/2010/04/20104514253379 4297.html

8 www.nytimes.com/2010/04/07/world/europe/07moscow.html

9 Several months later, a reporter from *The Guardian* newspaper interviewed the family; Luke Harding, "Dagestan: My Daughter

the Terrorist," *The Guardian*, June 19, 2010, www.guardian.co.uk/
world/2010/jun/19/dagestan-suicide-bombers-terrorism-russia

10 www.rttnews.com/Content/GeneralNews.aspx?Id=1304458&SM=1

11 www.rttnews.com/Content/GeneralNews.aspx?Id=1304458&SM=1;
www.timesonline.co.uk/tol/news/world/europe/article7125906.ece

†   A Brief History of Terror and the Logic of Oppression

1 Cited in Deeana J. Resse, "The Trouble between us: an uneasy
history of white and black women in the feminist movement."
Women's History Review, Vol. 18, issue 3, July 2009, p.513.

2 "Ulrike Meinhof calls for a move from protest to resistance," http://germanhistorydocs.ghi-dc.org/sub_document.
cfm?document_id=895&language=english.

3 Mia Bloom, *Dying to Kill: The Allure of Suicide Terror*, New York:
Columbia University Press, 2005, chapter 1.

4 Philip K. Hitti, "The Assassins," in George Andrews and Simon
Vinkenoog (eds.), *The Book of Grass: An Anthology on Indian Hemp*,
London: Peter Owen Press, 1967, writes that the whole mysterious
legend of the Assassins was most fancifully presented by Marco Polo,
who passed through Persia in 1273. For the full text see Charles E.
Nowell, "The Old Man of the Mountain," *Speculum: A Journal of
Mediaeval Studies*, vol. 22, no. 4, October 1947, pp. 497 passim.

5 Bernard Lewis, *The Assassins: A Radical Sect in Islam,* New York:
Oxford University Press, 1987, p. 127.

6 Mako Sasaki, "Who Became Kamikaze Pilots, and How Did
They Feel towards Their Suicide Mission?" Quoted by Roman
Kupchinsky, in "Smart Bombs with Souls," in *Organized Crime and
Terrorism Watch* 3, no. 13, April 17, 2003.

7 Ibid, p. 1.

8 Scott Atran, "Genesis and Future of Suicide Terrorism,"
Interdisciplines, 2003, www.interdisciplines.org/terrorism/papers/1/6
see also *Science,* March 7, 2003, vol. 299, no. 5612, pp. 1534–39.

9 Peter Hill, "Kamikaze: Pacific War, 1943–45," Department of
Sociology, University of Oxford, unpublished manuscript, pp. 2–4.

10 Maximilien Robespierre, "Principes de morale politique," speech to French National Convention, February 5, 1794, http://membres. lycos.fr/ discours/1794.htm

11 U.S. Department of State, National Counter Terrorism Center, www.state.gov/s/ct/rls/crt/2006/82739.htm

12 Richard B. Jensen, "The United States, International Policing of the War against Anarchist Terrorism," *Terrorism and Political Violence* 13, 1 (Spring 2001), pp. 15–46.

13 Bruce Watson, *Sacco and Vanzetti: The Men, the Murders, and the Judgment of Mankind*, New York: Viking Press, 2007, p. 77.

14 Beverly Gage, *The Day Wall Street Exploded: A Story of America in Its* 2003; Betsy Reed, *Nothing Sacred: Women Respond to Religious Fundamentalism and Terror*, New York, NY: Nation Books, 2002; Anne Cubilie, *Women Witnessing Terror: Testimony and the Cultural Politics of Human Rights*, New York: Fordham University Press, 2005.

First Age of Terror, New York: Oxford University Press, 2009.

15 David Rapoport, "Four Waves of Rebel Terror and September 11," *Anthropoetics* 8, no. 1 (Spring/Summer 2002), www.anthropoetics. ucla.edu/ap0801/terror.htm#b3

16 Ibid.

17 www.almaqdese.net/r1?i=3552&x=x483iubf. See also Nelly Lahoud, *The Jihadis Path to Self Destruction*, New York: Columbia University Press, 2010.

18 Bloom, *Dying to Kill*, op. cit.

19 Yoni Fighel, "Palestinian Islamic Jihad and Female Suicide Bombers," October 6, 2003, http://212.150.54.123/articles/ articledet.cfm?articleid=499 (accessed July 14, 2008)

20 Sophie Claudet, "More Palestinian Women Suicide Bombers Could Be on the Way: Analysts," *Middle East Times,* March 1, 2002.

21 Robert Baer, *The Cult of the Suicide bomber*. Documentary Film, New York: Disinformation Studios, 2005.

22 Scott Atran argues that as a result of Akras's martyrdom, Saudi Arabia sent 100 million dollars to fund the Al 'Aqsa Intifada.

23 Graham Usher, "At 18, Bomber Became Martyr and Murderer," *The Guardian*, March 30, 2002, www.guardian.co.uk/world/2002/mar/30/israel3

24 Cited by Bloom, *Dying to Kill*, op. cit., pp. 3–4

25 Shanthikumar Hettiarachchi, "Tamil Tiger Martyrdon in Sri Lanka: Faith in Suicide for Nationhood?" *Politics and Religion*, Vol. 2, www.politicsandreligionjournal.com/images/pdf_files/srpski/godina1_broj2/Shanthikumar_Hettiarachchi.pdf.

26 Paul Gill, *Marketing Martyrdom: The Political Psychology of Suicide Bombings*, Forthcoming, Philadelphia: University of Pennsylvania Press.

27 Alisa Stack O'Connor, "Picked Last: Women and Terrorism," *JFQ*, issue 44, 2007, NDU Press, p. 95.

28 Robin Kirk, *Untold Terror: Violence Against Women in Peru's Armed Conflict*, New York: Human Rights Watch, 2002; Ammu Joseph, *Terror and Counter Terror: Women Speak Out*, London: Zed Books,

29 Interviews with former bombers, Belfast, August 2009.

30 Eileen McDonald, *Shoot the Women First*, New York: Random House, 1992.

2 The Black Widow Bombers

 1 Gunmen Release Chilling Video, CNN http://archives.cnn.com/2002/WORLD/europe/10/24/moscow.siege.video/

 2 Robert Mackey, "Chechen Rebel Leaders Speaks via Youtube," April 1, 2010, http://thelede.blogs.nytimes.com/2010/04/01/chechen-rebel-leader-speaks-via-youtube/

 3 Margaret Ziolkowski, *Alien Visions: The Chechens and the Navahos in Russian and American Literature*, Newark, DE: University of Delaware Press, 2005, p. 41.

 4 Kerim Fenari, "The Jihad of Imam Shamyl," www.masud.co.uk/ISLAM/misc/shamyl.htm

 5 Moshe Gammer, *Muslim Resistance to the Tsar: Shamil and the Conquest of Chechnia and Daghestan*, London: Routledge, 2003.

 6 Bülent Gökay, "Russia and Chechnia: A Long History of Conflict,

Resistance and Oppression," *Alternatives*, vol. 3, no. 2 (Summer 2004).

7 Richard Pipes, *The Formation of the Soviet Union: Communism and Nationalism 1917–1923*, Cambridge, MA: Harvard University Press, 1997, p. 95.

8 Chechnya: A Time Trail, www.time.com/time/europe/chechnyatrail/chechnyatrail.html

9 Clare Doyle, "The Chechen Russian Conflict: Today and Yesterday," *Socialism Today*, www.socialismtoday.org/87/tolstoy.html.

10 1 AD–1721, A Mountain of Languages, January 1, 2001, www.telegraph.co.uk/news/1399566/1-AD-1721-A-mountain-of-languages.html.

11 Kerim Fenari, "The Jihad of Imam Shamyl," www.masud.co.uk/ISLAM/misc/shamyl.htm

12 Jeremy Putley, "Crime Without Punishment: Russian Policy in Chechnya," Open Democracy News Analysis (www.opendemocracy.net), July 27, 2003 www.opendemocracy.net/node/1388/pdf (p. 2)

13 Ibid.

14 Amnesty International, Chechnya—A Report to the Council of Europe, AI Index: EUR 46/001/2001, http://asiapacific.amnesty.org/library/Index/ENGEUR460012001?open&of=ENG-366

15 BBC, "Britons killed 'by Bin Laden Ally,'" November 18, 2001, http://news.bbc.co.uk/2/hi/uk_news/1663278.stm

16 Reports vary about the number of people inside. The theater had sold 711 tickets that night, and members of the cast and crew were also taken hostage, but an exact figure does not exist. Russian sources cite 912 hostages but as many as 979 have been reported. Russian sources are extremely unreliable on many of the details concerning the events at the theater.

17 Adam Dolnik and Keith M. Fitzgerald, *Negotiating Hostage Crises with the New Terrorists*, Santa Barbara, CA: Praeger, 2007, p. 61.

18 Oleg Petrovsky, "The Dagestan Route for Barayev's Terrorists," Moscow, www.ulto.ru (December 11, 2002)

19 One person died in the blast. It was initially assumed to be a Russian

Mafia operation. There is a view that the failure was the result of deliberate sabotage by Chechens who were secretly working with the FSB.

20 Roman Fomishenko, "Moscow. A Vile Blow Against the Innocent," *Moscow Krasnaya Zvezda* (in Russian), October 25, 2002.

21 John Giduck, *Terror at Beslan: A Russian Tragedy with Lessons for American Schools*, Golden, CO: Archangel Group, 2005, pp. 77–78.

22 Pavel Dulman, "Yanderbiyev Sought in Qatar," *Moscow Rossikaya Gazeta* (in Russian), November 1, 2002, p. 3.

23 http://archives.cnn.com/2002/WORLD/europe/10/24/moscow. siege.video

24 Baku Zerkalo, October 26, 2002, cited in Dolnik and Fitzgerald, op. cit., p. 182.

25 Kazantsev was named in 2000 as the presidential envoy to the Southern Federal District (2000–2004). This is why he should have conducted the negotiations in Dubrovka.

26 "Hostages speak of storming terror," BBC News, October 26, 2002.

27 The terrorists learned a great deal from their mistakes at Dubrovka, and were better prepared for the later attack on Beslan. Because the authorities used gas to neutralize the gunmen during the Dubrovka operation, the attackers in Beslan came equipped with gas masks, and smashed all the windows after entering the school to improve ventilation.

28 Chemical toxicology tests at the time showed that the drug was one that acted like carfentanyl but did not leave its signature residue. There was only one possible explanation: The Russians had developed a new, undetectable version of carfentanyl, possibly by adding BMU8 to create a powerful knockout gas.

29 Nick Paton Walsh, "Siege Rescue Carnage as Gas Kills Hostages," *The Guardian*, October 27, 2002, www.guardian.co.uk/world/2002/ oct/27/chechnya.russia3

30 "Mission Accomplished," *Moscow Gazeta*, October 30, 2002, pp. 1–6.

31 Movsar B. Suleimov (Barayev), Ruslan Elmurzayev, an Arab

mercenary called "Yassir," A.N. Baihatov, R. Baihatov, Muslim Adilsultanov, Selikat Aliyeva, Yupayeva, Kurbanova, Tagirov, the Khadjiyeva sisters—Ayman and Koku, Husainov, Zura Bitsiyeva (Barayeva), the Ganiyeva sisters—Khadizhat and Fatima, Aset Gishnurkayeva, Mutayeva, Bairakova, Madina Dugayeva, Tatayev, Shidayev, Arslanbek Abdulsheykhov, S. S. Elmurzayeva, Ahmetov, Bimurzayev, Husenova, M. B. Hadjiyeva, Bisultanova, Vitaliyeva, Luiza Bakuyeva, R. A. Hashanov, Tushayeva, Saidov, as well as terrorists using counterfeit documents in the names of Jabrailov, Turpal Khamzatov, Musayev, and three male corpses (corpses 2007, 2028, and 2036) whose identities were not determined.

32 Dolnik and Fitzgerald, op. cit., p. 65.

33 CNN, October 25, 2002, Gunmen Release Chilling Video, www.archives.cnn.com/2002/world/europe/10/24/moscow.siege.video/.

34 Simon Jeffrey, "The Moscow Theater Siege," *The Guardian*, October 28, 2002, www.guardian.co.uk/world/2002/oct/28/chechnya.russia6

35 BBC "Hostage Takers Ready to Die," October 25, 2002, news.bbc.co.uk/2/hi/europe/2360735.stm

36 Soldiers found eighteen new Russian passports, nine old Soviet passports, and dozens of police department–issued temporary Chechen IDs. In addition to fake IDs there were also authentic documents with other people's names. Many of the men carried real passports with other names; Barayev had the passport of Shamikhazi Akhmatkhanov. However, the female terrorists all possessed passports with their real names.

37 Viv Groskop, "Chechnya's Deadly 'Black Widows,'" *The New Statesman*, September 6, 2004, www.newstatesman.com/200409060023

38 Viv Groskop, "Women at the Heart of Terror Cells," *The Guardian*, September 5, 2004, www.guardian.co.uk/world/2004/sep/05/russia.chechnya1

39 Ibid.

40 Ibid.

41 Ibid.

42 Chechens often have an official name (for passport purposes) and another name that is commonly used within the family and that may be completely different. Sometimes the grandparents will give the children another completely different name, without informing the parents. Thus the inconsistencies in several of the Dubrovka accounts. Sources identify the bomber as Khadijat, although her parents call her Ayshat or Fatimat. There are lots of different name spellings depending on the source.

43 Kim Murphy, "A Cult of Reluctant Killers," *Los Angeles Times*, February 4, 2004.

44 Internal Displaced Monitoring Centre, "Women and Children Suffer Violence and Abuse (2008)," October 5, 2009, www.internal-displacement.org/idmc/website/countries.nsf/(httpEnvelopes)/88CA 1F1C7BDED7D2802570B8005AA947?OpenDocument

45 Murphy, "A Cult of Reluctant Killers," op. cit.

46 Anna Nugzarova and Natalya Khetagurova, "'Basayev Asked Me How My Sisters Ended up at Nord-Ost'; Man Charged with Preparing Acts of Terrorism Acknowledges His Guilt," *Moscow Gazeta*, January 10, 2005, p. 4.

47 Interview with Zarema Muzhakhoyeva, Ren TV, Moscow, June 24, 2004.

48 Sophie Shihab, "Black Widows of Chechnya," *Le Monde*, October 29, 2003, web.radicalparty.org/pressreview/print_right.php?func=detail&par=6859.

49 Elizabeth Frombgen, "Burkas, Babushkas, and Bombs: Toward an Understanding of the 'Black Widow,'" unpublished ms, prepared for the Pacific Northwest Political Science Association, 2008, p. 4.

50 Anna Politkovskaya, *A Small Corner of Hell: Dispatches from Chechnya*, translated by Alexander Burry and Tatiana Tulchinsky, Chicago: University of Chicago Press, 2003.

51 Murphy, "A Cult of Reluctant Killers," op. cit.

52 Ruslan Isayev, "The Chechen Woman and her Role in the New Society," Prague Watchdog, June 21, 2004, www.watchdog.cz/index.php?show=000000-000015-000006-000008&lang=1

53 Anne Speckhard and Khapta Akhmedova, "Black Widows, Chechen Female Suicide Terrorists," *Terrorism and Political Violence*, 2006, pp. 67–68.

54 Groskop, "Women at the Heart of Terror Cells," op. cit.

55 Amnesty International, "Urge Putin to Stop Violence Against Women in Chechnya," AIUSA, http://takeaction.amnestyusa.org/site/c.goJTI0OvElH/b.1157849/k.928E/Urge_Russian_President_Putin_to_Stop_Violence_Against_Women_in_Chechnya.htm

56 Svideteli: Cherniyye Vdovy ("Witnesses: Black Widows"), RTR TV Russia, October 14, 2004, 7:20 P.M.

57 Groskop, "Women at the Heart of Terror Cells," op. cit.

58 Human Rights Watch, "Rape Allegations Surface in Chechnya," January 20, 2000, available at www.hrw.org/press.2000/01/chech0120.htm

59 www.internal-displacement.org/8025708F004BE3B1/(httpInfoFiles)/BCA90FF82910EA0BC125764D0056508F/$file/Russian+Federation+-+October+2009.pdf.

60 Tom Parfitt, "Meet Black Fatima—She Programmes Women to Kill," *Daily Telegraph*, July 20, 2003, www.telegraph.co.uk/news/worldnews/europe/russia/1436622/Meet-Black-Fatima---she-programmes-women-to-kill.html

61 Laura Sjoberg and Caron E. Gentry, *Mothers, Monsters and Whores*, London: Zed Books, 2007, p. 91.

62 Nabi Abdullaev, "Women to the Forefront of Chechen Terrorism," International Relations and Security Network, 2005, p. 1, www.isn.ethz.ch/news/sw/details.cfm?ID=97812005

3 The "Pregnant" Bomber

1 DM Daugherty, "The Women Hunger Strikers of Armagh Prison." October 2002, http://irelandsown.net/armaghwomen.html

2 Laura E. Lyons, "At the End of the Day": An Interview with Mairead Keane National Head of Sein Fein Women's Department." *Boundary 2* 19:2, 1992.

3 Not her real name.

4 "Baby Bomb Bid at Airport," *Ulster News Letter*, April 30, 1990, p. 5.

5 www.pbs.org/wgbh/pages/frontline/shows/ira/conflict

6 John Horgan, "From War of Maneuver to War of Position: A Brief History of the Provisional IRA and the Irish Republic," in *Combating Terrorism in Northern Ireland*, James Dingley (ed.), London: Routledge, 2009, p. 228.

7 Ibid, p. 230.

8 Eunan O'Halpin, *Defending Ireland: The Irish State and Its Enemies Since 1922*, Oxford: Oxford University Press, 1999, p. 151.

9 Robert Kee, *Ireland: A History*, London: Time Warner Books, 1980 (revised edition, 2005), p. 237; Peter Berresford Ellis, *Eyewitness to Irish History*, Hoboken, NJ: John Wiley & Sons, 2004, p. 281.

10 www.pbs.org/wgbh/pages/frontline/shows/ira/conflict

11 Catholics in Ireland were underemployed or unemployed. As families grew, the state would not grant permission to build new apartments or housing estates. Most families lived several to one home, and housing for Catholics was not increased commensurate with their growing population. Any new developments were built almost exclusively for Protestants, further exacerbating the relations between the two communities.

12 Bernadette Devlin, *Price of my Soul*, London: Pan Books, 1969, foreword and chapter 12.

13 Richard English, *Armed Struggle: A History of the IRA*, New York: Oxford University Press, 2003, p. 106.

14 Seán Mac Stíofáin, *Memoirs of a Revolutionary*, London: Gordon Cremonesi, 1975 (second edition, Free Ireland Book Club, 1979), p. 146.

15 John Horgan, *Divided We Stand: The Strategy and Psychology of Ireland's Dissident Terrorists*. New York: Oxford University Press, forthcoming in 2011.

16 Dr. Raymond McClean, *The Road to Bloody Sunday*, Derry, Northern Ireland: Guildhall Press, 1983.

17 Bishop Edward Daly, in an interview shown in "Secret History: Bloody Sunday," broadcast by Channel 4 Television, UK, on January 22, 1992, http://cain.ulst.ac.uk/events/bsunday/sum.htm

18 www.pbs.org/wgbh/pages/frontline/shows/ira/conflict

19 Margareta D'Arcy, *Tell Them Everything: A Sojourn in the Prison of HMS Queen Elizabeth II at Ard Macha (Armagh)*, London: Pluto Press, 1981, p. 66.

20 Father Denis Faul, "Beating Women in Prison: Black February, Armagh Prison," special report, February 1980.

21 Some cells were eight feet by eleven feet.

22 D'Arcy, op. cit., pp. 54–55. However, the sheets and pillows were removed as punishment after the February 7 incident.

23 Nell McCafferty, *The Armagh Women*, Dublin: Co-op Books, 1981, p. 10.

24 D'Arcy, op. cit., p. 57.

25 Interviews with female ex-prisoners, Belfast, August 2009.

26 Mark Hoffman, "Perspectives on the Northern Ireland Women's Coalition," p. 72, passim www.sit.edu/SITOccasionalPapers/ops03.pdf#page=72

27 Interviews with female ex-prisoners, Belfast, August 2009.

28 Faul, "Beating Women in Prison: Black February, Armagh Prison," op. cit., p. 15.

29 D'Arcy, op. cit., p. 81.

30 Interview with Mary Doyle, Belfast, August 2009.

31 "The diary of Bobby Sands," available online at www.pbs.org/wgbh/pages/frontline/shows/ira/readings/diary.html.

32 "Women in the Irish National Liberation Struggle," *Radikal*, no. 145, February 1992, www.hartford-hwp.com/archives/61/291.html

33 Interview with Mairéad Farrell's cell mates, August 13, 2009.

34 Seán Mac Stíofáin, *Revolutionary in Ireland*, London: Gordon Cremonesi, 2005, p. 218, cited by Mary Corcoran, *Out of Order: The Political Imprisonment of Women in Northern Ireland 1972–1998*, Devon, UK: Willan Publishing, 2006, p. 6.

35 Jenny McGeever, "The Story of Mairéad Farrell," *Magill Magazine*, October 6, 1986, p. 9.

36 "IRA girl went to 'set up' sergeant," *Irish News*, August 11, 1975.

37 Interviews with female ex-prisoners, Belfast, August 2009.

38 Mary Corcoran, *Out of Order: The Political Imprisonment of Women in Northern Ireland 1972–1998*, Devon, UK: Willan Publishing, 2006, p. 5.

39 Interviews with female ex-prisoners, Belfast, August 2009.

40 Viviane Hewitt, "Special Branch Men Threatened to Rape Me," *Sunday News*, April 27, 1975, and "Police Deny Rape Threats," *Sunday News*, May 4, 1975.

41 Conflict Archive on the Internet, CAIN web services, "Internment: Summary of Main Events," http://cain.ulst.ac.uk/events/intern/sum.htm

42 Eoin Clarke, "Women and Irish Republicanism, 1914–1974," Part 1, http://searchwarp.com/swa54344.htm.

43 "IRA Attempt to Recruit Bomb Girls," *Daily Telegraph*, September 28, 1972.

44 Mark Hoffman, "Perspectives on the Northern Ireland Women's Coalition," p. 72 passim, p.8, www.sit.edu/SITOccasionalPapers/ops03.pdf#page=72

45 Interviews with the author, Belfast, August 2009.

46 www.parliament.the-stationery-office.co.uk/pa/cm199697/cmhansrd/vo961217/text/61217w19.htm

47 Interview with the author, Belfast, August 11, 2009.

48 Interview with the author, Belfast, August 12, 2009.

49 Ibid.

50 Mia Bloom and John Horgan, "Missing Their Mark: The IRA's Proxy Bomb Campaign," *Social Research: An International Quarterly*, vol. 75, no. 2 (Summer 2008).

51 A twelfth civilian was in a coma for thirteen years before dying.

52 In fact, "Sunday Bloody Sunday" is not a nationalist song at all. According to U2 drummer Larry Mullen, "We're into the politics of people, we're not into politics. Like you talk about Northern Ireland,

'Sunday Bloody Sunday,' people sort of think, 'Oh, that time when 13 Catholics were shot by British soldiers'; that's not what the song is about. That's an incident, the most famous incident in Northern Ireland and it's the strongest way of saying, 'How long? How long do we have to put up with this?' I don't care who's who—Catholics, Protestants, whatever. You know people are dying every single day through bitterness and hate, and we're saying, Why? What's the point? And you can move that into places like El Salvador and other similar situations—people dying. Let's forget the politics, let's stop shooting each other and sit around the table and talk about it ... There are a lot of bands taking sides saying politics is crap, etc. Well, so what! The real battle is people dying, that's the real battle," Interview, *White Lily*, April 1, 1983, http://u2_interviews.tripod.com/id18.html

53 In the 1970s, other women had gone on hunger strike, including the Price sisters, who staged a 206-day strike in order to arrange their transfer to Armagh prison.

54 "We Go Ahead with Hunger Strike, Say Women Prisoners," *Irish News,* November 29, 1980.

55 John J. O'Connor, "An IRA Member from Several Angles," *New York Times*, June 13, 1989, www.nytimes.com/1989/06/13/movies/review-television-an-ira-member-from-several-angles.html

56 "British Obstruct Gibraltar Action," *An Phoblacht/Republican News*, April 26, 1990, p. 5.

4   The Scout

1 Izz al Qassem Brigades' website dedicated to Ahlam Al Tamimi, www.qassam.ps/prisoner-96-Ahlam_Mazen_Al_Tamimi.html

2 Ahlam Al Tamimi interview with Shimon Dotan, HaSharon Prison, 2006; *Hot House*, Alma Films, Meimad Barkai production, December 2005.

3 Robert Fisk, "We Cannot Report Gaza Like a Football Match," www.mwaw.net/2009/01/08/fisk-on-gaza

4 Robert Fisk, "Fifteen Dead in Jerusalem Suicide Bomb," *The Independent*, August 10, 2001.

5 Martin Sicker, *Reshaping Palestine: From Muhammed Ali to the British Mandate, 1831–1921*, Westport, CT: Praeger, 1999, p. 4.

6 "More than forty Jewish communities could be traced to the sixth century … twelve on the coast, in the Negev, and east of the Jordan and thirty-one villages in Galilee and in the Jordan Valley," www. eretzyisroel.org/~peters/presence.html

7 Moshe Dayan, *Story of My Life*, New York: De Capo Press, 1992.

8 Article 22, The Covenant of the League of Nations, http://avalon. law.yale.edu/20th_century/leagcov.asp#art22 "Mandate for Palestine," *Encyclopedia Judaica*, vol. 11, p. 862, Keter Publishing House, Jerusalem, 1972.

9 The text of the agreement is located at Brigham Young University Archives, wwi.lib.byu.edu/index.php/Sykes-Picot_Agreement

10 Jeremy Wilson, *Lawrence of Arabia: The Authorized Biography of T.E. Lawrence*, New York: Athenaeum, 1990.

11 James Gelvin, *The Israeli-Palestine Conflict: One Hundred Years of War*, New York: Cambridge University Press, 2005, pp. 82–83.

12 Balfour Declaration. www.knesset.gov.il/lexicon/eng/ BalfourDeclaration_eng.htm

13 David Fromkin, *A Peace to End All Peace: The Fall of the Ottoman Empire and the Creation of the Modern Middle East*, New York: Owl Books, 1989 (reprinted by Holt, 2001 and 2009).

14 Gudrun Krämer, *A History of Palestine: From the Ottoman Conquest to the Founding of the State of Israel*, Princeton, NJ: Princeton University Press, 2008.

15 Peel Commission Report Cmd. 5479, 1937, p. 97.

16 Matthew Hughes, "The Banality of Brutality: British Armed Forces and the Repression of the Arab Revolt in Palestine, 1936–39," *English Historical Review*, vol. CXXIV, no. 507, 2009, pp. 314–54.

17 Brief History of Palestine and Israel and the Israeli Palestinian Conflict, www.mideastweb.org/briefhistory.htm#Modern%20 History

18 Benny Morris, *The Birth of the Palestinian Refugee Problem, 1947–49,* New York: Cambridge University Press, 1987, pp. 149, passim; see also Simha Flapan, *The Birth of Israel: Myths and Reality,* New York: Pantheon Press, 1988, and Avi Shlaim, *Collusion Across the Jordan: King Abdullah, the Zionist Movement and the Partition of Palestine,* New York: Columbia University Press, 1988.

19 Said K. Aburish, *Arafat, From Defender to Dictator.* New York: Bloomsbury Publishing, 1998, pp. 41–90.

20 Dan Fisher, *Los Angeles Times,* December 23, 1987.

21 John Kifner, "Burial Alive of Palestinians," *New York Times,* February 16, 1988.

22 Ray Hanania, "Sharon's Terror Child," www.counterpunch.org/hanania01182003.html

23 www.mideastweb.org/hamashistory.htm

24 Palestine TV broadcast, August 9, 2001.

25 www.arabicnews.com/ansub/Daily/Day/010810/2001081005.html

26 Suzanne Goldenberg, "The Street Was Covered with Blood and Bodies: The Dead and the Dying," *The Guardian,* August 10, 2001, www.guardian.co.uk/world/2001/aug/10/israel1

27 Brian Whitaker, "Who Carried Out Suicide Bombing?" *The Guardian,* August 10, 2001, www.guardian.co.uk/Archive/Article/0,4273,4236794,00.html

28 Jerusalem Bomber 'driven by despair' *Sunday Tribune,* August 10, 2001, www.sundaytribune.co.za/index.php?fSectionId=1028&fArticleId=ct20010810092510430M323911.

29 Barbara Victor, *Army of Roses: Inside the World of Palestinian Women Suicide Bombers,* New York: Rodale Press, 2003, p. 144.

30 Joyce Davis, *Martyrs: Innocence, Vengeance, and Despair in the Middle East,* New York: Palgrave Macmillan, 2004, p. 130.

31 Al Masri's sister did name the baby after him two days later. When asked what hopes she had for the child, she said she wanted him to be "like his uncle." "Paradise—Hollywood Style," agsconsulting.com/articles/ab060120.htm

32 Brian Whitaker, "Who Carried Out Suicide Bombing?" *The Guardian*, August 10, 2001, www.guardian.co.uk/Archive/Article/0,4273,4236794,00.html

33 The last-will-and-testament video was broadcast on Al Manar TV; CNN provided a detailed transcript, http://edition.cnn.com/TRANSCRIPTS/0601/23/ywt.01.html

34 Jailed bomber, interview with Shimon Dotan 2006; *Hot House*, Alma Films, Meimad Barkai production.

35 *Al Masa'a* Egyptian Newspaper, January 2, 2004, translated by MEMRI, www.memri.org/report/en/0/0/0/0/0/0/1057.htm.

36 abcnews.go.com/Nightline/story?id=128515&page=1

37 Sara Helm, "The Human Time Bomb. What Motivates a Suicide Bombing?" *Sunday Times Magazine*, January 6, 2002, p. 54.

38 *Al Masaa* (Egypt), January 2, 2004, cited by MEMRI www.memri.org/bin/articles.cgi?Page=archives&Area=sd&ID=SP65804#_edn1

39 Ahlam Al Tamimi interview, Shimon Dotan, HaSharon prison, 2006; *Hot House*, Alma Films, Meimad Barkai production.

40 Pierre Conesa, "The Suicide Terrorists," *Le Monde Diplomatique*, June 2, 2004.

41 "Just Married and Determined to Die," *BBC*, October 13, 2008.

42 Robert Fisk, "What Drives a Bomber to Kill an Innocent Child?" *The Independent*, August 11, 2001.

43 Interview with Shimon Dotan 2006; *Hot House*, Alma Films, Meimad Barkai production.

44 Ariel Merari, Jonathan Fighel, Boaz Ganor, Ephraim Lavie, Yohanan Tzoreff, and Arie Livne, "Making Palestinian 'Martyrdom Operations' 'Suicide Attacks': Interviews with Would-Be Perpetrators and Organizers," *Terrorism and Political Violence*, 22: 1, December 2009, pp. 102–19.

45 Ibid.

46 Matthew Gutman, "Who Is a Target? 9/11 One Year Later," *Jerusalem Post* supplement, http://info.jpost.com/C002/Supplements/911_OneYearLater/story_03.html

47 Laura Blumenfeld, "In Israel, A Divisive Struggle Over Targeted Killings," *Washington Post*, August 27, 2006, p. A1.

48 International Middle East Media Center, "Assassination as Official Israeli Policy," November 22, 2008, www.imemc.org/article/57755

49 Joshua Hammer, "This Land Is My Land: How Arafat and Sharon Have Debased the Very Societies They Claim to Serve," *Washington Monthly*, September 2004.

50 Laura Blumenfeld, op. cit.

51 Pierre Conesa, op. cit.

52 Judith Miller, "The Bomb Under the Abaya," *Policy Review*, Hoover Institution, June–July 2007.

53 Khaled Mish'al, speech, Gaza, Al Aqsa satellite television channel (in Arabic), June 25, 2009.

54 Interview with Shimon Dotan 2006; *Hot House*, Alma Films, Meimad Barkai production.

55 Judith Miller, op. cit.

56 *Al Quds*, April 7, 2008, quoted by PMW www.pmw.org.il/Bulletins_july2008.html

57 www.tau.ac.il/jcss/haaretz021206.html

58 Tim McGirk, "Palestinian Moms Become Martyrs," *Time*, May 3, 2007.

59 Frimet Roth, "The Once and Future Child Murderer," *The Jerusalem Post*, July 21, 2008.

60 www.metimes.com/2K2/issue2002–4/women/fadlallah_condones_female.htm (accessed November 14, 2003)

61 Ariel Merari et al, op. cit.

62 Judith Miller, op. cit.

63 Other accounts place responsibility with the Nabil Masoud Unit of the Al Aqsa Martyrs' Brigades.

64 Judith Miller, op. cit.

65 Manuela Dviri, "I Wanted to Kill 20, 50 Jews. Yes, even Babies," *Daily Telegraph*, June 25, 2005, www.telegraph.co.uk/news/world-news/middleeast/israel/1492836/My-dream-was-to-be-a-suicide-bomber.-I-wanted-to-kill-20-50-Jews.-Yes-even-babies.html

66 Muhammed Doura was killed at the beginning of the Al ʿAqsa Intifada and became a symbol for the resistance. Recent investigations have questioned whether Doura was killed by the Israelis or accidentally shot by Palestinian police in a crossfire, but the powerful images captured on French TV have become synonymous with the Second Intifada.

67 *Intervue avec la Mère de Wafa Al Bas* (in French), February 20, 2006, You Tube, www.youtube.com/user/Tazda

68 Tim McGirk, op. cit.

69 Barbara Victor, *Army of Roses*, op. cit. p.126.

70 Ibid.

71 Ibid, pp. 129–33.

72 Interview with Shimon Dotan 2006; *Hot House*, Alma Films, Meimad Barkai production.

73 Interview with Barbara Victor cited by Frimet Roth in "The Once and Future Child Murderer," *The Jerusalem Post*, July 21, 2008.

74 Yoram Schweizter, *Dying for Equality*, JCSS Study, 2006, p. 9.

75 Judith Miller, op. cit.

76 International Gay and Lesbian Human Rights Commission (IGLHRC), "Palestinian Women Subjected to Sexual Harassment and Abuse in Detention," June 21, 2002, www.iglhrc.org/cgi-bin/iowa/article/takeaction/globalactionalerts/623.html

77 NGO Alternative Report in Response to the List of Issues and Questions With Regard to the Consideration of Periodic Reports (CEDAW/PSWG/2005/II/CRP.1/Add.7). Israel's Implementation of the U.N. Convention on the Elimination of All Forms of Discrimination Against Women (CEDAW) in the Occupied Palestinian Territories (OPT). May 2005, p. 5.

5 The Future Bombers

1 "Homage to the Black Tigers: A Review of *Sooriya Puthalvargal 2003 Memorial Souvenir*" by Sachi Sri Kantha (Tamil Nation), cited in Tisaranee Gunasekara, "The Inimitable Tiger," *Asian*

Tribune, April 30, 2006, www.asiantribune.com/news/2006/04/30/ inimitable-tiger-0

2 Mia Bloom, "Mother. Sister. Daughter. Bomber," *Bulletin of the Atomic Scientist*, 2005.

3 "Lady with the Poison Flowers," *Outlook*, India, August 29, 2005.

4 http://news.bbc.co.uk/1/hi/world/south_asia/340717.stm and members.tripod.com/~sosl/gandhi.html news.bbc.co.uk/2/hi/south_asia/5122032.stm

5 Allissa Stack O'Connor, "Lions, Tigers and Freedom Birds: How and Why the Liberation Tigers of Tamil Eelam Employs Women," *Terrorism and Political Violence*, vol. 19, Issue 1, March 2007, pp. 43–63.

6 For a full account see Mia Bloom, *Dying to Kill*, op. cit., chapter 3.

7 Interview with the author, personal correspondence, June 2005.

8 David Little, "Religion and Ethnicity," in Robert I. Rotberg, *Creating Peace in Sri Lanka: Civil War and Reconciliation*, Washington, DC: Brookings Institution Press, 1999, p. 45.

9 Stanley J. Tambiah, *Sri Lanka: Ethnic Fratricide and the Dismantling of Democracy*, Delhi, India: Oxford University Press, 1986, p. 78.

10 Ibid, pp. 66–68.

11 Kumari Jayawardena, *Ethnic and Class Conflicts in Sri Lanka*, Madras, India: Kaanthalakam, 1987, p. 14.

12 Passed in 1956 by a margin of 56 to 29. Bandaranaike was assassinated three years later in 1959 by a nationalist dressed as a Buddhist monk, and succeeded by his wife, Sirimavo; Kingsley M. de Silva, *Reaping the Whirlwind*, London: Penguin Books, 1996, p. 58 passim.

13 Neil DeVotta, "Ethno Linguistic Nationalism and Ethnic Conflict in Sri Lanka," in Michael Brown and Sumit Ganguly (eds.), *Fighting Words: Language Policy and Ethnic Relations in Asia,* Belfer Center for Science and Information, JFK School of Government, Cambridge, MA: MIT University Press, 2003, p. 115.

14 David Little, "Religion and Ethnicity," in Robert I. Rotberg, *Creating Peace in Sri Lanka: Civil War and Reconciliation*, Washington, DC: Brookings Institution Press, 1999, p. 48.

15 Kingsley M. de Silva, *Managing Ethnic Tensions in Multi Ethnic Societies*, Lanham, MA: University Press of America, 1986, p. 228.

16 Rohan Gunaratna, *Sri Lanka: A Lost Revolution, The Inside Story of the JVP*, Institute of Fundamental Studies, Sri Lanka, 1990, pp. 92–105; see also Tambiah, op. cit., p. 13.

17 Kingsley M. de Silva (ed.), *Conflict and Violence in South Asia: Bangladesh, India, Pakistan, and Sri Lanka*, Kandy, Sri Lanka: International Centre for Ethnic Studies, 2000, pp. 381–82.

18 Different sources place the formation date of the LTTE between 1972 and 1978. Edgar O'Ballance, *The Cyanide War: Tamil Insurrection in Sri Lanka 1973–88*, London: Brassey's, 1989, pp. 12–17.

19 Bruce Hoffman, *Inside Terrorism*, New York: Columbia University Press, 2006, p. 139.

20 Tambiah, op. cit., pp. 42–43.

21 http://blog.amnestyusa.org/iar/sri-lanka-end-impunity-for-human-rights-violations/ see also, blog.amnestyusa.org/asia/lessons-learnt-or-not-in-sri-lanka

22 The assassination of the SFLP mayor of Jaffna, Alfred Durayappah, by future LTTE leader Velupillai Prabhakaran occurred on July 27, 1975. "This act gave him terrorist standing and prestige, making him the unquestionable leader of his group, and enabled him to formalize the TNT into the broader LTTE." Edgar O'Ballance, *The Cyanide War*, op. cit., p. 13. The Tamil Tigers also claimed responsibility for at least eleven assassinations in 1978, including that of a member of the TULF who had defected to the UNP, as well as a number of policemen.

23 Little in Rotberg, op. cit., p. 51, and Neelan Tiruchelvam in *Autonomy and Ethnicity: Negotiating Competing Claims in Multi Ethnic States*, Yash Ghai, (ed.), Cambridge, UK: Cambridge University Press, 2000, p. 200.

24 Anita Pratap, *Island of Blood: Frontline Reports from Sri Lanka, Afghanistan and Other South Asian Flashpoints*, New York: Putnam Press, 2001, pp. 76–77.

25 H.P. Chattopadhyaya, *Ethnic Unrest in Modern Sri Lanka: An Account of Tamil–Sinhalese Race Relations*, New Delhi: MD Publications, 1994, p. 68.

26 Tamil sources estimated 2000 dead and between 80,000 and 100,000 refugees, who abandoned their homes and were placed in "care and welfare" centers; O'Ballance, op. cit., p. 25.

27 Tambiah, op. cit., pp. 15–16.

28 Kingsley M. de Silva (ed.), *Conflict and Violence in South Asia: Bangladesh, India, Pakistan, and Sri Lanka*, Kandy, Sri Lanka: International Centre for Ethnic Studies, 2000, p. 235 passim.

29 Tambiah, op. cit., p. 27.

30 Elizabeth Nissan, "Some Thoughts on Sinhalese Justifications for the (1983) Violence," in James Manor, (ed.), *Sri Lanka: In Change and in Crisis*, New York, 1984, pp. 176–177, cited in Little, op. cit., p. 51.

31 Chris Smith, "South Asia's Enduring War," in Rotberg, op. cit., p. 17.

32 Interview with the author, Colombo, Sri Lanka, October 28, 2002.

33 H.P. Chattopadhyaya, *Ethnic Unrest in Modern Sri Lanka: An Account of Tamil–Sinhalese Race Relations*, New Delhi, India: MD Publications, 1994, pp. 36, 40 passim. Chris Smith alleges the connection was between the People's Liberation Organization of Tamil Eelam (PLOTE) and Al Fatah; Rotberg, op. cit., p. 32.

34 The LTTE rebuffed several offers from Al Qaeda to share their suicide bombing technology. In interviews with the author they explained, "We did not want to kill Americans."

35 www.lacnet.org/srilanka/issues/kumari.html#a (accessed October 24, 2009)

36 The accord was opposed by Sinhalese fundamentalists in the JVP, according to Kingsley M. de Silva (ed.) in *Conflict and Violence in South Asia*, op. cit., p. 197. The theme of JVP propaganda was the alleged "betrayal of the motherland" which the occupation of part of the country by an alien army was seen to represent. Eventually the Tamil separatists likewise opposed the IPKF, leading to its departure in 1990.

37 K.T. Rajasingham, *Sri Lanka: The Untold Story*, chapter 35; "Accord Turns to Discord," *Asia Times*, n.d., www.atimes.com/ind-pak/ DD13Df02.html

38 Tiruchelvam, op. cit., pp. 199–200.

39 Smith in Rotberg, op. cit. p. 20.

40 Rohan Gunaratna, *Sri Lanka: A Lost Revolution, The Inside Story of the JVP*, Institute of Fundamental Studies, Sri Lanka, 1990, http://nesohr.org/inception-sept2007/human-rights-reports/ StatisticsOnCiviliansAffectedByWar.pdf Chris McDowell, *A Tamil Asylum Diaspora: Sri Lankan Migration, Settlement and Politics in Switzerland (Studies in Forced Migration)*, London: Berghahn Books, 1996, p. 181.

41 Prabhakaran wrote letters dated 12/10/1987, 14/10/1987, and 13/01/1988.

42 "Thamil National Liberation Struggle and National Leader Prabhakaran," chapter 4, *Indo–Thamil Eelam War*, nakkeran.com/ Thalaivar11.htm

43 Darini Rajasingham-Sananyake, in Robert Rotberg, *Creating Peace in Sri Lanka*, op. cit., p. 62.

44 Charu Lata Joshi, "Sri Lanka Suicide Bombers," *Far Eastern Economic Review*, June 1, 2000, www.feer.com/_0006_01/ p64currents.html (accessed November 26, 2003)

45 Little in Rotberg, op. cit.

46 Adele Ann, *Women Fighters of the Liberation Tigers*, Jaffna, Sri Lanka: Thasan Publication Department of the LTTE, January 1, 1993, p. 17.

47 Prabhakaran quote provided by Tamil sources. Personal correspondence, September 2008.

48 Peter Schalk, "On the Sacrificial Ideology of the Liberation Tigers," 1993. www.tamilnation.org/ltte/93schalk.htm

49 Peter Schalk, "Resistance and Martyrdom in the Process of State Formation of Tamililam," Joyce Pettigrew (ed.), *Martyrdom and Political Resistance*, Amsterdam, Netherlands: 1997 pp. 61–83.

50 Alex Perry, "How Sri Lanka's Rebels Build a Suicide Bomber," *Time*, May 12, 2006, www.time.com/time/world/article/0,8599,1193862,00.html/#ixzz0zJltxVrG

51 Neloufer de Mel, "The Body Politics, (Re)presenting the Female Suicide Bomber in Sri Lanka," citing M.R.N. Swamy, *Inside an Elusive Mind: Prabhakaran*, Fremont, CA: Literate World, 2003, pp. 243–44.

52 Adele Ann, *Women Fighters of the Liberation Tigers*, op. cit., p. ii.

53 Tamil sources, personal correspondence with the author, November 26, 2003.

54 Frances Harrison, "Up Close with the Tamil Tigers," *BBC World*, January 29, 2002, http://news.bbc.co.uk/2/hi/south_asia/1789503.stm

55 Charu Lata Joshi, "Sri Lanka Suicide Bombers," *Far Eastern Economic Review*, June 1, 2000.

56 Beate Arnestad interview with Darshika and Puhalchudar in the film *My Daughter the Terrorist: Black Tiger Suicide Cadres Tell Their Story*, 2008.

57 Ibid.

58 Ibid.

59 John Horgan, *The Psychology of Terrorism*, London: Routledge, 2005.

60 Beate Arnestad interview, op. cit.

61 Ibid.

62 Alex Perry, "How Sri Lanka's Rebels Build a Suicide Bomber," *Time*, May 12, 2006, www.time.com/time/world/article/0,8599,1193862,00.html

63 LTTE statement issued in December 2007 after the aerial bombardment and targeted assassination of second-in-command Tamilchelvam.

64 Beate Arnestad interview, op. cit.

65 Sachi Sri Kanthi, "Homage to the Black Tigers," www.tamilnation.org/ltte/black_tigers/index.htm

66 Beate Arnestad interview, op. cit.

67 Ibid.

68 Ibid.

69 Ibid.

70 *New York Times*, May 29, 1995.

71 Beate Arnestad interview, op. cit.

72 www.tamilnation.org/ltte/vp/070423us.htm

73 Jan Goodwin, "When the Suicide Bomber Is a Woman," *Marie Claire* magazine, www.marieclaire.com/world-reports/news/international/female-suicide-bomber

74 "At the time, each family living under LTTE control was required to provide a child to the separatist forces fighting for an independent Tamil homeland for three decades." "Former Female Fighters Strive for Better Life," *Daily Times*, September 30, 2010, http://www.dailytimes.com.pk/default.asp?page=2010%5C09%5C30%5Cstory_30-9-2010_pg20_9.

75 Jan Goodwin, op. cit.

76 Ibid.

77 Ibid.

78 Ibid

79 Ibid.

80 Ibid.

81 Ibid.

82 According to Tamil sources, and the LTTE's Peace Secretariat.

83 www.island.lk/2007/06/10/news13.html

84 Tamil Guardian, "Admired Female LTTE Leader Killed in Battle," June 4, 2008, p. 13.

6 The Crucial Links

1 http://us.detiknews.com/read/2008/10/23/150550/1024886/10/paridah-abas-bungkam-usai-besuk-muklas

2 Paridah Abas, *orang bilang ayah teroris,* Jakarta: Jazeera Abas, 2004, p. 87.

3 Kelly McEvers, "The Terrorist's Wife," *Slate*, October 31, 2005, http://audiojournal.com/paridah.html

4 Paridah Abas, *orang bilang ayah teroris,* op. cit., p. 99.

5 International Crisis Group, *Jemaah Islamiya in South East Asia: Damaged but Still Dangerous*, ICG Report no. 63, August 26, 2003, p. 32.

6 Agence France Presse, March 17, 2003.

7 Kelly McEvers, *Straits Times*, January 19, 2004.

8 The Indonesian *Ikhwan' ul-Muslimin* began in the mid-1980s and derived most of its ideas, tactics, and practices from the *Ikhwan Al Muslimun* movement in Egypt. The Indonesian *Ikhwan* was comprised mostly of student returnees from Egypt and other Arab countries. R.P. Mitchell, *The Society of the Muslim Brothers*, Oxford: Oxford University Press, 1969, and *Ikhwan Al Muslimin: Inspirasi Gerakan Tarbiyyah*, in *Suara Hidayatullah*, Jakarta, August 2001, cited by Farish A. Noor, "Women in the Service of the Jundullah: The Case of Women Supporters of the Jama'ah Islamiya of Indonesia," paper for the workshop on "Female Suicide Bombers and Europe" organized by the International Institute for Strategic Studies (IISS), Arundel House, London, March 12, 2007.

9 S.Q. Fatimi, *Islam Comes to Malaysia*, Malaysian Sociological Research Institute (MSRI), Singapore. 1963; see also Norani Othman and Virginia Matheson Hooker (eds.), *Islam Society and Politics*, Institute of Southeast Asian Studies, 2003.

10 Noor, op. cit.

11 Sidney Jones, interview with the author, December 16, 2009.

12 International Crisis Group, *Jemaah Islamiya in South East Asia*, op. cit., p. 2.

13 Maria A. Reesa, *Seeds of Terror: An Eyewitness Account of Al Qaeda's Newest Center of Operations in Southeast Asia*, New York: Free Press, 2003.

14 www.historycommons.org/entity.jsp?entity=noralwizah_lee_binti_abdullah_1

15 Deborah Snow, "Race for Hambali's Secrets," *Sydney Morning Herald*, August 16, 2003, www.smh.com.au/articles/2003/08/15/10 60936061339.html

16 Arabinda Acharya, *The Bali Bombings: Impact on Southeast Asia*. Center for Eurasian Policy, Occasional Research Paper, Series II, no. 2. p.1.

17 Marc Sageman, *Understanding Terror Networks*, Philadelphia: PA: University of Pennsylvania Press, 2004, p. 91.

18 Malhadi, "Konsep Jihad Jemaah Islamiyah" ("JI's Concept of Jihad"). Surabaya, *Suara Hidaytulah*, September 1, 2009.

19 U.S. District Court for the Eastern District of Virginia, Alexandria Division, 3/8/2006 court transcripts. Sufaat's company Green Laboratory Medicine SDN BHD purchased four tons of ammonium nitrate (four times as much the amount used in the Oklahoma City bombing), which has never been located. Simon Elegant, "Untangling the Web," *Time*, January 28, 2002, www.time.com/time/asia/news/magazine/0,9754,197713,00.html

20 AP, "Family Ties Bind Muslim Militants Together," *Taipei Times*, September 3, 2003, p. 5.

21 Christopher S. Bond, "Indonesia and the Changing Front in the War on Terrorism," Heritage Foundation Lectures, no. 875, April 28, 2005.

22 Rohan Gunaratna, "The Links That Bind Terror Groups," *The Guardian*, October 15, 2002.

23 Kelly McEvers, "The Terrorist's Wife," op. cit.

24 William M. Wise, *Indonesia's War on Terror*. USINDO United States Indonesia Society, August 2005, www.usindo.org/publications/reports/pdf/WarOnTerror.pdf (p. 3).

25 Samudra has multiple aliases, including Qudama and Abdul Aziz.

26 Imama Samudra, *Aku Melawan Teroris* ("I Fight the Terrorists"), cited by Acharya, op. cit., p. 2.

27 Kelly McEvers, "The Terrorist's Wife," op. cit.

28 DHS profile of Huda bin Abdul Haq (Mukhlas) Global Security, www.globalsecurity.org/security/profiles/huda_bin_abdul_haq.htm

29 The two hotels were hit simultaneously by suicide bombers who had assembled their bombs in the guest rooms.

30 Anthony L. Smith, "The Politics of Negotiating the Terrorist Problem in Indonesia," *Studies in Conflict and Terrorism* 28:1, January 2005, pp. 33–44.

31 Between 2003 and 2005 JI suffered from internal fractures, with some members calling for a more sectarian-centered approach while others argued for attacks against the Indonesian government and Western targets. JI pursued both strategies. Documents captured during a police raid showed that sectarian violence is in fact central to JI tactics.

32 "CIA, Mossad Infiltrated Muslim Organizations," *The Daily*, Pakistan, December 28, 2008, www.daily.pk/world/middleeast/ cia_mossad_infiltrated_muslim_organizations.html

33 Estimates of JI membership vary from two hundred to several thousand members at the time of the Bali bombings. However, most sources tend to agree that JI has a membership of around five hundred.

34 "Jemaah Islamiya Declared Terrorist Organization, Alleged Military Chief Given 15 years," AP, *Jakarta Post*, April 21, 2008, www.the jakartapost.com/news/2008/04/21/jemaah-islamiya-declared- terrorist-organization-alleged-military-chief-given-15-years

35 Sally Neighbour, *The Mother of Mohammed: An Australian Woman's Extraordinary Journey into Jihad*, Melbourne, Australia: Melbourne University Press, 2009, pp. 148–59.

36 In 1982 Abu Bakar Ba'asyir opened a Madrassa in Johor, Malaysia. During this time JI began to court the support of other Southeast Asia Islamists who had gone to Afghanistan as mujahideen. Members of the Afghan Mujahideen International Brigade made up the first rank and file of the organization. Zachary Abuza, *Militant Islam in Southeast Asia: Crucible of Terror*, Boulder, CO: Lynne Rienner, 2003, and Greg Barton, *Jamaah Islamiya: Radical Islam in Indonesia*, Singapore: National University of Singapore (NUS), 2005.

37 Kelly McEvers, "The Terrorist's Wife," op. cit.

38 Sally Neighbour, op,cit. p.158.

39 Carlyle A. Thayer, "Leadership Dynamics in Terrorist Organizations in Southeast Asia," Centre for Defence Leadership Studies, 3/2005, April 2005, p. 18.

40 Elena Pavlova, "From Counter-Society to Counter-State: Jemaah Islamiya According to PUPJI," Working Paper, no. 117, Institute of Defence and Strategic Studies, Singapore, November 14, 2006, p. 2.

41 Ibid., p. 6. The oath of allegiance, or *bay'ah*, can only be given to the leader of all of the Muslims, and it is given by the decision makers— i.e., the scholars and people of virtue and status. It is not intended to be a form of personal allegiance to an individual terrorist-cell leader.

42 The chain of transmission for the Hadith was: Al Hakim narrated it in the Mustadrak (1:116, 177) with a sound (sahih) chain as well as Tirmidhi (gharib) #2256, Cairo ed. 'Aridat Al Ahwadhi (11:9). See www.sunnah.org/fiqh/usul/ijma.htm

43 Muhammed Salih Al Munajid, "Did Shaikh Muhammad ibn 'Abd Al Wahhaab rebel against the Othmani Caliphate and what was the reason for its fall?" www.islamqa.com

44 Interview with the author, December 16, 2009. Top and Azahari created the Banten Ring, which was a precursor to their violent JI splinter.

45 Interview in Jakarta, name withheld, July 2007.

46 Sally Neighbour, op. cit., p. 157.

47 Interview in Jakarta Prison, 2005, Noor Huda Ismail, cited in "Al Qaeda's Southeast Asia, Jemaah Islamiya and Regional Terrorism: Kinship and Family Links," *Japan Focus*.

48 Scott Atran, "A Chilling Message for the Infidels," *The First Post*, June 18, 2006; BBC News, "Profile: Abu Bakar Ba'asyir," June 14, 2006, news.bbc.co.uk/2/hi/asia-pacific/2339693.stm

49 "Ba'asyir: Indonesia Hrus Kirim Psukan" ("Ba'asyir: Indonesia to Send Troops"), *Hizbut Tahrir*, Jakarta, November 2, 2009.

50 Arabinda Acharya, "The Bali Bombings: Impact on Southeast Asia," op. cit., p. 5.

51 Author interview with John Horgan, Jakarta, June 2007.

52 David Montero, "In Her Boarding Schools, Lily Munir Teaches Women and Children Their Religion Supports Gender Equality," *Christian Science Monitor*, October 28, 2008.

53 Renier Hendrik Van Der Merwe, "Jemaah Islamiya—Critical Discussion of Tactics and Threats," *NewsBlaze*, November 22, 2009, newsblaze.com/story/20091122185010iiis.nb/topstory.html

54 His aliases include Mukhlas and Huda bin Abdul Haq.

55 Farish A. Noor, "Women in the Service of the Jundullah," op. cit.

56 Kelly McEvers, "The Women of Jemaah Islamiah," BBC, *East Asia Today*, January 10, 2004.

57 Ibid.

58 "Jemaah Islamiyyah in South East Asia: Damaged but Still Dangerous," International Crisis Group (ICG) Report. August 26, 2003, p. 2; see also Wong Chun Wei and Lourdes Charles, "More Than 100 marriages Involve Key JI Members," *The Star Online*, September 7, 2004, www.thestar.com.my/news/list. asp?file=/2004/9/7/nation/8791437&sec=focus

59 Noor Huda Ismail, "Al Qaeda's Southeast Asia, Jamaah Islamiyah and Regional Terrorism: Kinship and Family Links," *Japan Focus*, January 19, 2007.

60 Noor Huda Ismail, *Understanding How Jihadis in Indonesia Rejuvenate Themselves*, paper for the IRRI-KIIB conference, Brussels, March 30, 2006, p. 7.

61 Her aliases include Acang, Lee Yen Lan, and Awi.

62 Hambali is in extrajudicial detention in a Guantánamo Bay detainment camp in Cuba.

63 Ken Conboy, *The Second Front: Inside Jemaah Islamiya, Asia's Most Dangerous Terrorist Network*, London: Equinox, 2005, pp. 55–56 and "Highly Covert U.S.-Thai Operation Nabbed Hambali," International Regional Security Agency, www.irs-agency.us/recent_captures.htm

64 Marc Sageman, *Understanding Terror Networks*, Philadelphia, PA: University of Pennsylvania Press, 2004, p. 113.

65 Zainah Anwar, *Islamic Revivalism in Malaysia: Dakwah among the Students*, Kuala Lumpur: Pelanduk Press, 1987; Lenore Manderson, *Women, Politics and Change: The Kaum Ibu UMNO of Malaysia 1945–1972*, Oxford: Oxford University Press, 1980.

66 Noor, op. cit.

67 Interview with Sidney Jones, December 2009.

68 Sally White, "The Wives of Noordin Top, "*Inside Indonesia*, 2009, www.insideindonesia.org/content/view/1254/47

69 E-mail correspondence with Sally White, December 17, 2009.

70 Abdul Khalik, "Noordin's Wife Privy to Terror Plans: Police Source," *Jakarta Post*, October 11, 2004.

71 Sally White, "The Wives of Noordin Top," op. cit.

72 Sally Neighbour, op. cit., pp. 173–74.

73 BBC World, "Al Qaeda's Surf Chick," August 13, 2009, www.bbc.co.uk/worldservice/programmes/2009/08/090804_outlook_rabiah_hutchinson.shtml

74 Tom Allard and Cynthia Banham, "ASIO Took Mum's Passport of Terror Suspects," *Sydney Morning Herald,* November 3, 2006.

75 "Jemaah Islamiya Recruiting Women for Bombing Missions," ABS–CBN News, July 13, 2007.

76 Simon Elegant, "Untangling the Web," *Time*, January 28, 2002, www.time.com/time/world/article/0,8599,197713,00.html

77 Renier Hendrik Van Der Merwe, "*Jemaah Islamiya—Critical Discussion of Tactics and Threats,"* NewsBlaze*, November 22, 2009 http://newsblaze.com/story/20091122185010iiis.nb/topstory.html

78 Zoe Murphy and Yoki Sari, "Bali Bomber Ali Imron Becomes Comic Book Character," BBC News, August 6, 2010, www.bbc.co.uk/news/world-asia-pacific-10893889

79 Ibid.

7 The Recruiters and Propagandists

1 "Al Qaeda's Stance on Women Sparks Extremist Debate," Associated Press, May 31, 2008, www.nytimes.com/aponline/world/AP-Al-Qaidas-Women.html?pagewanted=print.

2 Canadian Embassy of Afghanistan, Bulletin 2031, Afghan News 06/01/2008, www.afghanemb-canada.net/en/news_bulletin/2008/june/01/index.php.

3 Interview with the author (name withheld), January 2010.

4 French senior counter-terrorism magistrate Jean-Louis Bruguière, quoted in *The New York Times*, May 28, 2008, www.covenentzone. blogspot.com

5 CNN "One Woman's War," Part 1, http://edition.cnn.com/video/#/video/international/2009/02/10/wus.one.womans.war.bk.b.cnn

6 Marie Rose Armesto, *Groot Bijgaarden de Standaard*, December 22, 2007.

7 CNN, "One Woman's War," op. cit.

8 On May 12, 2009, Ayachi was charged with being the leader of a logistical support team for Al Qaeda in Europe. Wiretaps suggested his involvement in a plot against Charles de Gaulle Airport in Paris.

9 Mark Eeckhaut, "Bastin's Muslim Elite," *Groot Bijgaarden De Standaard*, November 23, 2004.

10 Malika, veuve du Moujahid Shahid (Insha'Allah) Dahmane Abdessater (RA), *Les Soldats de la Lumière*. 2003 available at www. archive.org/details/lumiere_580

11 Neil J. Kressel, "When Moderate Religion Fails: Some Social and Psychological Roots of Extremist Faith," paper presented at the 30th Annual Scientific Meeting of the International Society of Political Psychology, Portland Oregon, July 6, 2007, p. 4.

12 CNN, "One Woman's War," op. cit.

13 *Wall Street Journal*, September 11, 2002; *Los Angeles Times*, September 11, 2002.

14 Lawrence Wright, "My Trip to Al Qaeda." HBO Documentaries, September 7, 2010.

15 Sid Ahmed Hammouche, La Prison pour Malika el Aroud, icone D'Al Qaeda en Europe, Rue 89, La Liberte, May 11, 2010, www. rue89.com/2010/05/11la-prison-pour-malika-el-aroud-icone-dal-qaeda-en-europe-150963

16 Stephen Wright, "Woman Who Preached Jihad on the Internet Charged with Five Other al Qaeda Militants Over Plot to Kill EU Leaders," *Mail Online*, December 12, 2008.

17 Scott Stewart, STRATFOR, the Curious Case of Adlène Hicheur, ee-online, www.stratfor.com; www.eesti.ca/?op=article& articleid= 25664

18 Nic Robertson, "Belgian Al Qaeda Cell Linked to 2006 airline plot," CNN, www.cnn.com/2009/WORLD/europe/02/10/belgium.terror/ index.html "Alerta en la Inteligencia europea ante posibles nuevos atentados de Al Qaeda en Francia y Bruselas," May 16, 2009, http://globedia.com/alerta-inteligencia-europea-posible-atentado-qaeda-francia-brusela

19 Cited by Paul Cruickshank, "Love in the Time of Terror," *Marie Claire* magazine, May 18, 2009.

20 CNN, "One Woman's War," op. cit.

21 Elaine Sciolino and Souad Mekhennet, "Al Qaeda Warrior Uses Internet to Rally Women," *New York Times*, May 28, 2008, www. nytimes.com/2008/05/28/world/europe/28terror.html

22 Malika el Aroud's signature line from her jihadi website, www. minbar-sos.com

23 Malika el Aroud, www.minbar-sos.com, December 13, 2007.

24 Malika el Aroud, *Les Soldats de la Lumière*.

25 Panorama Program, *Al Arabiyah* television, December 16, 2008.

26 Claude Moniquet, president of the Brussels-based European Strategic Intelligence and Security Center, cited by Elaine Sciolino and Souad Mekhennet, "Al Qaeda Warrior Uses Internet to Rally Women," *New York Times*, op. cit.

27 CNN, One Woman's War, op. cit.

28 Sciolino and Mekhennet, op. cit.

29 "European Gang Trained for Terror," CNN, July 31, 2009, http:// edition.cnn.com/2009/CRIME/07/30/robertson.al.qaeda.europe/ index.html

30 "8 jar cel voor Malika el Aroud," (8-year sentence for Malika el Aroud), DeMorgen.be, Belgium, May 10, 2010, www.demorgen.be/

dm/nl/989/Binnenland/article/detail/1104029/2010/05/10/8-jaar-cel-voor-Malika-El-Aroud.dhtml

31 David Cook, "Women Fighting Jihad?" *Studies in Conflict and Terrorism*, vol. 28, pp. 375–84, p. 375.

32 "Milanese Wife Converts to Islam for Love," *La Stampa*, Milan, November 14, 2003, http://archivio.lastampa.it/LaStampaArchivio/main/History/tmpl_viewObj.jsp?objid=4841320

33 http://media.nbcphiladelphia.com/documents/JihadJane.pdf

34 "Al Qaeda puts bounties on heads of Swedes," AFP, in *The Local*, September 15, 2007, www.thelocal.se/8498/20070915

35 "Al Khansa'a, Poetess of Courage and Pride," *Arab News,* 5/27/1998, www.arabicnews.com/ansub/Daily/Day/980527/1998052703.html

36 Javid Hassan, "Women Come Out Against Extremist Internet Magazine," *Arabic News*, September 7, 2004, http://archive.arabnews.com/?page=1&section=0&article=51115&d=7&m=9&y=2004

37 Quoted in Loch Johnson, *Strategic Intelligence,* vol. 1, London: Praeger Security International, 2006, p. 173.

38 Farhana Ali, "Rising Female Bombers in Iraq, An Alarming Trend," http://counterterrorismblog.org/2008/04/rising_female_bombers_in_iraq.php

39 Interviews with Iraqi war veterans, USMC, and Special Forces, November 2009.

40 Craig S. Smith, "Raised as Catholic in Belgium, She Died as a Muslim Bomber," *New York Times*, December 6, 2005, www.nytimes.com/2005/12/06/international/europe/06brussels.html?_r=1&th&emc=th

41 Anthony Browne and Rory Watson, "The girl who went from baker's assistant to Baghdad bomber," *The Times,* December 2, 2005, www.timesonline.co.uk/tol/news/world/iraq/article744833.ece

42 Paul Wilkinson, "Zarqawi's Death and the Iraqi Insurgency," National Public Radio, www.npr.org/templates/story/story.php?storyId=5459914

43 Interviews with the author, Fort Bragg, 2007.

44 "Increase in Female Bombers Raises Concern," CBS News, January 4, 2008, www.cbsnews.com/stories/2008/01/04/iraq/main3677485.shtml

45 *Al Arabiya* Television, July 29, 2008.

46 Farhana Ali, op. cit.

47 "Iraqi TV Broadcasts Statements of Women who Reportedly Attacked Checkpoint," Fox News, April 4, 2003, www.foxnews.com/story/0,2933,83169,00.html

48 Mia Bloom, "Female Suicide Bombers: A Global Trend," *Daedalus* (Winter 2007), p. 7.

49 "Sisters in Jihad," www.iraqi-alamal.org/Doc/somaya.pdf

50 Aqeel Hussein and Damien McElroy, "Mother of All Suicide Bombers Warns of Rise in Attacks," *Daily Telegraph*, November 15, 2008, www.telegraph.co.uk/news/worldnews/middleeast/iraq/3464411/Mother-of-all-suicide-bombers-warns-of-rise-in-attacks.html

51 Uthman al Mukhtar, "Al Arab Opens the File of Female Suicide Bombers in the Land of the Two Rivers," *Al Arab* Online, Doha, June 25, 2008.

52 Farhana Ali, op. cit.

53 *Al Arabiya* Television, July 29, 2008.

54 *Al Arabiya* Television, "The Death Industry," October 3, 2008.

55 In one recent story she was referred to as Rania Al Anbaki. Ali Mohammed, "Would be suicide bomber recalls failed mission." ICR Issue 348, August 5, 2010, http://iwpr.net/report-news/would-be-suicide-bomber-recalls-failed-mission

56 Muhammed Al Tammimi, "Concern Over the Kidnapping of Girls for Use in Suicide Attacks," *Al Hayah*, London, October 10, 2008.

57 Niqash article, "Sumaya, A Fortunate Iraqi Female Suicide Bomber Among Al Qaida's Women," *Awan*, Kuwait, August 23, 2008.

58 Khoulud Ramzi, "Sumaya Reluctant Suicide Bomber," August 12, 2008, www.iraqi-alamal.org/Doc/somya.pdf also at www.niqash.org/content.php?contentTypeID=75&id=2275&lang=0

59 *Al Arabiya* Television, July 6, 2008.

60 Several Halliburton employees (e.g., Jaime Lee Jones) are claiming to have been raped by U.S. soldiers. Also, many of the returning soldiers have come home with post-traumatic stress disorder, which has resulted in an upsurge of domestic violence, suicide, and killing of spouses. The 4th Infantry's Second Battalion (the "Lethal Warriors") have had eight members accused of murder or attempted murder since 2007. Upon his return from Iraq, one soldier from the company, Robert Marko Hull, raped and slit the throat of a nineteen-year-old learning-disabled woman. See Tim McGirk, "The Hell of PTSD," *Time,* November 30, 2009, pp. 41–43.

61 In Algeria, Al Qaeda-affiliated groups have had male recruits raped to prepare them to be suicide bombers. Intense social stigma and fear of more gay sex attacks leaves Muslims prepared to die. According to news reports, there was a large tear in the terrorist's anus to confirm the allegations of sexual abuse. One of the young terrorists was aged twenty-two, from Diar El Djemaâ, El Harrach, and was supposed to execute a suicide operation in the region of Boumerdes. "Al Qaeda accused of using male rape to 'create' suicide bombers," *Pink News,* February 4, 2009, www.pinknews.co.uk/news/articles/2005-11023.html

62 Steven Lee Myers, "Iraq Arrests Woman Tied to Bombings," *New York Times*, February 4, 2009.

63 Ibid.

64 "16 Killed as Veiled Female Bomber Hits Police Station," *Kuwaiti Times*, April 11, 2007, www.kuwaittimes.net/read_news.php?newsid=NDI2MTY1NTE2

65 Islamic Front for Iraqi Resistance, JAMI, August 8, 2008.

66 *Al Arabiyah* Television, July 6, 2008.

67 The name derives from the *Qur'an*—Asma, Abu Bakr's daughter and Aisha's sister, cut a piece of cloth from her waist belt and tied the mouth of the leather bag with it; she tore it in two and gave one piece to the Prophet Muhammed (PBUH). For that reason she was named *dhat al nitaqayn,* the "One with Two Waist Belts."

68 Kaishan al Bayati, "Supervision Is Tightened against Women; Officials Fear Female Suicide Bombers in Baghdad," *Al Arab* online, Doha, June 25, 2008.

69 Lawrence Wright, *The Looming Tower: Al Qaeda and the Road to 9/11*, New York: Knopf, 2006; see also Steve Coll, *The Bin Ladens: An Arabian Family in the American Century*, New York: Penguin, 2008.

70 "Women plead with Al Qaeda to join jihad: report." *Al Arabiya*, June 2, 2008, www.alarabiya.net/articles/2008/06/02/50858.html.

71 Umayma Al Zawahiri, "Risalat illah al Akhawat al Muslimat" (Letter to my Muslim Sisters), www.jihadica.com/wp-content/uploads/2010/02/umayma-al-zawahiri-risala-jan-2010.pdf. See also Nelly Lahoud, "Umayma Al Zawahiri on Women's Role in Jihad," February 26, 2010, the-real-islam.org/forum/viewtopic.php?f=6&t=315

72 Bin Ladin, www.tawhed.ws/pr?i=7839

73 *9/11 Commission Report: Final Report of the National Commission of Terrorist Attacks Upon the United States,* New York: W.W. Norton, 2004.

74 www.forsanelhaq.com/showthread.php?t=49656 (p. 27).

75 Nelly Lahoud, *The Jihadis Path to Self-destruction*, New York: Columbia University Press, 2010.

76 "Martyr Operations: A Means of Jihad," Bayynat, the website of the religious authority Sayyid Muhammed Hussein Fadlallah, http://english.bayynat.org.lb/news/martyr.htm

77 Islam on-Line, Ask a Scholar, Dr. 'Abdel Fattah Idrees, professor of Comparative Jurisprudence, Al Azhar University, "Muslim Women Participating in Jihad," www.islamonline.net/servlet/Satellite?pagename=IslamOnline-English-Ask_Scholar/FatwaE/FatwaE&cid=1119503544310

78 Annette Ramelsberger, "Converted to Female Warrior," *Sueddeutsche Zeitung*, Munich, June 1, 2006.

79 "Fatwa of Doctor Yusuf al Qaradawi regarding the employment of women in Martyrdom operations" www.palestine-info.info/arabic/fatawa/alamaliyat/qaradawi1.htm

80 Forum posted on a jihadi website by the UK-based cleric Hani al Siba'i, August 1, 2008.

81 Dr. Muhammed al Habash, *Al Thawrah*, Damascus, May 8, 2009.

8 The Four Rs plus One

1 Peter Bergen, "The Battle for Tora Bora: How Osama bin Laden Slipped from Our Grasp: The Definitive Account," *The New Republic*, December 22, 2009.

2 Jessica Stern, "When Bombers Are Women," *Washington Post*, December 18, 2003.

3 Author interviews with U.S. Marines deployed in Diyala Province 2006–2007, names withheld for security reasons, November 2009.

4 Eric Schechter, "Where Have All the Bombers Gone?" *The Jerusalem Post*, August 9, 2004.

5 Michael J. Mazarr, Review of Assaf Moghadam's *The Globalization of Martyrdom*, *Perspectives on Politics*, vol. 7, Issue 4, December 2009, p. 992.

6 Clara Beyler, "Using Palestinian Women as Bombs," *New York Sun*, November 15, 2006.

7 Anat Berko and Edna Erez, "Gender, Palestinian Women, and Terrorism: Women's Liberation or Oppression?" *Studies in Conflict and Terrorism*, vol. 30, Issue 6, June 2007, pp. 493–519.

8 Ibid.

9 "Taliban Puts Afghan Boy in Suicide Vest," *USA Today*, www.usatoday.com/news/world/2007-06-25-afghan-boy-bomber_N.htm

10 David Montero, "In Her Boarding Schools, Lily Munir Teaches Women and Children Their Religion Supports Gender Equality," *Christian Science Monitor*, October 28, 2008.

SELECT BIBLIOGRAPHY

Adele Ann, *Women Fighters of the Liberation Tigers*. Publications Section of the LTTE, January 1, 1993.

Amnesty International, Chechnya—a report to the Council of Europe. AI Index: EUR 46/001/2001, http://asiapacific.amnesty.org/library/Index/ENGEUR460012001?open&of=ENG-366

Scott Atran, "Genesis and Future of Suicide Terrorism." *Interdisciplines*, 2003, www.interdisciplines.org/terrorism/papers/1/6; see also *Science* 7, March 2003, vol. 299. no. 5612, pp. 1534–39.

Anat Berko, *The Path to Paradise: The Inner World of Suicide Bombers and their Dispatchers*. New York: Praeger, 2007.

Anat Berko and Edna Erez, "Gender, Palestinian Women, and Terrorism: Women's Liberation or Oppression?" *Studies in Conflict and Terrorism*, vol. 30, issue 6, June 2007, pp. 493–519.

Clara Beyler, "Using Palestinian Women as Bombs," *New York Sun*, November 15, 2006.

Mia Bloom, *Dying to Kill: the Allure of Suicide Terror*. New York: Columbia University Press, 2005, chapter 1.

———, "Female Suicide Bombers: A Global Trend." *Daedalus*, Winter 2007.

———, "Mother. Sister. Daughter. Bomber." *Bulletin of the Atomic Scientist*, 2005.

Mia Bloom and John Horgan, "Missing Their Mark: The IRA's Proxy Bomb Campaign." *Social Research: An International Quarterly*, vol. 75, no. 2, Summer 2008.

CNN "One Woman's War," Part 1. http://edition.cnn.com/video/#/video/international/2009/02/10/wus.one.womans.war.bk.b.cnn

David Cook, *Understanding and Addressing Suicide Attacks: The Faith and Politics of Martyrdom Operations*. Santa Barbara, CA: Praeger, 2007.

———, *Understanding Jihad*. Berkeley, CA: University of California Press, 2005.

———, "Women Fighting Jihad?" *Studies in Conflict and Terrorism*, vol. 28, pp. 375–84.

Mary Corcoran, *Out of Order: The Political Imprisonment of Women in Northern Ireland 1972–1998*. Devon, UK: Willan Publishing, 2006.

Kim Cragin and Sara A. Daly, *Women as Terrorists: Mothers, Recruiters and Martyrs*. Santa Barbara, CA: Praeger, 2009.

Martha Crenshaw, *Explaining Terrorism: Causes, Processes and Consequences*. London: Rputledge, 2010.

Paul Cruickshank, "Love in the Time of Terror." *Marie Claire*, May 18, 2009.

Karla J. Cunningham, "Cross-Regional Trends in Female Terrorism." *Studies in Conflict and Terrorism*, Vol. 26, Issue 3, May 2003, pp. 171–195.

Margareta D'Arcy, *Tell Them Everything: A Sojourn in the Prison of HMS Queen Elizabeth II at Ard Macha (Armagh)*. London: Pluto Press, 1981.

Joyce Davis, *Martyrs: Innocence, Vengeance, and Despair in the Middle East*. New York: Palgrave Macmillan, 2004.

Bernadette Devlin, *The Price of My Soul*. London: Pan Books, 1969.

Adam Dolnik and Keith M. Fitzgerald, *Negotiating Hostage Crises with the New Terrorists*. Santa Barbara, CA: Praeger, 2007.

Paige Whaley Eager, *From Freedom Fighters to Terrorists*. London: Ashgate, 2008.

Richard English, *Armed Struggle: A History of the IRA*. New York: Oxford University Press, 2003.

David Fromkin, *A Peace to End All Peace: The Fall of the Ottoman Empire and the Creation of the Modern Middle East*. New York: Owl Books, 1989 (reprinted by Holt, 2001 and 2009).

Diego Gambetta, *Making Sense of Suicide Missions*. New York: Oxford University Press, 2006.

James Gelvin, *The Israeli–Palestine Conflict: One Hundred Years of War*. New York: Cambridge University Press, 2005.

Paul Gill, *Marketing Martyrdom: The Political Psychology of Suicide Bombings*. Forthcoming, Philadelphia: University of Pennsylvania Press .

Jan Goodwin, "When the Suicide Bomber Is a Woman." *Marie Claire*, September 2007, www.marieclaire.com/world-reports/news/international/female-suicide-bomber

Viv Groskop, "Women at the Heart of Terror Cells," *The Guardian*, September 5, 2004, www.guardian.co.uk/world/2004/sep/05/russia.chechnya1

Sara Helm, "The Human Time Bomb. What Motivates a Suicide Bombing?" *Sunday Times Magazine*, January 6, 2002.

Bruce Hoffman, *Inside Terrorism*. New York: Columbia University Press, 2006.

John Horgan, *Divided We Stand: The Strategy and Psychology of Ireland's Dissident Terrorists*. Forthcoming, New York: Oxford University Press, 2011.

———, *The Psychology of Terrorism*. London: Routledge, 2005.

International Crisis Group, *Jemaah Islamiya in South East Asia: Damaged but Still Dangerous*. ICG Report no. 63, August 26, 2003.

Alison Jamieson, *The Heart Attacked: Terrorism and Conflict in the Italian State*. London: Marion Boyars, 1989.

Nelly Lahoud, *The Jihadis Path to Self-destruction*. New York: Columbia University Press, 2010.

Seán Mac Stíofáin, *Memoirs of a Revolutionary*. London: Gordon Cremonesi, 1975(second edition, Free Ireland Book Club, 1979).

Raymond McClean, *The Road to Bloody Sunday*. Derry, Northern Ireland: Guildhall Press, 1983.

Eileen McDonald, *Shoot the Women First*. New York: Random House, 1992.

Ariel Merari, *Driven to Death: Psychological and Social Aspects to Suicide Terrorism*. New York: Oxford University Press, 2010.

Judith Miller, "The Bomb Under the Abaya," *Policy Review*, Hoover Institution, June–July 2007.

Assaf Moghadam, *The Globalization of Martyrdom: Al Qaeda, Salafi Jihad, and the Diffusion of Suicide Attacks*. Baltimore, MD, Johns Hopkins University Press, 2008.

Sally Neighbour, *The Mother of Mohammed: An Australian Woman's Extraordinary Journey into Jihad*. Philadelphia: University of Pennsylvania Press, 2010.

Edgar O'Ballance, *The Cyanide War: Tamil Insurrection in Sri Lanka 1973–88*. London: Brassey's, 1989.

Alisa Stack O'Connor, "Lions, Tigers and Freedom Birds: How and Why the Liberation Tigers of Tamil Eelam Employs Women." *Terrorism and Political Violence*, vol. 19, Issue 1, March 2007, pp. 43–63.

Ami Pedahzur, *Suicide Terrorism*. Cambridge, UK: Polity Books, 2004.

Anna Politkovskaya, *A Small Corner of Hell: Dispatches from Chechnya*, translated by Alexander Burry and Tatiana Tulchinsky. Chicago: University of Chicago Press, 2003.

Anita Pratap, *Island of Blood: Frontline Reports from Sri Lanka, Afghanistan and Other South Asian Flashpoints*. New York: Putnam Press, 2001.

David Rapoport, *Terrorism: Critical Concepts in Political Science*. London: Routledge, 2006.

Maria A. Reesa, *Seeds of Terror: An Eyewitness Account of Al Qaeda's Newest Center of Operations in Southeast Asia*. New York: Free Press, 2003.

Walter Reich, *Origins of Terrorism: Psychologies, Ideologies, Theologies, and States of Mind*. Washington, DC: Woodrow Wilson Center Press, 1999.

Robert I. Rotberg, *Creating Peace in Sri Lanka: Civil War and Reconciliation*. Washington, DC: Brookings Institution Press, 1999.

Marc Sageman, *Understanding Terror Networks*. Philadelphia, PA: University of Pennsylvania Press, 2004.

Laura Sjoberg and Caron E. Gentry, *Mothers, Monsters and Whores*. London: Zed Books, 2007.

Rosemarie Skaine, *Female Suicide Bombers*. Jefferson, NC: McFarland and Company, 2006.

Jessica Stern, *Terror in the Name of God*. New York: Ecco Press, 2004.

———, "When Bombers Are Women." Washington Post, December 18, 2003.

Stanley J. Tambiah, *Sri Lanka, Ethnic Fratricide and the Dismantling of Democracy*. New York: Oxford University Press, 1986.

Lawrence Wright, *The Looming Tower: Al Qaeda and the Road to 9/11*. New York: Knopf, 2006.

Debra D. Zedalis, *Female Suicide Bombers*. Honolulu, Hawaii: University Press of the Pacific, 2004.

INDEX